ESSAYS ON

EVOLUTIONARY ASTROLOGY:

The Evolutionary Journey
of the Soul

Jeffrey Wolf Green

Edited by Deva Green

The Wessex Astrologer

Published in 2011 by
The Wessex Astrologer Ltd
4A Woodside Road
Bournemouth
BH5 2AZ
England

www.wessexastrologer.com

ISBN 9781902405520

A catalogue record of this book is available at The British Library

Cover design by Tania at Creative Byte, Poole, Dorset

CONTENTS

Foreword

Kristin Fontana

When I learned that a compilation of teachings by Jeffrey Wolf Green would be available to expand the book shelf of Evolutionary Astrology, I waited with eager anticipation. Jeffrey's daughter, Deva pulled from the archives and unearthed a gold mine of priceless wisdom to share with us all - a true gift for anyone interested in deepening their understanding of Evolutionary Astrology. While all of it is packed with profound Evolutionary Astrology teachings on various subjects, what makes this compilation of work so special are the 'live' exchanges where Jeffrey is engaging with his audience. This interaction gives the reader an experience to 'meet the man' the master behind the work, offering a window into the heart and soul of Jeffrey Wolf Green. For those of you who did not have the opportunity to experience his teachings firsthand, you will come to better know the spirit of this God Soul as his heart, humor and humility shine through the pages.

Jeffrey's knowledge of history and natural spiritual laws prove to open additional inner doors, expanding the awareness of the studying astrologer. You will find, as in all of his teachings, either written or spoken, that not a word is wasted. Studying this rich and profound science called Evolutionary Astrology, the body of work put forth on this planet by Jeff Green, offers far more than an intellectual process. It shines the light on the path of the journey of every Soul who is ready to return. It is about the discovery of who you are, where you have been, how you were created by God/dess, and an opportunity to uncover and embrace your intended destiny. All of EA ultimately is a call to return home, back to your nature, back to your roots.

Jeffrey has an art in getting to the bottom line signature for any Soul, to the very essence of who you are and why you are here, which includes helping to uncover dynamics that have been preventing necessary growth. *Essays on Evolutionary Astrology* helps to further de-code the mystery by teaching new levels and layers of this understanding. There were many topics that Jeffrey taught in all of his international travels while he was on the road teaching, many of which never made it to print. Thankfully some of those lectures were turned into transcripts and are now available for us to glean a new and deeper understanding of the journey of the Soul.

You will find chapters dedicated to often sought-out subjects of interest where very little is available in the astrological world of study. Jeffrey dials in on all the sensitive subjects, topics such as Medical Astrology, Sexuality and Trauma. He was always known for going places others would never dare to tread and with the consciousness he was given he was able to teach on these topics with such an inherent wisdom and a compassion that allowed the student or client to be deeply reached and validated. There is no greater gift for a searching and suffering Soul.

Another unique offering in *Essays on Evolutionary Astrology* is in Jeffrey's teaching on the planetary Nodes. He shares how the Nodes of all the planets, not just the Moon, unveil with more detail the past as well as the intended future for the Soul in question. He shares chart examples using the Nodes of all the planets in such a way as to take you deeper into the history of the individual, expressing far more than could ever be gleaned in the natal birth chart. This offers an extraordinary dimension of awareness.

The planetary Nodes do not just reflect the individual's journey but generational themes and the collective implications for us all. There is a karmic link that we all share simply by being on the planet together today. Jeffrey describes how the North Nodes of those outer planets reflect our collective role in facilitating the evolution of the species. With a high degree of focus in Cancer, we must go back in order to move forward, back to our Mother root, the Matriarchal time when humans were aligned with Natural Law. Jeffrey used to teach that any Soul's most important work starts with themselves. Like dandelions in the wind, together we can make the kind of change necessary to restore a more natural state of balance and being. This book will show you the way back and the way in.

Evolutionary Astrology has touched the lives of countless people all over the globe. The precision and unparalleled depth of the EA paradigm and all of its workings never ceases to amaze me in its ability to penetrate to the core of the issue and the heart of the story, inevitably opening a healing door. The way back is rarely easy but reversing your direction only to have to walk down this road again or staying static and simply marking time is hardly an option for evolution. For anyone who aches to know, and who wants a tool that will never let you down in its ability to answer those perplexing questions, you have found it. It will leave you spell bound, awestruck and hungry for more, even if it hurts.

What else can I say, except it's pure genius !

Introduction

When my father retired and went into seclusion he left me with everything that he had ever written which included drafts of various manuscripts which he had intended to publish at various points. This also included every audio tape, video, dvd, and transcript of his lectures delivered over a lengthy career.

He gave me his business and asked me to carry on with it. This book reflects my desire to continue to disseminate his work as widely as possible. In *Essays on Evolutionary Astrology: The Evolutionary Journey of The Soul* there is a combination of transcribed lectures with parts of various manuscripts. Typically when my father lectured he would always encourage those who came to ask as many questions as they had. I have tried to leave as much of those two way interactions as I can in this book.

The origins of evolutionary astrology started when my father had a dream one night in which the entire astrological paradigm that measures the Soul's growth, and evolutionary intent, from life to life was given. At that time my father's spiritual teachers were Paramahansa Yogananda, and his guru Sri Yukteswar. Sri Yukteswar was an astrologer in his own right, and a galactic one at that. The dream that my father was given came from Yukteswar. In fact the entire book *Pluto Volume 1: The Evolutionary Journey of the Soul* was given to my father in that dream. That dream happened in 1977.

My father began to apply the evolutionary paradigm of the Soul to all of his clients, and lectured on it from that point forwards. Wherever he went to lecture the lecture halls would be packed due to the nature of this topic. It was the first time in the long history of astrology that a paradigm that was able to measure the evolutionary journey of the Soul had ever been given.

After seven years of practical application of this paradigm to his clients, at that point numbering in the thousands, my father felt it was finally time to write his now famous book *Pluto Volume I: The Evolutionary Journey of the Soul*. He wrote that book in just sixty days. It came out in 1985 and has been in continuous print since that time. It has been translated into many, many languages. It is literally all over the world. My father lectured all over the world from 1977 until 2004. Wherever he went he found people who were Soul-thirsty for this knowledge. He established schools at various points, with the help and cooperation of various students of his, in the USA, Canada, England, Germany, Holland, Israel, and Chile. He also established a video correspondence course in 1994 for Souls that desired to become certified Evolutionary Astrologers. He also established the Jeffrey Wolf Green conferences on Evolutionary Astrology that are held from time to time.

By the time he retired he had counseled over 30,000 clients from all over the world. He wrote his second volume, *Pluto Volume II: The Evolutionary Journey of the Soul Through Relationships* in 1996 that focused on the evolutionary and karmic reasons for being in the relationships that we are in. And now this book has been edited by me. Upon his retirement he left it to me to continue the spread of this work. I have started the Council of Evolutionary Astrologers to do so. We have a website at http://www.schoolofevolutionaryastrology.com; it has a tremendous message board that has become its own international community of evolutionary astrologers. We continue to offer my father's original Evolutionary Astrology correspondence course for those who wish to become certified as evolutionary astrologers, and we continue to have our conference on evolutionary astrology which is held at different times.

I have written my own book called *Evolutionary Astrology*, and there are now other books by wonderful authors such as Patricia Walsh (*Understanding Karmic Complexes*, The Wessex Astrologer) and Rose Marcus (*Insights into Evolutionary Astrology*, Llewellyn) who have written on evolutionary astrology as well. And there are other new authors who will be writing soon. I deeply hope that you find *Essays on Evolutionary Astrology: The Evolutionary Journey of the Soul* interesting, and that it will in some way help the evolutionary journey of your own Soul.

God Bless,
Deva Green,
Ashland, Oregon, Fall of 2010

1

A Review of the Key Principles in Evolutionary Astrology

For most of you a review of the key astrological principles involved in Evolutionary Astrology will be useful. And, again, I highly recommend that you read the first two volumes of *Pluto: The Evolutionary Journey of the Soul* if you have not already done so. The key principles that we will be reviewing are (1) the natural law of evolution and the two primary ways it manifests, (2) exactly what is a 'Soul', (3) how the natural law of evolution manifests from within the Soul, (4) the 'ego' that the Soul manifests in each life and (5) the four natural evolutionary conditions or stages of a Soul's evolution.

Evolution

The simplest way to validate the natural law of evolution is based on the universal human experience in which all of us know that we are in a continuous state of becoming. This is not a function of belief, or needing to believe it. It is simply a fact. Of course any of us can observe the natural law of evolution in countless ways as applied to the totality of the Creation. We can observe it relative to the evolution of the human life form, we can observe it in the life of plants and animals, we can observe it through the fundamental changes over great lengths of time to the Earth itself as an evolving planet. We can observe it through our telescopes pointed out into the universe, we can observe it even at a molecular level of life. Evolution simply means the changing of form, the changing of structure, the changing of energy, and the change of anything. The very word change implies evolution.

Evolution is always preceded by another natural law called involution. What this means is that for a change, or evolution, to occur relative to some structure, form, energy pattern, dynamics etc., it is always preceded by the ending or destruction of something that pre-exists. That which pre-exists, when evolution or change becomes necessary, is promoting a state of stagnation or non-growth. In all life forms, in anything that exists as phenomena within the totality of the Creation, there exists another natural law called survival. When this natural law is ignited or stimulated, for whatever reasons, it will always cause the natural law of involution leading to evolution to occur, so that the ongoing survival of a life form, structure and so on can occur.

The natural laws of evolution and involution have two ways of manifesting. One is as a slow, progressive, non-cataclysmic process of change that Darwin called uniformity. The other is cataclysmic change in which the very nature of involution leading to evolution is intense and abrupt. These two natural ways of evolution are observable by anyone as facts and do not require any belief at all. The natural law of evolution and involution correlate astrologically to Pluto.

The Soul

'Soul' has been a word in almost every human language system that has ever been on Earth. So what is it? Can we open up the brain and find it? No, obviously we can not. We can not open up the physical body and find emotion either, yet we know we all have emotions. Can we open up the brain and find thought? No. Yet, we all know we at least have a thought or two in our heads. Can we open up the body and find sadness, or depression, or happiness, or love? No. Yet, we all know that these things exist within us. So obviously we are dealing with the nature of energy. The Soul is energy no different than the energy of consciousness itself. Again, we can't open the brain and find it. Consciousness is one of the greatest mysteries of all to scientists for they can not explain its origins or even how it came to be. Consciousness correlates astrologically to Neptune. This is exactly the starting point for what we call religion and philosophy: the human need to contemplate and consider, within the desire to know, where we come from and why. In turn this becomes the causative factor for 'beliefs' where beliefs are the result of the human pondering upon the origin of life itself. But is there a difference between beliefs and actual knowing? Is there a way to know the answer to the big cosmic questions versus the need to believe in an answer? The happy news is that there is. By the sheer fact that there is a manifested Creation that exists as fact there must also be *truths that inherently exist* because of the fact of the manifested Creation in the first place. By the fact of its existence most of us can reason that there has to be something that is the origin of the Creation. In generic language we could call that something the Origin of All Things, or The Source, and in religious terminology it is called God or the Goddess.

Consciousness is certainly part of the manifested Creation. It exists. And that which is the origin of consciousness, of itself, must also be conscious. Thus the totality of consciousness emanates from this Source. As an observable fact we know that consciousness is in all living things: all life forms. And all of these life forms have the appearance of being separate from all other life forms yet are simultaneously connected to them: two plants next to each other appear separate yet are connected by the sheer fact of being plants. So, on the one hand there is the individualizing aspect of consciousness, and, on the other, the universal aspect of consciousness which binds all the individual aspects of consciousness together.

Another way of illustrating this is the famous story of the wave and the ocean. Most of us would agree that it is the ocean that is the origin of the wave. Yet from the point of view the wave, if the individualizing aspect of consciousness were centered there, the wave appears and seems separate. In other words if the center of gravity for consciousness were within the wave then from that center of gravity the wave appears, and is experienced, as something separate from its own source: the ocean. On the other hand if the center of gravity within consciousness were the wave itself then the ocean simultaneously experiences its totality while at the same time experiencing the individualizing aspects of itself as manifested in the waves that emanate from it.

In the very same way the Universal Consciousness, which is the origin of all consciousness, has created and manifested the totality of the manifested Creation, which includes the human being and the consciousness within it. And within human consciousness there exists a natural individualizing aspect that occurs as a natural result of the human life form having distinct and individual forms relative to its root: the human life form as a seed, so to speak, that produces many other branches.

Thus, each human life form has its own individualizing consciousness that is called the Soul. The Soul, then, is an immutable consciousness, or energy, that is naturally part of the Universal Consciousness that created it in the first place. Immutable here means that which can not be destroyed. Why? Because energy can never be destroyed, it can only change form. To evolve.

So how does the Soul evolve? What dynamics are inherent within it that are the cause of its own evolution? Within all human souls there exist two antithetical desires *where desire is the determinant of evolution*. One desire is to *return* to that which is the origin of us, of all of Creation, in the first place. The other desire is to *separate* from that which is the Origin of All Things. This simple inner dynamic within the Soul is also the natural cause, or law, of free choice, or free will.

The evolution of the Soul is simply based on a progressive elimination of all separating desires to the exclusion of only one desire that can remain: to return to the Origin Of All Things. This does not require any belief system at all, or any religion that one must belong to. This simple truth, because it is a function of natural law, can be validated by anyone through their own life experience. Is it not true for example that any of us can have whatever separating desire that one can imagine? For example a desire for a new lover, or a new career post, the new possession, and so on. And we may have the ability to manifest that which we desire. And when we do there is in fact a sense of satisfaction of actualizing that which we have desired. But what soon replaces it? Is it not the sense of dissatisfaction, the sense of something more? It is precisely this sense of dissatisfaction, the sense of something more, that 'echoes' the ultimate desire to return to the Origin Of All Things, the only desire that will bring to us that ultimate satisfaction. All of us have this universal experience.

So how can we know, independent of belief systems, that there in fact exists an Ultimate Source? The human being knew long, long ago, before the manifestation of religions and complicated cosmologies, that through inner contemplation, inner 'looking', that when the breath in the body, inhale and exhale, became very, very shallow, even stopped, that there would appear within the interior of their consciousness a *light*. This occurred as a natural function of the breath becoming shallow or stopping. Naturally. Much later in human history this became known as the famous 'third eye'. And it is this very Light that symbolized and connected the individual consciousness reflected in the Soul to the Universal Consciousness that is the Origin of All Things. The human being also learned long ago that by merging its own individual consciousness, or Soul, with that Light, that its consciousness would expand in such a way that the individual consciousness itself became Universal and was able to consciously experience that Ultimate Source of All Things: the wave had returned to the ocean.

The point here, again, is that any human being can know and validate these natural laws through their own actual experience that does not require belief systems of any kind. The key to do this, again, is to progressively shallow and stop the breath all together. Any one can do this. If you doubt it, or wonder how, simply try the following natural method. On your inhaling breath mentally affirm the number one. On your exhaling breath mentally affirm the number two. The secret here is to concentrate as hard as you can simply on the numbers one and two. It is this act of concentration intensified by desire manifesting as will that progressively your breath will begin to shallow and even stop. Remember that consciousness is energy and can not be destroyed. It can only change form. When the breath is stopped it does not mean that you have to die. Consciousness is *not* dependant on the human form. So when the breath is stopped the inner *light* which is intrinsic to consciousness will soon begin to appear. And as it does so, simply move into it with a conscious act of surrender. Surrendering to it will allow for a merging of your own consciousness with that Universal Consciousness as symbolized in the Light. *Anyone can do this and then know for themselves this natural truth.*

It is this natural law of breath, when stopped or becoming very shallow, that validates what all the great teachers of relatively recent centuries, (when compared to how long the human being has actually been on the planet), have said; including Jesus: "When thy eye is single one's whole body is full of light". Symbolically speaking our two physical eyes correlate to the two motions of breath: inhale and exhale. It is the inhaling and exhaling of the breath that keeps one's consciousness utterly involved and enmeshed in the duality, or polarity, of life itself. Likes and dislikes, happiness and sadness, love and hate etc, correlate too and demonstrate this natural law. The numbers one and two illustrate the natural law of finitude and duality: cause and effect. Yet between one and two there exists an interval, or zero. The interval or zero correlates to the Universal Consciousness or infinity. Thus when the breath stops or becomes very, very shallow the interval is perceived. And what is perceived in the single eye, or what has been called the 'third eye' that naturally exists within the interior of consciousness, can be accessed and merged with our Soul. When this occurs the law of duality ceases to exist. The ultimate satisfaction is then realized. The Soul correlates astrologically to Pluto.

From the point of view of natural laws it is interesting to note, historically speaking, that advanced mathematics like algebra, trigonometry, quantum physics and so on, could not have been realized unless there was an 'idea' or conception called zero. This occurred in the third century AD in India. It was the Indian mathematicians that conceived of the number zero. And from the point of view of Indian cosmologies this occurred as a direct extension of their natural understanding of the origin of Creation: out of nothing, or zero, the manifested Creation occurred: the un-manifested/ manifested, or the causeless cause.

The Ego

Coming into human form the Soul will then manifest what is known as the ego. The ego correlates astrologically to the Moon. The ego is also pure energy. We can not open the brain and find it. Unlike the energy of the Soul which is sustained from life to life until the final merging with the Source occurs, the energy of the ego in any life is dissolved after each life is lived. The analogy of the wave and the ocean again serves to illustrate this point. The ocean can be equated with the Soul, and the wave can be equated with the ego. Of course the ocean, Soul, is manifesting the waves, ego, life after life. And just as the waves can rise and fall, any given life that the Soul creates, the ocean is sustained. In other words the egos that the Soul manifests in each life rise from birth but finally dissolve back into the ocean, Soul, upon the completion of each life. Its energy is not destroyed but simply absorbed back into the energy that created it in the first place.

The ego created by the Soul thus allows for the individualizing aspect of the Soul in each life. In each life the ego is created by the Soul in such a way as to serve as the vehicle through which the evolutionary intentions of the Soul in any life occurs. Each ego that the Soul creates is oriented to reality in such a way that the very nature of the orientation serves as the vehicle through which the life lessons occur and are understood by the Soul. In each life the ego allows for a self image of the Soul to occur relative to the individualizing aspect of the Soul.

An analogy to a movie projector will suffice to illustrate this point. If I have a movie projector, a reel of film on the back, and a screen in front of the movie projector, and then turn on the machine generating light from it, I will have no distinct imagery on the screen unless I also have a lens within the projector. Without the lens what manifests from the machine is simply diffuse light. Thus the lens serves as a vehicle through which the inherent images on the film can be focused and given distinct shape and form. In the very same way the ego that the Soul generates in each life allows for a vehicle, or lens, through which the inherent images that exist with our Soul to take form. This natural law of consciousness is thus the cause that allows for individual self perception and the word 'I' itself.

The Soul, Pluto, also correlates to the genetic code, RNA and DNA, chromosomes, and enzymes. In each life the Soul *is the determinant for the entire genetic code of the life, human form, that it is being born into*. Each life that the Soul chooses is a continuation of that which has come before where each new life taken correlates to the ongoing evolutionary lessons or intentions of any given Soul. Thus the body type, including the race to be born into, the appearance, the culture, the parents, the specific and individual nature of the emotions, feelings, psychology, desires, and so on correlate to the Soul's intentions reflected in the genetic code in total in each life. This is all then given individual form via the egocentric structure, Moon, that the Soul creates in each life. Any person can then say things like "this is who I am", "this is what I need", "this is what I am feeling", "this is what I am trying to learn", and so on: the individualizing aspect of the ego that the Soul creates in each life.

When 'death' occurs in any given life, the ego that the Soul has created dissolves back into its origin: the Soul. Since both are energy, and energy can not be destroyed, where does the Soul go upon the physical death of the body? In other words where is it on an energetic level? Most of us have heard the words the 'astral plane' or heaven and hell. Obviously these types of words refer to other realities or planes of existence, and there are in fact other energetic realities or planes of existence. Simply speaking, the astral plane is an energetic plane of existence that all Souls go to after the completion of physical lives on places like Earth. Energetically this plane is much less materially dense than places like Earth. After physical death the Soul 'goes to' the astral plane in order to review the life that has just been lived, and to prepare for yet another birth on places like Earth. Upon the completion of a life on Earth the ego dissolves back into the Soul in such a way that the center of gravity within the consciousness, within the astral plane, is the Soul itself. For most folks living lives in the material plane we call Earth the center of gravity of consciousness is the ego itself. This is why the vast majority of people living feel within themselves that they are separate from everything else: the center of gravity being the egocentric 'I'. In the astral plane the center of gravity shifts to the Soul so that when death occurs in any given life the memory of the ego of that life is sustained.

This memory of the ego is necessary for the Soul for it is the memory of the ego that allows the Soul to not only review the life that has just been lived, but also to serve as a basis for the next life to be lived relative to the continuing evolution of the Soul itself: in each life we pick up where we have left off before. Thus, this memory of the ego in each life serves as the causative factor of what type of egocentric structure the Soul needs to create in the next life. In essence it is the memory of the ego that the Soul draws upon, the 'images' contained therein, that serve as the basis of the next ego that the Soul needs to generate in each successive life that promotes its ongoing evolution.

Astrologically speaking this is symbolized by Pluto, the Soul, and the South and North Nodes of the Moon. The South Node of the Moon correlates to the prior egocentric memories of the Soul that determine the natal placement of the Moon in each life, the current ego; whereas the North Node of the Moon correlates to the evolving ego of the Soul: the nature and types of inner and outer experiences that the Soul needs and desires to facilitate its ongoing evolution. In turn this will constitute the new egocentric memories and images that the Soul will draw upon when a life has been lived and terminated at physical death.

Most of us are aware that the Moon also correlates to one's family of origin in any given life. It should be clear then that upon the death of the physical body the Soul 'goes to' the astral plane and meets again important family members, and others close to the Soul. This is also why, for many Souls, we meet again those family members upon rebirth into yet another physical life on places like Earth. It is the memory of the ego now combined with the memory of family that is the determinant in this phenomenon. And this phenomenon is sustained until there is no longer any evolutionary or karmic need to sustain such relationships.

The Evolutionary Conditions or States

A very, very important principle to review concerns the four natural evolutionary conditions, or stages, of a Soul's evolution. One of the great problems of modern astrology is a total ignorance of this natural law. As a result, much if not most of astrological understanding is the 'one size fits all' approach, which does a total disservice not only to astrology in general, but to the very people it attempts to help. This approach flies in the face of common sense, not to mention life itself. It's like saying if I have Venus square Pluto then the meaning of that astrological pairing would be the same for all. It never takes into account the *individual context* of anything. Let us remember a core truth about astrology: it only works relative to observed context. If the 'one size fits all' approach were in fact true then, for example, when Uranus transited Pisces in the 1920s the same social themes would have existed all over the planet. In reality they did not because of individual context. In Germany, for example, following World War One it manifested as an almost total breakdown in the social order where literally one had to haul wheel-barrows of money just to buy a loaf of bread. Yet, at the same time, in the United States it manifested as the 'Roaring 20s' because of the individual context of America at that time. This was in essence fueled by the 'invention' of the non-secured credit card.

Again, the evolution of the Soul is based on the progressive elimination of all separating desires to the exclusion of the only desire that can remain: to return 'home' to that which is the Origin of all Souls in the first place. Based on this natural law there are four natural evolutionary conditions, with three subdivisions in each, that correlate to the Soul's evolutionary journey. And, again, if you doubt this simply stand back in a Uranian way from any society, country, culture, or tribe and observe it. Any detached observer will notice these four natural evolutionary conditions: (1) That roughly three to four percent of all Souls are in what I call the 'dimly evolved' state. This means one of two things. Either Souls that are evolving into human consciousness from other forms of life such as animals and plants, or Souls that are 'de-evolving' backwards into this condition due to karmic causes. (2) Souls that have evolved into what can be called the 'consensus' state of evolution which comprises roughly seventy percent of all Souls on the planet at this time. (3) The 'individualized' state of evolution where individualized is used in the Jungian sense of the word and comprises roughly twenty percent of all Souls. And (4) the 'spiritual' state of evolution that comprises roughly four to six percent of all Souls on the planet.

It is extremely important to understand that no astrologer can determine which evolutionary condition exists for any Soul by simply looking at the birth chart alone. The astrologer must observe and interact with the client in order for this determination to be made. A good way to do this in a counseling situation is to simply ask the client why they are there, and what questions they have. Generally, the very nature of the questions will clue the astrologer as to what evolutionary condition exists for that client. For example if one client asks "when can I expect enlightenment?" and another asks "when will I have my new BMW?" there clearly is an observed difference reflecting the level of evolutionary progression of the Soul.

The Dimly Evolved State: Those Souls that are evolving into human consciousness from other forms of life, typically animal and plants since these essentially have the same emotional and nervous systems as humans, are characterized by a very limited sense of self-awareness. This self-awareness is typically limited to the time and space that they personally occupy. When one looks into such Souls' eyes they express a density within the pupils, like a film effect. These Souls are very joyous, very, very innocent, and can bring great love to those who are close to them. Modern terminology that reflects these types of Souls are words like cretinism, very low intelligence, mongoloidism, metal retardation, and the like. The root desire within this evolutionary stage or state is the desire to be 'normal' where normal means to be like most other people: the consensus state.

Conversely, it can occur due to karmic causes that Souls can be de-evolved, which means that such Souls are forced back into this state. This then becomes very problematic for such Souls because they had previously evolved beyond this stage. Such Souls now experience great and humiliating limitations because of the de-evolution and as a result these Souls are very, very angry and some go about creating great disturbances for other people. These souls can also be classified through the modern terminology as above. But the difference is that when one looks into the pupils of these Souls' eyes one will notice a great white light manifesting from the pupil: piercing-like. And within that light one will inwardly experience the intense anger within such a Soul.

The Consensus State: Astrologically speaking this state correlates to Saturn because of the underlying desire to conform to the consensus of any society, culture, tribe or country. Thus such Souls' entire orientation to reality including their values, the sense of meaning for life, moralities, customs, norms, taboos, what is right and wrong and so on, are simply an extension of the prevailing consensus of whatever society they are born into.

In essence the 'reality' for such Souls is merely an extension of the external conditioning that any consensus group of people provides. They can not step out of the box, so to speak. For example if a scientist claims that "astrology is bogus" then all those who are within the consensus state will have the same opinion. Within the consensus state, like all the other states, there are three subdivisions that we must account for. Each subdivision reflects the ongoing evolution of a Soul through the entire evolutionary state which then leads to the next evolutionary state with its three subdivisions until the final 'liberation' of a Soul occurs. This is relative to exhaustion of all separating desires ultimately reflected in the third subdivision of the Spiritual State of evolution.

The way that evolution occurs is by exhausting all the desires that are intrinsic to the nature of each evolutionary state or condition. Within the consensus state the root desire that propels the evolution of the Soul forwards, from the first subdivision through the third, is characterized by the desire to get ahead: to get ahead of the system, which of course means the consensus society that they belong to. Souls within the first subdivision of the consensus state are characterized by a limited sense of self-awareness that is essentially limited to the time and space they occupy, a limited awareness of the dynamics of the community that they inhabit, and an even more limited awareness of the dynamics of the country that they live within. And yet they are incredibly self-righteous relative to the values, moralities, consensus religion of the existing society of birth, how life is interpreted according to those beliefs, the judgments issued because of those beliefs, and so on. There simply is no ability to separate themselves from any of this: it is as if they are like social automatons. An apt analogy for these Souls is the worker bees in a bee hive. Typically, they are in the lowest social strata of the society of birth.

As evolution proceeds for these Souls relative to the desire to get ahead, it will lead them into the second subdivision. Their root desire means that they will want more from society than simply remaining within its lower strata. These Souls of course perceive from the point of view of the lower strata that there are others who have more than they have. This perception is more or less limited to others having more possessions of a grander nature than they have, social positions within society that they do not have, thus more social freedom, and so on. Yet that limited perception fuels the root desire to get ahead and to have more. In order for this desire to be realized they must learn ever more how society, its dynamics, work. This then requires an expansion of their personal awareness. It is the very fact of the evolutionary necessity to expand their awareness that propels the evolution of the Soul into the second subdivision within the consensus state.

In the second subdivision it becomes necessary for the Soul to learn ever more about the nature of society in order to use the social system to its own evolutionary advantage: to get ahead. The reality for such Souls is still totally defined by the consensus of society: its values, moralities, religions, judgments, what is right and wrong, and so on. Yet by desiring to get ahead the Soul must expand its personal awareness of the nature of the dynamics of how its society is put together: its rules, regulations, what is required for this ambition or that to be actualized, and so on. The Soul thus becomes ever more aware of others, of the community that it is part of, and the country that it lives within. This expanding awareness also includes the beginning of an awareness of other countries and the difference in values, moralities, religions, and so on as reflected in other countries and societies. Personal awareness, self-awareness, expands because of the heightened awareness of others relative to the Soul's desire to get ahead. This evolutionary stage correlates to the middle strata within the social order of any given society. As the Soul evolves through this state it increasingly becomes aware of the upper strata of society, of those that are in positions of power and leadership, of those that have great material abundance, and, as result, the desire to get ahead fuels the ongoing evolution of the Soul into the third subdivision within the consensus state.

In order for the Soul to evolve into the third subdivision it demands an ever increasing awareness of how society works in total. Because of this, personal awareness expands through evolutionary necessity in order for the Soul's desires, defined by ambitions to get ahead, to be realized. The Soul's personal awareness has expanded to the point that it is now very aware of the totality of the community and society that it belongs to and the country that it lives within. And this also includes a progressive awareness of other countries, other cultures, and of the relativity of moralities, values, religions, and so on. Even though this awareness progressively includes the relativity of moralities and values it does not mean that the Soul in this subdivision considers other countries, values, beliefs, and religions equal to its own: the society and country of birth. If fact within this subdivision the self-righteousness born out of conformity, the underlying hallmark of the consensus state in total, is sustained: we are right, and they are wrong. In total the consensus state correlates to what is called nationalism.

In this final subdivision within the consensus state the Soul desires to be 'on top' of society, to have positions of social importance and relative power, prestige, and material abundance: the politicians, the CEOs of corporations, important positions in the business world, mainstream religious leaders, and so on. As a result these Souls constitute the upper strata of society. As the Soul evolves through this last subdivision it will finally exhaust all the desires that are inherent within it. The meaning to life itself will be progressively lost as those desires no longer hold any meaning, and at the very end of the journey through this state the Soul will finally ask the question "there must be more to life than this". This very question implies an awakening alienation from the consensus, from 'normal' life as defined by the consensus. It is this awakening alienation from normalcy defined by the consensus of any society that triggers the beginning of a new desire that will propel the Soul into the Individuated Evolutionary State: the desire to liberate from all external conditioning that has previously defined the Soul's sense of reality in general, and its sense of personal identity, or individuality, specifically.

The Individuated State: Astrologically speaking the individuated state correlates to Uranus because the Soul now desires to liberate or rebel against the consensus state from which it is evolving away from. Instead of the Soul being defined by the consensus to shape its sense of reality in general, and its personal identity specifically, the Soul now desires to discover who and what it is independent of such conditioning. Earlier it was stated that if a Soul were in the consensus state, and the scientist said "astrology is bogus", this would then be the automatic belief of those Souls who are within the consensus state. If that same scientist said this to a Soul within the individuated state the response would be something like "no thank you, I will think for myself". Souls in this evolutionary state inwardly feel 'different': different than the majority of the society and country of birth. Because of the desire to liberate from the consensus, the awareness of Souls in this state progressively expands to include ever larger wholes, or frames of reference.

This expansion of awareness begins because the Soul no longer can identify with the consensus of the society of birth. The Soul now feels a progressive detachment from society: like standing on the outside and looking in. This allows the Soul to objectify itself relative to personal awareness and self perception. Rebelling against consensus beliefs, values, moralities, what constitutes 'meaning' for life itself, and so on, the Soul begins to question the assumptions that most people hold dear to their heart that correlate to what reality is and is not. As a result such Souls now begin to experiment by investigating other ways of looking at and understanding the nature of life. And it is through this independent thinking and investigating all kinds of different ways of understanding life, including investigating ideas, beliefs, and philosophies from other lands and cultures, that allows for an ever increasing expansion of their consciousness and, thus, their sense of personal awareness. As a result of this such Souls no longer feel 'home' in their own land, their country of birth.

In the first subdivision the Soul will typically try to compensate for this inner feeling of being different, of not belonging to the consensus, and the inner sense of alienation, by trying to appear normal. This compensation will cause the Soul to structure their outer reality much as Souls do in the consensus state: normal kinds of work, normal kinds of friends, the normal appearance, and so on. Yet inwardly they feel and know that they can no longer personally identify with that compensatory reality that they attempt to sustain. This compensation manifests in this subdivision because, after all, the consensus is just where the Soul has been. It constitutes a sense of security relative to the inner feeling of being detached and different. We must remember that for most people the sense of security for life is a function of self-consistency. And self-consistency is a function of the past. As a result the compensation manifests as a reaction to this increasingly new feeling of being different, of not belonging anymore to the consensus. This feeling creates a sense of insecurity in this subdivision because is it brand new: the Soul has not been here before. Yet this very act of compensation creates a very real state of being in a 'living lie'.

Even as this compensatory behavior occurs the Soul will nonetheless be questioning everything deep within themselves: the privacy of their own inner life. Typically, they will read all kinds of books that contain ideas that go way beyond the norm as defined by the consensus. Many, depending on cultural possibilities, will take classes or workshops that have the same theme or intention. Some will seek out these kinds of 'alternative' environments in order to find and bond with others of like mind: others who feel just as they do. This compensatory behavior will progressively give way, involution, as the Soul evolves further through this subdivision. The Soul will progressively distance itself from the consensus and begin to form relationships with other alienated Souls just like itself. Because of the necessity of work, or a job, most of these Souls will either do any kind of work just to get by without identifying with such work in any way, or they will actualize a work that is individualistic and symbolic of their own individuality.

In the second subdivision the underlying archetype of Uranus as it correlates to rebellion is at its highest. This rebellion is so extreme that the Soul has now thrown off almost any idea or philosophy that has come before at any level of reality. Such Souls end up in a kind of existential void and typically hang out with other such alienated Souls, having the effect of reinforcing the total state of rebellion from all of reality other than the reality that they have now defined through the existential void.

These Souls will exhibit a deep fear of integrating into society in any kind of way for the fear suggests that if they do so somehow that very same society or reality will absorb their hard won, at least to them, individuality which is defined through the act or rebellion in this stage. As a result these Souls typically hang out on the avant-garde of society hurling critical atom bombs at it so as to reinforce their sense of personal righteousness defined by their alienation from the consensus. Because of the natural law of evolution, which is always preceded by an involution, these people at some point realize that their fear of integrating into reality, into society, is just that: a fear only. Once this is realized they begin to make the effort to integrate back into society but with their individuality intact. Once this is realized the Soul will evolve into the third subdivision within the individuated state.

In the third subdivision the Souls will begin to manifest within society or reality as truly unique and gifted people from the point of view of the consensus. This means that such Souls will have in some way a unique gift, or capacity, to help the consensus itself evolve by integrating that capacity or gift within the consensus. Yet these people will not inwardly feel identified with the consensus: they are standing inwardly very distant from it. The consciousness of these Souls has progressively expanded through the individuated state in such a way that they are aware of the entire world and the relativity of beliefs, values, moralities, and so on. As a result they will feel themselves to be world citizens much more than being a singular citizen of the country of birth. The inner pondering as to the very nature of existence, the nature of Creation, the nature of who they 'really' are essentially defines the nature of their consciousness. Progressively these people begin to open up their consciousness to the universal, the cosmos, to God/ess. Not the God/ess defined through consensus religions but the real or natural God/ess. A perfect example in recent history that reflects such a soul is Albert Einstein. Another example would be Carl Jung.

The Spiritual State: Astrologically speaking this evolutionary state correlates to Neptune because now the root desire becomes to consciously *know*, not just believe in, and unite with the Source of All Things: the universal, God/ess. Because of this root desire the consciousness now progressively expands into the universal, the cosmos, in such a way that the very nature of the interior consciousness within the Soul becomes conscious of the living universe within: the wave within the ocean, and the ocean within the wave. Progressively in this spiritual state of evolution the very center of gravity within the Soul's consciousness shifts from the subjective ego to the Soul itself. Once the center of gravity shifts to the Soul then in the context of any given life the Soul is able to simultaneously experience its specific individuality as reflected in the ego while at the same time experiencing, being centered in, the Soul: the ocean that is aware of the waves that it manifests.

The Soul contains within itself all the prior life memories that it has ever lived. And the Soul has its own identity or ego. This identity or ego is not the same as the ego that the Soul creates in any given life on places like Earth. The ego of the Soul is one's eternal identity. An easy way for any of us to understand this occurs when we dream. Obviously when we dream we are not identified with our subjective ego. After all we are asleep. The subjective ego has temporarily dissolved back into the Soul when we sleep. So the question becomes "who and what is doing the dreaming?" Obviously it can only be the Soul with its own ego that thus allows the Soul to know itself as a Soul that is eternal. Another way to validate the same thing occurs when we sometimes wake up from sleeping and can not immediately remember who we are: the current subjective ego, the 'I', of this life. It takes some effort to actually remember the subjective 'I' when this occurs. So, again, the question becomes "who and what must make the effort to remember the subjective 'I' in the current life?" Obviously it can only be our Soul.

So, again, as evolution proceeds in this spiritual state there is a progressive shift in the center of gravity within the Soul's consciousness. When this shift firmly takes hold then the Soul, in any given life, is simultaneously experiencing its eternal self or ego while at the same time experiencing the subjective ego, and the individuality attendant to it that it has created for its own ongoing evolutionary reasons and intentions. This is very similar to when we stand on a beach at the moment of sunset when the Sun is equally half above and below the horizon. In this state of consciousness the Soul is aware from within itself of all the prior lives that it has lived and at the same time aware of the specific life, ego, that it is currently living.

Progressively as evolution proceeds in the spiritual state of evolution the Soul also becomes consciously aware of the Source of All Things. This occurs as the consciousness of the Soul becomes truly universal: the inner experience of the entire universe within one's own consciousness. This state of cosmic consciousness allows one to actually experience the very point of the manifested Creation itself: the interface between the un-manifested and the manifested. As this occurs the Soul also becomes aware of all the natural laws that govern and correlate to the very nature of Creation. In the most advanced states of evolution the Soul now being utterly identified with these natural laws of Creation is able to harmonize with those laws so as to use them at will in conjunction with the Will of All Things: that which is the very origin of those natural laws.

In the first subdivision within the Spiritual State the Soul progressively becomes aware of just how small it is because of the increasing universal dimensions that are occurring within its consciousness. This is vastly different than being the center of one's own universe as reflected in the consensus state for example. Of itself this has a naturally humbling effect to the Soul and thus to the current subjective ego, Moon, that it has created. It is exactly this naturally humbling archetype that allows progressively for the center of gravity to shift within the Soul's consciousness from the subjective ego to the Soul itself, and ultimately to a conscious union with the Source of All Things.

As a result the Soul desires to progressively commit itself to the desire to reunite with the Source. As this occurs the Soul will commit itself to devotional types of spiritual practice in this subdivision. Within this the Soul desires to commit itself to various forms of work that all correlate to being of service to the larger whole, of service to others in some way. Many will naturally want to orient to various forms of the healing arts or to start centers in which the healing arts become the focus of the center. The core issue here is that the Soul desires to do a work on behalf of the Source of All Things and to use the work as a vehicle through which The Source can be inwardly experienced because of the nature of the work. In the East this is called karma yoga.

In this first subdivision the Soul becomes progressively aware of all that it needs to improve upon within itself. A heightened state of awareness occurs that makes the Soul aware of all its imperfections and, as a result, the Soul can now become highly self-critical. Even though this is natural it creates a potential danger or trap to the Soul in that this heightened state of critical self-awareness can cause the Soul to not feel 'good enough' or 'ready' to do the task, or work, that it is being inwardly directed to do. This then sets in motion all kinds of excuse making, always manifesting as perfectly rational arguments, of why the Soul will not do what it should do when it should do it. The way out of this trap is to realize that the path to perfection occurs by taking one step at a time.

As evolution progresses through this first subdivision the Soul will increasingly have direct perception of the single eye, or the third eye, which is inherent to consciousness. As a result this perception allows the Soul to merge with that single eye in such a way that various types and states of cosmic consciousness will occur which will lead into the second subdivision within the spiritual state or state of evolution.

The second subdivision: As the Soul evolves into this subdivision it has already had various kinds of inner cosmic or universal kinds of experiences within its consciousness. Yet in this state the final shift in the center of gravity within consciousness from the subjective ego to the Soul itself has yet to occur. In this state the shift manifests more like a rubber band wherein the gravity points keep going back and forth from the subjective ego to the Soul. The problem that this generates is that the progressive inner experiences within consciousness of the universal, the cosmic Source, fuels the subjective ego in such a way that the Soul feels more evolved than it actually is. This can then set in motion in varying degrees of intensity 'spiritual delusions of grandeur' from an egocentric and Soul point of view. When this occurs such Souls will feel they have a spiritual mission to fulfill on behalf of others, of the world itself.

It is important to remember in trying to understand this subdivision that as the Soul gets ever closer to the Source, The Light, that whatever egocentric impurities remain within the Soul must be purged. As a result, the closer the Soul becomes to re-uniting with its own Origin these impurities will manifest through the current life subjective ego that the Soul's own ego contains.

These impurities can be many things depending on the specific nature of each Soul but all Souls in this subdivision will share one common impurity: the ego of the Soul that is still identifying itself as somehow separate from that which has created it. This ongoing delusion is thus reflected in the subjective ego that the Soul creates. This common impurity will then be exhibited in specific psychological behaviors that essentially boil down to such Souls pointing the way to themselves as the vehicle of salvation, or to know God/ess, while at the same time pretending that they are not. In other words they are extremely good salespeople that peddle God/ess as the hook in order to have themselves revered as the way to actually know God/ess. There is always a hidden or secret egocentric agenda within these Souls that is masked by the overlay of whatever spiritual or religious teaching they are representing. Examples of this point, in recent modern history, would be Bagawan Rajneesh, Claire Prophet, ZZ Knight (Ramtha), Da Free John, Rasputin, and the like.

As the Soul evolves through this subdivision it finally realizes the nature of this root impurity. As a result it experiences a natural guilt and this guilt is then used by the Soul to create its own downfall in order to atone for that guilt. The downfall can occur in many different ways depending on the specific nature of the circumstantial life that the Soul has generated. This downfall caused by guilt and the need to atone for that guilt thus serves as the final evolutionary development that allows the Soul to evolve into the third subdivision within the spiritual state.

In the last subdivision the Soul is now finally and firmly identified with that which has created it: The Source of All Things. The center of gravity within consciousness has finally centered within the Soul, not the subjective ego created by the Soul. At this point in the evolution of the Soul all subsequent evolution through this final subdivision will be focused on the elimination of any separating desires that the Soul still has. Because of this final shift within consciousness to the Soul itself the Soul is inwardly attuned to the Source of All Things in such a way that it perceives itself as but a singular manifestation of the Source. Simultaneously the Soul perceives all others, all of Creation, as manifestations of that Source. Thus the Soul's inner and outer responses to life itself, how life is understood and interpreted, how it comes to understand the nature of the life it is currently living, how it understands the purpose for the current life, and how it comes to make decisions relative to the life being lived, are all based on this inner attunement and alignment with that which has Created it.

As evolution begins in this final subdivision the Soul inwardly feels and knows that it is here to serve The Source in some way. It knows that it can not just live for itself. It knows that it has some kind of work to do on behalf of the Source. The consciousness of the Soul at this point is entirely structured to give to others, and to give purely without any ulterior agenda or motive involved. The nature of the work will always involve the theme of teaching or healing in some way. Because the Soul is now consciously identified with the Source the very nature of the Soul's own vibration radiates in such a way that many others are drawn to it like a magnet. Many other Souls are drawn magnetic-like to these Souls because they also reflect and radiate a fundamental wisdom of life, of a deep compassion at the human condition. This occurs because, after all, these Souls have traveled a very long evolutionary journey which has taken them through almost every kind of life experience imaginable. Such Souls are naturally very unassuming, naturally humble, and have no desire whatsoever for any kind of acclaim to their ego. Quite the opposite: they shy away from such things and always remind anyone who tries to give them acclaim of any kind for that which they do that all things come from God, or the Source. They only point the way Home, and never to themselves.

Conversely these Souls can attract to themselves others who project onto them all manner of judgments, projection of motives, intentions, of 'who they really are', and wholesale persecution. The reason this occurs is because the very nature of these Souls is fundamentally pure and full of the inner Light of the Source. As a result their own inner light has the effect of exposing the impurities in others, of others' actual reality versus the persona that is created, of others' actual intentions and motives for anything. Accordingly, those who do this kind of projection and so on feel threatened by these types of Souls for they know that they are themselves fundamentally dishonest, and that they are invested in having others believe in whatever persona they are creating to hide their actual reality. Feeling threatened thus causes these types of people to manifest this type of behavior at these Souls.

In the beginning of this subdivision the nature of the work that the Soul does, the amount of people that it is destined to help in some way through the vehicle of teaching or healing is relatively small and limited to the immediate area of community in which they live. Progressively this will evolve from this limited application to involve increasingly larger circles in which the nature of the work on behalf of the Source increases. In the end this increasing circle will include the entire world. And at the very end of evolution in this subdivision the Soul will be remembered by countless others long after the physical life of the Soul is over: the nature of their life and the teachings that they represented. Examples of these types of Souls are individuals like Jesus, Yogananda, Lao-Tzu, Buddha, Mohammed, Saint Teresa, and so on.

It is important to remember, again, that these are the natural evolutionary conditions that reflect the current reality of all peoples on Earth. For those who wish to use evolutionary astrology it is essential that you make the necessary observations of any given person to determine their evolutionary state, and to then orient yourself to their natal chart accordingly. Again, one size does not fit all. We will now discuss the four natural ways that the Soul, Pluto, affects its evolutionary intentions and necessities.

Pluto's House, Sign and Polarity Point

Pluto's house and sign placement describe two simultaneous phenomena. On the one hand, the natal position of Pluto describes the generational vibration that a person comes in with, as well as the specific individualized patterns in identity association implied from the evolutionary past: the desires, beliefs, thoughts, perceptions, values and orientation to reality itself. On the other hand, the natal position of Pluto points to the evolutionary desire, intent, or cause of this life as seen in Pluto's opposite house and sign.

Whether the individual is conscious of this intent or not does not matter because the Soul, not the personality, is the ultimate causal factor, or determining force, behind each life. The lesson will occur in some way through evolutionary necessity. If we are conscious of the intent for this life we can foster it through cooperation and non-resistance. As the life unfolds the inherent patterns of identity association, seen in the natal position of Pluto, will be reborn to a new level of expression described by Pluto's opposite house and sign. The implied limitations of the past will be experienced in some way so that the evolutionary point will transmute these limitations into new levels or horizons of awareness and expression. When we link these principles to the coexisting desires inherent in the Soul, we will see that there is an implied tension between the past, present and future. The potential for internal conflict is enormous. The desire for separateness can lead to an effort to maintain the past, while the desire for return to the Source promotes a focusing on the future (the polarity point of Pluto). The tension or conflict, if there is subconscious resistance, occurs in each moment of our lives.

Some simple examples will illustrate these principles. The sign that Pluto is in, i.e. Pluto in Leo, represents the generational vibration that we come in with. Pluto was in Leo from 1937 to 1958. Obviously, millions were born with Pluto in Leo. In general, this generation has natural desires and pre-existing orientations for creative self-actualization. Pluto in Leo individuals need enough freedom to actualize, in a creative way, their own unique purpose for living. This need implies a deep self-orientation, a more or less narcissistic orientation to life. Pluto in Leo implies a creative generation that needs to be in charge of their own lives, and able to take destiny by the hands and create it out of the strength of their own wills. Yet, the polarity sign for the generation is Aquarius. As a generation then, they must realize Aquarian lessons that involve developing an awareness of the whole, of humanity, versus an awareness of just themselves.

By developing this awareness, the generation could then creatively realize their specific purposes by linking their work or identities to the socially relevant needs of the whole. This process demands evolving an attitude of objectivity versus subjectivity, of detachment versus over involvement with personal concerns. We are rapidly moving toward the Aquarian Age.

In general, all Pluto in Leo people must learn Aquarian lessons. The specific house placements of Pluto will begin to indicate the specific and individualized lessons for each person. An example: Pluto in Leo in the 9th house. Let's say this person, in a prior life, desired to understand life in a cosmological, metaphysical, or religious context by intuitively sensing that there was more to reality than meets the tactile senses. Commonly this individual, from a prior-life point of view, needed to initiate a wide variety of experiences in order to discover or realize the knowledge that she or he was seeking. This need or desire became part of the individual's own creative self-actualization process from an evolutionary point of view. The individual would come into this life with not only a highly developed intuition, but also a rigid organization of reality (beliefs) that reflected the desire for self-understanding in a cosmological sense. The polarity point would be the 3rd house and the sign Aquarius. Simply stated, the general Aquarian lessons mentioned above would be earned through 3rd house kinds of experiences. Thus, the individual would necessarily experience internal and external philosophical and intellectual confrontations in order to realize the limitations of his or her own organization of reality (beliefs). This does not necessarily imply that those beliefs are wrong, but that they are limited. The individual would progressively learn that the paths to truth (9th house) are relative, and thus learn to communicate in a variety of ways depending on the people or circumstances encountered.

Keep in mind how the two coexisting desires in the Soul, and the potential tension or conflict, can impact on this illustrated process. As an example, it would be very common for this individual, coming into this life, to defend the personal beliefs and the organization of reality relative to those beliefs. The individual commonly would attempt to convince or convert other people to his or her own point of view. The need to defend reflects the desire to maintain separateness. On the other hand, the desire to evolve, or grow, leads toward the intellectual or philosophical confrontation implied in the 3rd house polarity. The interaction of these dual desires, and the resulting behavior, will be a primary theme underlying the individual's entire life. The potential for tension and conflict reflected in these dual desires of the Soul can be equated with the basic psychological phenomenon of attraction and repulsion. We can be attracted to the very thing that we are repulsed by, or we can be repulsed by the very thing that we are attracted to.

In the above example the Soul intends or desires to evolve. This is demonstrated, again, by the polarity point of the natal position of Pluto. As this desire reflects itself through the consciousness of the individual (ego), the individual is attracted to intellectual or philosophical discussions. Yet this very attraction will guarantee, because of the implied limitations from the evolutionary past, intellectual or philosophical confrontations with other people. The individual will experience his or her own philosophical or intellectual limitations because of these confrontations which will ignite the dynamic of repulsion through these experiences. In terms of behavior, the individual will alternately attempt to convince or convert others to their personal point of view, or withdraw altogether from this kind of experience to avoid dealing with this perceived and experienced conflict. Withdrawal creates an internal volcano of confrontation that induces intuitive thoughts or ideas that directly challenge the pre-existing beliefs or philosophical orientation that the individual brought into this life. Because the Soul (Pluto) desires to evolve (3rd house) it will lead the individual into conversations with others in order to affect the necessary challenges that allow for a transmutation of existing beliefs. In other words, the individual will subconsciously be attracted to, and thus draw to them, those kinds of people who will have this effect upon his or her beliefs and philosophical orientation.

As this process unfolds throughout life, the individual may come to realize the evolutionary lessons involved and acknowledge the relativity of his or her own point of view. At this point they could participate in philosophical and intellectual discussions in a non-defensive way, learning from as well as teaching others. The individual would learn to understand and respect individual differences in beliefs, philosophies, religions and intellectual organization. Conversely, the individual may succeed in repulsing the evolutionary pressure or intent. In this case, the behavior would manifest in defensiveness and rejection of anyone who did not agree with his or her own point of view. This attraction/repulsion dynamic linked with the dual desires inherent in the Soul will manifest in any natal house position of Pluto. Allow yourself to take a few moments to reflect on your own natal position of Pluto to see this principle operating in your own life. From an ultimate point of view, repulsion will automatically be a consequence of any desire and attraction to anything other than to return to the Source.

From a purely psychological point of view, Pluto correlates to the deepest emotional security patterns in all of us. These security patterns are unconscious. Most of us automatically gravitate to the path of least resistance. The patterns in identity association that are carried over from the evolutionary past are directly linked to the path of least resistance and, therefore, to our security needs at an unconscious level. The past represents familiarity and that which is known. Our lessons, or the evolutionary intent described by Pluto's polarity point are not known. They are the unknown, the uncharted. The unknown as described by our evolutionary intentions directly challenges that which is known or familiar, and therefore challenges our security at the deepest possible level: the Soul, our core. How many of us are aware of our security needs at an unconscious level? How many of us are aware of how these patterns and needs control or dictate our behavior? I think most of us would agree that many of us are not. If this is true, then how many clients are aware of these patterns? Again, not many. These deep-seated security needs drive us to approach certain areas in life in exactly the same way over and over again. These areas are specifically linked to the natal position of Pluto. If we remain stuck in the old way (the past) for security reasons, problems will arise in these areas because the Soul in each of us desires to grow and evolve.

The natal position of Pluto represents an area of natural gravitation for security reasons and is thus given tremendous power. Pluto implies a compelling force to maintain that area (house and sign) in the familiar ways of operating: the past. This compelling force can be called compulsion or obsession if the resistance (desire) is strong enough. The strength of the resistance determines the magnitude of problems or confrontations experienced in Pluto's natal house and sign position. Because the evolutionary force of the Soul is to grow, the individual will either experience cataclysmic growth (evolution) because of the problems experienced through resistance to the evolutionary intent or slow, yet progressive growth because of the relative non-resistance to the evolutionary intent. These areas of natural gravitation will be the stumbling blocks to the individual's development and growth. The intense degree of power and identification of Pluto (the Soul) is the cause of the problem. Because Pluto represents an essentially unconscious process, the individual is basically unaware of the motivational patterns of the Soul, and may feel stagnated, frustrated, or wonder why the same lessons, the same mistakes, the same kind of relationships, the same problems occur over and over again. Eventually the person may ask the question "Why am I here?", "What am I supposed to be doing?", and "What can I do about these things?" These questions are a natural response to the desire for ultimate identification with the Creator, although the individual may not recognize it as such.

At this point, the astrologer can indicate ways to help the individual become freer and more growth-oriented. Once the person becomes aware of the problems, motivations, needs, desires, attitudes and security issues dictating his or her experiences, the necessary changes may occur: if the individual desires to initiate them. Everything begins with desire. Again, the path to change rests in the polarity point of Pluto by house and sign. As change begins to occur there will be an automatic redefinition, evolution, and evolution in the natal house of Pluto. The individual will approach that area differently and will be reborn at a new level through death of the old behavioral patterns.

We can take these ideas about Pluto and apply them to anyone. Through observing and listening to the client, and analyzing the chart, we can determine the reality of that person as it exists for them. The ways in which we communicate or express these principles to another person are determined by the individual's level of understanding. It is extremely important to understand a person's evolutionary past. In the many years that I have been doing astrological charts I have observed that seventy-five to eighty percent of any individual's behavior is directly conditioned by the past. Even modern psychologists refer to 'unconscious forces' or 'memories' that influence the thoughts, feelings, moods and desires in our subjective consciousness. It is important to understand the past because it explains the here and now, why this kind of life, and for what reasons. It explains everything from the point of view of evolutionary necessity and karmic causes. Why this parent, this lover, this experience, why these conditions in my life, and so forth. By understanding that we are in charge of that which we have been, are, and are in the process of becoming, we have choices at every step, and at every moment, in our lives. The choices are reflected in our desires, and desire determines everything that occurs, individually and collectively. By understanding life in this way, we can more thoroughly understand the 'lessons' that we must learn. We can understand the 'why' of those lessons, and by so doing, create a willingness to accept, not resist, these lessons because of the knowledge gained about the past causes. If you are a student of astrology these ideas can lead to the objective understanding of these issues in your own life. If you are an astrological counselor, then you may be able to use these ideas on your client's behalf.

Why is it a common experience to have a difficult time during the first Saturn return? The first twenty-eight to thirty years of life is spent living out the conditions represented by the evolutionary and karmic past. As the Saturn return approaches, the individual commonly begins to feel restricted, frustrated, or depressed by the reality or conditions of his or her life. The Saturn return is a natural growth period that is a condensed reflection upon the past and, therefore, accelerated because of the new evolutionary cycle that is in the process of emerging. As Saturn comes closer and closer to its natal position, the individual experiences two simultaneous states: a sense of restriction, frustration and depression based upon the old conditions (karmic heredity), but also the emerging instinctive sense of needing to redefine and recreate the life conditions. In other words, the past and future (the evolutionary intent of the Soul) begins to collide in each moment of the individual's life. As the evolutionary forces converge upon the existing reality (security) that is defined by the past (Pluto), the individual is presented with extremely important choices that will determine the experiences of the next twenty-eight years.

Of course there are other planetary cycles that influence this natural evolutionary process. Saturn has a natural seven-year cycle within the complete twenty-eight year cycle. Jupiter has a twelve-year cycle of growth and expansion. The nodal axis of the Moon has a natural eighteen-year cycle, Uranus forms a square to itself at twenty one years of age, an opposition between thirty-nine and forty-two, another square at sixty-three, and returns at approximately eighty-four years. Neptune forms a square to itself at forty-two years of age. Depending on its elliptical path, Pluto can also form a square to itself during the life of an individual. During these natural cycles the evolutionary forces relative to the future are accelerated relative to the conditions represented by the past. Those evolutionary forces represented by the past define the total reality of the moment both individually and collectively.

Creation is in a continual process of birth, death and rebirth. We can observe this natural evolutionary process all around us: from the changing seasons to the solar system and universe beyond. So it should not be so surprising to consider that all of us are part of this process. To understand the past is to understand the moment. This understanding allows for positive choices relative to our individual and collective futures. We can help ourselves, and we can help humanity and the Earth in doing so. The natural cycles of evolutionary acceleration allow for maximum growth opportunities. If those opportunities are resisted because of the cumulative forces of the past, then the potential for cataclysmic phenomena exists.

Pluto and the Nodal Axis

Most astrologers have learned that the South Node of the Moon represents a composite of issues, i.e. value systems, beliefs, needs and so forth from the past that are relied upon or gravitated to in this life. We have also learned that the North Node of the Moon represents lessons to be learned in this life. A few professional astrologers insist that this correlation is wrong, that the North Node is the past and the South Node the future. Despite the insistence of these few, historical observations over centuries validate the correlation of the South Node with the past and the North Node with the future. Based on my own observations over many years, and reading thousands of charts, history seems to be correct. Meditate on these symbols in your own chart, and then reflect on your own life, and I think this correlation will be born out. The relationship between the North and South Nodes and Pluto is very important. We have correlated Pluto to desires based on evolutionary factors. The natal position of Pluto describes the preexisting patterns in identity association that the individual naturally gravitates to in this life. The South Node describes, from a prior life point of view, the mode of operation that allowed the individual to actualize or fulfill the desires or intentions described in the natal position of Pluto.

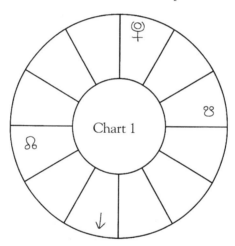

Chart 1

A simple example using the 9th house Pluto discussed earlier will illustrate this point (see chart 1). Let's put the South Node in the 7th house. The individual's desire to understand his or her life in a larger cosmological context would be the essence of the life. With the South Node in the 7th house, how would we expect the person to actualize or fulfill that desire? From a prior life point of view, the mode of operation would have led to the initiation of many kinds of relationships through which the individual was seeking the knowledge implied by the 9th house Pluto. Relationships would typically be formed with others who could serve as 'teachers' to the individual. These prior patterns imply a dependency on that kind of orientation coming into this life. Thus, the person would tend to draw, through relationships, others to them who would attempt to convince or convert that person to their points of view. In this way, the individual would have collected a variety of teachings from a variety of people. Which one is right, which one wrong? Is one more right than the other? Are they all wrong?

These are questions this person might now be asking. In this case the North Node, the mode of operation, would be in the 1st house, and Pluto's polarity point in the 3rd house. What are the evolutionary lessons here? Simply stated, the individual would acknowledge the relativity of varying points of view, yet by using the mode of operation symbolized by the 1st house North Node, learn to develop his or her own voice, own identity, own vision, own knowledge, and would learn to ask and answer questions from within the self. This transformation would then progressively, yet totally, change the approach and orientation to relationships. Rather than depending on teacher-type relationships, they would subconsciously want to become the teacher. Further down the road the individual would desire a situation of equality in a relationship. Both partners would then be simultaneously student and teacher to each other by encouraging mutual independence in each.

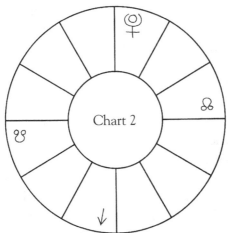

Let's take the same 9th house Pluto and put the South Node in the 1st house (see chart 2). The polarity point of Pluto remains in the 3rd house. The mode of operation to actualize or fulfill the evolutionary intent of Pluto is the 7th house North Node. The bottom line is still the 9th house

Pluto and the desire for the individual to understand him/herself in a larger cosmological context. From a prior-life point of view, the individual fulfilled that desire by maintaining independence and freedom from involvement in relationships in order to initiate whatever experiences that he or she deemed necessary in order to fulfill the desire for cosmological knowledge. The individual was dependent only upon the self. They would come into this life with the ability to ask and answer his or her own questions. It is from exactly this orientation that the evolutionary limitations and intentions are reflected. Yes, the individual is learning the lessons of intellectual and philosophical beliefs symbolized by the 3rd house polarity point of the 9th house Pluto. Yes, the individual is destined to experience intellectual or philosophical confrontations with others in order for this lesson to occur. How will this lesson occur specifically?

Through the 7th house North Node. The Soul of this individual would desire and need to be in relationships in this life. The individual will also be required to give to others, and must learn how to listen to other people in order to understand and identify another's reality as it exists for them. In this way they will be giving to another what is needed from the other's point of view (North Node in Seventh, polarity point of Pluto in the 3rd house) versus giving to others from the individual's own reality (South Node in the 1st, 9th house Pluto). Commonly this individual, when disposed to be involved with people at all from a prior-life point of view, would have been the teacher. They would have needed to be perceived by others as a leader, as special, because of the knowledge that the individual presents (9th house Pluto, South Node in the 1st). Because Pluto's 3rd house polarity point will lead to philosophical or intellectual confrontation in order to expose the limitations of the individual's own belief structure, the 7th house North Node creates a mode of operation through which the individual will also be taught by other key individuals on a cyclical basis throughout life.

Gradually, through confrontations, the individual will learn that he or she can learn from others. In addition, the individual will come to realize that he or she must learn how to be in relationships as an equal, that relationships are essential to his or her evolutionary growth. With this understanding, the individual will also realize, just as the person with the South Node in the 7th house did, that equality will occur through encouraging the independent self-actualization of the partner. The South and North Nodes thus correlate to the modes of operation that help the individual fulfill the evolutionary necessities and desires. The 9th house Pluto was used in both examples. Yet the modes of operation, past and present, needed to fulfill those 9th house desires were diametrically opposed. This principle can be applied to all combinations of Pluto and the nodal axis.

The next principle that we need to consider is this: What signs and houses do the planetary rulers of the South and North Node occupy? The planetary rulers of the nodes are the planets that 'rule' the sign that each node is in, i.e. with the South Node in Libra the ruler would be Venus. The house and sign position of each planetary ruler of the nodes act as facilitators that the individual has either used to develop the mode of operation from in the past or to develop the mode of operation relative to the evolutionary intent in this life. An example (see chart 3): The 9th house Pluto in Leo. South Node in Gemini in the 7th house. The ruler of Gemini, Mercury, is in Pisces in the 4th house. The North Node is in Sagittarius in the 1st house. The ruler of Sagittarius, Jupiter, is in Scorpio in the 12th house. Keeping in mind what has already been said about Pluto in the 9th house relative to the South Node in the 7th, how would Mercury in Pisces facilitate the mode of operation implied in the 7th house South Node in Gemini?

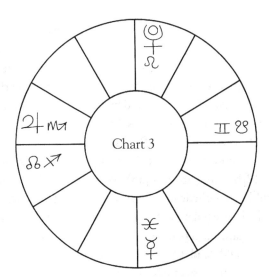

Chart 3

It would imply that the individual's 'teachers' were his or her parents in the early environment, and that the individual was extremely sensitive or impressionable to the impact of the parents' belief systems. For self-consistency and security reasons (4th house relative to the 9th house

Pluto) the individual may have drawn partners (7th house) who reflected the parents' belief system: Mercury in Pisces. The individual did not know what else to believe or how to think independently, so he or she took on the parents' beliefs because they reflected the individual's own desire to understand him/herself in a cosmological context. The individual may in turn pass along these teachings to his or her own children. With the South Node in Gemini, the individual will normally have a tremendous thirst for different ideas and experiences. Yet, in this case, the 9th house Pluto could have created a situation in which the individual denied the relevancy or legitimacy of any other point of view but his or her own, these being an extension of the parents' views, and later on, a partner's or mate's beliefs. The threat of other points of view would undermine the security structures and self-image: 4th house Mercury in Pisces. Yet, with the South Node in Gemini in the 7th house, the individual would naturally attract others who did have other points of view. So although the individual would attempt denial, he or she would take in this information on a subconscious level. There would be an awareness of something more than the beliefs taken on from the parents and mate. This awareness, from the prior-life point of view, 'sets up' this life.

The North Node is in the 1st house in Sagittarius, the polarity point of Pluto is in the 3rd house. The planet ruling the North Node is in Scorpio in the 12th house. Simply stated, the individual in this life would most likely choose parents who attempted to lay their beliefs upon the child. The child progressively would feel suffocated by those beliefs, and would not feel that the parents truly understood their individual needs. The child would progressively withdraw (Mercury in Pisces) into him/herself in order to begin the lesson of independence (North Node in the 1st house in Sagittarius, Jupiter in the 12th house in Scorpio). By emotionally withdrawing, the individual would also be learning internal security (Mercury in 4th house Pisces through 1st house polarity of North Node in Sagittarius). Progressively, as the individual matured, a personal vision, voice and independence would develop which would lead to an evolutionary consequence that would allow the individual to answer and ask his or her own questions. Through philosophical or intellectual confrontation (initially with the parents) the person would not only learn the relativity of beliefs, but also, through meditation (Jupiter in Scorpio in the 12th house), would learn the essential unity of all cosmological, metaphysical or religious systems.

The 12th house Jupiter in Scorpio would progressively dissolve all the old barriers separating one system from another showing the essential unity of all of them. With the North Node in Sagittarius, South Node in Gemini, the individual would see and experience this truth everywhere. The person would also commit to one system that he or she felt most drawn too intuitively because of a natural resonance with it. With Jupiter in Scorpio in the 12th house, this system would have to be experienced. It would have to offer techniques and methods through which the individual could directly experience the truth of the conceptual framework being utilized by the metaphysical/spiritual system. In this way the individual would learn to discriminate true teachings and teachers from false teachings and teachers: truth or revelation versus delusion or fiction. The individual would learn how to relate with others (South Node in Gemini, Pluto polarity point in the 3rd house) at whatever level of reality they were coming from and would give to them that which they needed.

The individual would be in a partnership that was equal and that encouraged freedom and independence, yet valued commitment. This transformed individual would now encourage independence and respect the individuality of his or her own children. These basic principles correlating the natal position of Pluto with its polarity point the North and South Nodes as modes of operation, the planetary rulers of the Nodes as facilitators to the modes of operation, all constitute the main karmic/evolutionary dynamic in the birth chart This dynamic will serve as the bottom line, the foundation that gives meaning to every other factor in the birth chart. Every other factor in the chart can be related to this dynamic and given new meaning relative to their contributing evolutionary roles implied in this main evolutionary/karmic dynamic.

Pluto in Aspect to the Nodal Axis

When we find Pluto in direct aspect to the nodal axis of the Moon in the birth chart (see chart 4), specific and unique evolutionary and karmic factors exist. The nature of the aspect determines what those factors are. Pluto conjunct the South Node indicates one of three possible conditions.

1. The individual is in an evolutionary and karmic reliving condition because of a failure to deal with, or resolve successfully, the issues described by the house and sign that Pluto and the South Node fall in. The planetary ruler of the South Node, by sign and house position, supplies an additional information concerning this issue and necessity.

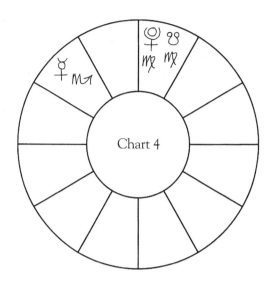

Chart 4

2. The individual is in an evolutionary and karmic fruition condition. In the past so much effort has been put into the area in question, and with such pure intentions, that the individual is reaping that which was sown before. The individual has some kind of special 'destiny' to fulfill. Look to the planet ruling the South Node, its sign and house locality, to supply additional information concerning this condition.

3. The individual is in a simultaneous evolutionary and karmic condition in which certain conditions from the past must be relived while other conditions are in a fruition state. The house and sign positions of Pluto and the South Node will describe these issues and conditions. Check the locality, by sign and house, of the planet ruling the South Node for additional information.

The first two conditions are rare. The third condition is the most common when Pluto is conjunct the South Node. How can we know which condition exists for that individual? In general, I would suggest you use the traditional astrological approach; observe or ask questions about the individual's life. This technique will allow for a rather quick understanding as to what conditions exists. It can be difficult to understand what condition exists for the individual by simply looking at the birth chart alone.

If you wish to ask questions about the individual's life, then these questions should revolve around the areas and experiences suggested by the polarity point of Pluto and the North Node. If you know the individual, then your observations as to what condition exists should also revolve around these dynamics.

If there seems to be a total blockage from being able to realize these polarity points, then condition one exists. If there seems to be something unique and special about the individual's life relative to the experiences and area (house) that the Pluto/South Node symbol is in, then condition two exists. If there are elements of both, then condition three exists.

On the other hand there are conditions in the birth chart that can help us understand the probability of karmic conditions. In general, non-stressful aspects to Pluto tend to indicate a fruition condition. Stressful aspects tend to indicate a relive condition. A combination of both kinds of aspects tends to indicate a dual condition. The non-stressful aspects formed by other planets would indicate, by sign and house locality, those conditions in a state of fruition. The stressful aspects formed by other planets would indicate, by sign and house locality, those dynamics in a relive condition.

In addition to the above, there are other contributing factors and principles to consider when Pluto is conjunct the South Node. In all three conditions, unless there are mitigating factors, the individual will be blocked from being able to realize fully the evolutionary issues described by the North Node until the second Saturn return. As stated earlier, the first Saturn return symbolizes the normal time cycle in which we fulfill, or live out the evolutionary and karmic conditions of the past. The mitigating factors that can reduce the amount of time spent fulfilling these past conditions are: (1) planets conjunct the North Node, or (2) planets in some kind of aspect to the North Node. With a planet or planets conjuncting the North Node, a situation exists wherein that planet has directly acted to evolve the individual out of past conditions in the last few lifetimes, sometimes the life just before this one. The specific nature of the planet or planets describes how this was done. With a planet in any other kind of aspect to the North Node, a situation exists wherein it obliquely acted to evolve the individual out of past conditions in the last few lifetimes, sometimes the very last life before this one. The number of aspects to the North Node relatively determines the reduction of time spent in fulfilling past conditions.

If other planets are conjunct the South Node with Pluto, then those functions (planets) are not only directly linked to the past, but are subject to the three possible evolutionary/karmic conditions mentioned above. Apply these same principles to these planets to help determine their condition.

If the planetary ruler of the North Node is conjunct Pluto and the South Node, conditions pertaining to the past are intensified two-fold.

Check aspects to the North Node itself to determine the time necessary for fulfilling these past conditions. If a planet is square the nodal axis and Pluto, that planetary function (by sign and house position) is interwoven

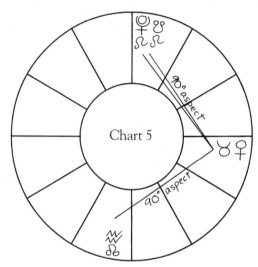

among issues of the past and future (see chart 5). The most common behavioral manifestation is a situation wherein the individual attempted to evade or escape those issues pertaining to the past. The evasion or escape was linked to the intense degree of conflict or tension that the individual experienced relative to the issues implied by the house and sign position of Pluto conjunct the South Node, and the house and sign position of the squaring planet. While avoiding the South Node problem, the individual attempted to solve problems related to the issues indicated by the house and sign position of the North Node. In so doing, the individual 'skipped steps'. The individual did not succeed in resolving the issues pertaining to the South Node and Pluto within the context of their house and sign positions.

In this life the individual must recover or relive those skipped steps. Only then will the full promise of the North Node be allowed full actualization. Until then the individual is torn in two simultaneous directions: at times manifesting behavior associated with the South Node and Pluto, and other times behavior associated with the North Node. The solution, again, is to fulfill those issues pertaining to the past within the context of the South

Node conjunct Pluto: then, and only then, will the promise of the North Node be realized.

In general, the number of aspects to the North Node will indicate the time necessary for fulfilling or reliving prior karmic conditions. In some cases this need is fulfilled at the time of the first Saturn return. This time factor is significantly decreased when the aspects are non-stressful in nature, for they imply a general understanding and partial resolution of these karmic issues in prior lives. A preponderance of stressful aspects tends to imply a lack of understanding or resolution of these karmic issues coming into this life. Thus, the time spent in reliving these conditions in this life is significantly increased relative to the first Saturn return. However, no hard and fast rules can be applied because this evolutionary and karmic analysis must take into account the natural evolutionary condition or station of the individual. In general, however, an individual's progression along the evolutionary scale will correlate to a decrease in the amount of time necessary for fulfilling prior karmic issues.

Pluto conjuncting the North Node indicates one evolutionary or karmic condition that applies to all charts. The individual has been working to transform the area represented by the house and sign locality of conjunction within the last few lifetimes, and is meant to continue in that direction. The results of the evolutionary transformation can create tremendous growth in this life. Every other contributing factor in the birth chart will be channeled or focused through the North Node conjunct Pluto. The principle of Pluto's polarity point does not apply in this particular condition.

However, there are mitigating factors that we need to consider. If a planet conjuncts or aspects the South Node, then the same three conditions under the discussion of Pluto conjunct the South Node can apply. Evaluate the stressful and non-stressful aspects to determine the probable condition of the planet. If that planet is in a fruition condition, then the specific nature of the planet, its sign and house location and the aspects to it from other planets, and their own house and sign locations, will contribute in a positive and integrated way toward the fulfillment of the evolutionary intent described by Pluto's conjunction to the North Node (see chart 6).

If a planet conjunct the South Node is in an apparent relive situation, then the specific nature of that planet, and the house and sign locality that it is in, will act as a conflicting force that to some degree blocks the individual's ability to fulfill the evolutionary impulse of Pluto's conjunction to the North Node (see chart 7).

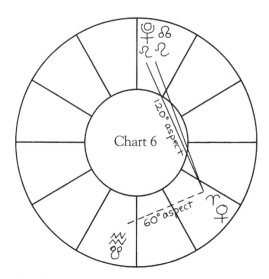

Example of a planet helping the development of Pluto conjunct
the North Node

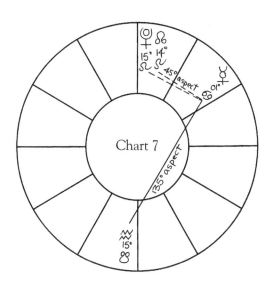

Example of a chart in 'relive' condition that in some way is blocking full
development of Pluto's conjunction to the North Node

The key to resolving this condition is for the individual to resist the desire or temptation to avoid this factor and its impact on his or her life. Instead, the individual should face those issues head on and integrate and resolve them in the context of Pluto's conjunction to the North Node. If there are planets in both conditions simultaneously, determine which planet forms non-stressful aspects to the South Node, and which form stressful aspects. The planets forming non-stressful aspects will contribute in a positive and integrated way to the fulfillment of the evolutionary intents described by Pluto's conjunction to the North Node, and the planets forming stressful aspects to the South Node must be faced head on and resolved within the context of Pluto's conjunction to the North Node.

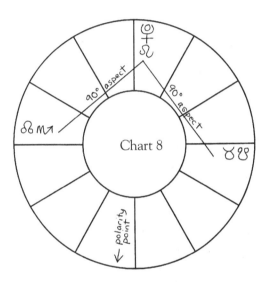

With Pluto square the nodal axis, the individual is in a unique evolutionary situation (see chart 8). The individual is equally torn between issues pertaining to the past and issues pertaining to the future. This division exists in each moment in the individual's life. This karmic/evolutionary condition indicates that the individual has neither succeeded in totally resolving or learning the issues pertaining to his or her evolutionary past (desires), nor the issues reflected through the North Node. Because Pluto is square both Nodes the issues pertaining to each have been acted upon prior to this life. Yet neither has been totally developed, understood, resolved, or integrated. The individual is upon an extremely important evolutionary threshold.

The choices that the individual makes relative to his or her desires are extremely critical, as they concern the evolutionary journey and progression. The individual is simultaneously attracted and repulsed by the issues, orientations and lessons of both Nodes. The issue of 'skipping steps' described before is magnified two-fold. The need to relive and resolve those skipped steps in order to integrate the issues with respect to the Nodes is magnified two-fold. The skipped steps apply in both areas. Until the individual consciously understands the lessons and how to approach and develop them, the behavior will alternately express the orientations implied by the South and North Nodes.

The polarity point of Pluto applies in this situation. This polarity point must be activated to begin the integration and resolution of this evolutionary condition. The mitigating factors to check for are these:

1. If Pluto applies to the South Node, then the polarity point of Pluto and planetary ruler, must be integrated through the South Node. The individual will have a consistent 'bottom line' upon which the evolutionary intentions described by Pluto's polarity point and the North Node and its planetary ruler, can be continually referred. Thus the South Node, and its planetary ruler, will transmute into new levels of expression.

2. When Pluto applies to the North Node, then the polarity point of Pluto and the South Node with its planetary ruler must be integrated through the North Node, with its ruling planet facilitating the process. In the same way, the individual will have a bottom line upon which the evolutionary intentions described by Pluto's polarity point, and the South Node and its planetary ruler, can be continually referred. The North Node, and its planetary ruler, can then evolve into new levels of expression.

In the case of other planets conjuncting or forming aspects to the nodal axis, apply the same techniques to determine their evolutionary condition. Determining the Node that Pluto is applying to will explain how to integrate and handle those issues. (See charts 9 and 10). In determining this keep in mind that the mean motion of the Nodes is retrograde. Thus the normal rules for determining what is applying to what are reversed. As an example, (see chart 9), let's say Pluto is in Leo at sixteen degrees, the South Node is in Taurus and North Node is in Scorpio at sixteen degrees respectively. Due to the retrograde motion of the Nodes, the North Node is moving toward Pluto. The South Node is moving away from Pluto. Thus the North Node is

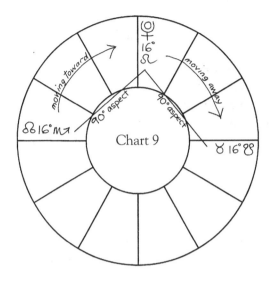

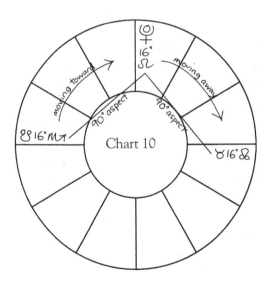

applying to Pluto and Pluto is applying to the South Node. In this example, then, the integration point would be the South Node. The Node that last formed a conjunction to Pluto is the Node that Pluto is applying to.

Planets in aspect to the Nodal axis

When planets aspect the nodal axis and Pluto has no direct aspect to the Nodes, then those planets have played a major role (by house, sign and aspect to other planetary functions) in shaping the kinds of experiences that the person has had for evolutionary and karmic reasons. The type of aspect determines how the individual responded to those experiences and will supply clues as to the probable evolutionary and karmic condition of those planets.

Pluto in Aspect to Other Planets

Any planet in aspect to Pluto indicates that those planets have been, and continue to be, subject to an intensified and accelerated evolutionary metamorphosis. The type of aspect determines the intensity of the evolutionary necessity to metamorphose that planetary (behavioral) function. The stressful aspects produce tremendous evolutionary intensity leading to cyclic cataclysms and restful states. The non-stressful aspects produce a non-cataclysmic evolutionary process of a relatively smooth yet continuous nature. When in the middle of a cataclysmic change, the individual will probably not understand why it is occurring. The 'why' will be understood, in most cases, after the change has occurred. The non-stressful aspects promote an understanding as to why the changes are occurring during the time frame that the changes are taking place.

The number of aspects Pluto forms to other planets determines the degree of evolutionary pace or change in any life. In other words, the number of aspects involving Pluto correlates with the intensity of the evolutionary state; how much they are trying to accomplish or work on in this life. The greater number of aspects, the more the individual is desiring to accelerate his or her evolutionary growth. This principle is clearly a relative phenomenon. Observe the lives of people who have many aspects to Pluto in their birth charts. Contrast this observation with those who do not. The lives of those who have more aspects will be characterized by more cyclic cataclysms than those who have fewer. The reason is that these individuals are desiring to confront, eliminate and transmute limitations, stagnations and the status quo at key junctures in their lives. This process is reflective of the desire to return to that which created the Soul.

Of course, the individual may not consciously identify this process as such. A few will understand it in this way, but most will not. Simply stated, the individual is desiring to get on with it. People with fewer aspects to Pluto are taking a break from the intensity of evolutionary and karmic necessities. It makes no difference whether these aspects are stressful or non-stressful in terms of the evolutionary process. On the other hand, the individual's ability to handle and understand this process is governed by the traditional attributes of the hard or soft aspects. The Sun in the birth chart represents how this evolutionary process is integrated and given meaning. The Moon represents how this purpose, meaning, and karmic/evolutionary conditions is applied and actualized on a daily basis. This symbolism should be clear when we consider Pluto to be the outermost planet in the solar system, and the Sun to be at the very center. Pluto represents the evolution of the Soul, and the changing natures of the personalities that it manifests. The Sun gives each new personality of the Soul a way to integrate and give meaning to its life. Since this drama is taking place on Earth, the Moon, because of its proximity to Earth, shows how the new purpose and lesson is applied on a daily, rhythmic basis. The Moon can be correlated to the ego, and on that basis, gives the personality a self image in order for it, the egocentric personality of the Soul, to feel secure, and to know itself.

The Three Reactions to the Evolutionary Impulse

People tend to react to their evolutionary necessities and karmic requirements in one of three ways. These three possible reactions determine how the evolutionary process will work in our lives. They are:

1. To resist the evolutionary/karmic requirements altogether.

2. To respond whole heartedly and desire to understand what the lessons are for this life and go for it in a totally non-resistant way.

3. To be willing to change in some ways, yet resist changing other dynamics because of fear of the unknown.

The first response is a reflection of the desire to maintain a separateness from the Source. The second response is a reflection of the desire to know the Source. The third response is a combination of both and is the most common choice. We change a little each lifetime. This is why evolution of the Soul, the progressive elimination of separating desires, is such a slow process for most.

The Four Ways Pluto Affects Evolution in our Lives

The four primary ways in which Pluto affects or instigates the evolutionary intent or process are:

1. By producing emotional shocks in which some behavioral pattern, or life situation, is forcefully removed from our lives. This process is associated with cataclysmic change and produces an evolutionary 'leap'. This situation always occurs when we have resisted the cumulative evolutionary forces to the extent that this effect must occur in order to enforce the required growth. A classic example is Nixon and the Watergate affair.

2. By forming a relationship to something we perceive that we need. This 'something' can be anything: a new friend, a new love, a body of knowledge contained in a book or seminar, the initiation of a new goal, and so forth. The point here is that by forming a relationship to something that symbolizes that which we think we need, an evolutionary process occurs. That which we think we need implies something that we do not already have. By forming a relationship to that 'something' we become that which we need. The psychological process involved here is one of osmosis: Pluto. By forming the relationship, we absorb into ourselves that which we need. A simple example of this process is this: You are now reading this book that you bought because it was relevant or sounded interesting to you. Perhaps the title piqued your curiosity. Maybe you thought you would learn something that you desired to learn. Beyond this book, astrology itself, as a subject, would have represented this to you. By forming a relationship to astrology or this book, through the process of osmosis, you nave learned something that you did not know before. By forming the relationship, your own personal limitations, your existing reality (self-definition, self-concept), were encountered. The relationships that we form in this way help us evolve, metamorphose, and grow beyond those existing limitation into new levels of awareness and self-definition. This process is associated with non-cataclysmic change: slow, progressive evolution.

3. By producing or creating situations in our lives in which we become aware of some external or internal source of stagnation or limitation

blocking further growth. This process is quite different than process number two, which involves no particular crisis. It is simple, yet steady, growth. The condition we are dealing with in process number three includes those cycles or times in which we become aware of some internal or external block preventing further growth, and need to find out the source of the block. This process implies a crisis in varying degrees of magnitude. The awareness of the block does not imply or mean that there is an awareness of the origin or source on which it is based. It is precisely this lack of awareness that induces the crisis. This process can have the effect of mobilizing our whole attention in order to focus on the block. This focus of attention can be so intense that everything else in our lives is excluded until we figure out the source of the block. This process is extremely similar to the dormant volcano that suddenly turns active. At some point an eruption will occur that has the effect of transforming the volcano and its surroundings. In the same way, the steady build up of pressure, and the singularity of conscious attention and focus, induces an eruption of the subconscious contents into our subjective consciousness. We become aware, through the knowledge produced during the eruption, of what the block is. As this occurs, we evolve because the source of the block has been removed. We proceed with our life in a new and transformed way because of this cataclysmic evolution.

4. By producing or creating a situation in which we become aware, of a new capacity or capability that has been latent or dormant. This process is triggered, at various points in our lives, through internal or external conditions that give birth to some new impulse, idea, thought, or desire. The process of actualizing or developing the new capacity creates an evolutionary or growth affect. A simple example: When President Carter became aware of his desire and perceived the capacity to be president when Pluto was transiting his 12th house Libra Sun. The process of fulfilling or actualizing that desire and capacity certainly produced growth and personal evolution for him. The process is associated with non-cataclysmic change but requires perseverance and will to actualize the perceived capability.

An important point is that these four processes do not necessarily occur as isolated or separate experiences. One process can trigger or lead to another. As an example, an individual may become aware of a latent capability or capacity at a certain juncture in his or her life. This awareness could then lead to the discovery of a block in a related area that may then lead to a crisis that forces the removal or metamorphosis of that block.

The three possible reactions to the evolutionary and karmic necessities described before are closely connected to these four ways that Pluto affects or instigates our evolutionary requirements. As an example consider an individual who has Pluto aspected to all the other planets and who reacts by resisting growth, change and the evolutionary requirements of his or her life. This reaction could clearly 'set up' the individual for the evolutionary process described in condition one: emotional shocks that lead to the forced removal of behavioral patterns or associations, and as a result, bringing about an evolutionary leap because of the forced removal. We all have choices to make in our lives. Those choices are reflected in our desires. Desires reflect our evolutionary state or condition, and the reasons for that state or condition. The responsibility for these conditions is our own. There are no 'victims'. President Nixon was not a victim. His life situation and experience reflected his own evolutionary condition, needs and lessons. The same is true for all of us. The assessment of an individual's general evolutionary condition and way of reacting to the evolutionary process must be correlated with the individual's socio/political context. This sociological consideration is important because environmental factors condition how we view ourselves and life in general. To better understand the karmic condition, we should determine why the individual chose the environment, and for what reasons.

2

The Leading Edge of the Soul's Evolution: The Mars and Pluto Interface

Jeffrey: This morning's lecture is called The Nature of Personal Evolution, and it is probably a pretty heavy topic to deal with this early in the morning. I don't know if I can deal with it! This topic is actually a spin-off on the Pluto material (*Pluto: The Evolutionary Journey of The Soul*), and we are going to make it quite specific to the planet Mars.

The first thing that we want to consider is the phenomenon of evolution itself. I think most of us would agree that through empirical observation we can notice that life seems to evolve. All forms of nature evolve including the human species. Is it not true that all of us, as a life experience, are in a continuous state of becoming? Is that not an experience that we all share? This seems to infer beyond debate the phenomenon of evolution. If we examine the nature of evolution we will in fact find that there are two types of evolution. There is Darwin's notion of uniformity, i.e. slow yet progressive change which does not of itself imply cataclysm; it is slow yet progressive.

Then there is the other kind of evolution which is cataclysmic. This is observed and experienced as earthquakes, volcanoes, political cataclysms, and individually as emotional shocks associated with loss, betrayal, etc. A quick example of this would be ex-president Nixon in the US and the Watergate Affair, which led to the specter of impeachment and the ultimate resignation by Nixon from the presidency. These are types of cataclysms. So the obvious question becomes: what is the casual factor of a cataclysmic event? Why would it occur? Why not just have non-cataclysmic evolution?

The clear answer is that cataclysmic evolution has two causal factors. Once cause is resistance to necessary change. Now why would one resist necessary change? The reason is that sometimes when changes are necessary they intrinsically threaten our existing state of security. The essence of security in most people is based on the need for self-consistency. So that when our self-consistency is challenged we tend to resist. The essence of self-consistency is familiarity: that which is already known. That which is familiar and known correlates with the past as the past continues to shape and define our present relative to the yet unknown future even though that future attempts to also define the present. Anytime an unknown challenges the known a dynamic state of stress occurs because the unknown causes a real sense of insecurity in most of us. As a result, we tend to resist the evolutionary forces that are reflected in the future because most of us do not want to feel insecure. Now my point is that if the event is necessary in order for the evolutionary factor in life to occur, then a cataclysmic event will occur in order to enforce the change. The nature and intensity of the cataclysm will be in direct proportion to the degree of resistance to the necessary change.

The other cause of cataclysmic events is karma. Karmic requirements. Let's try to remember that there are all kinds of karma. Most of us in this type of culture tend to think that karma is just an inherently negative thing, that karma is somehow always negative versus a positive thing. But the fact is that there are all kinds of karma. As an example, there can be the karma of disillusionment. The point here being that if you are living a certain period of years in your life and if you have created a reality that you have thought was true, and yet perhaps it is actually based on your own illusion, at some point in order to grow you will have to experience events associated with disillusionment. And this becomes a karmic/evolutionary requirement in order to become realigned with actual reality. Karma is simply the net results of prior actions, and it is the law of every action having a proportionate reaction. If I go out and kill somebody this very moment, I myself will be killed either in the next moment, two months from now, or in another life for example. If it occurs in another life, and I do not remember the life in which I was the one doing the killing, then you can imagine how I, and those close to me, would be shocked if I were killed for no apparent reason. It would seem cataclysmic.

So the next question becomes: What is the actual mechanism, at least linked with the human being, that creates and leads to growth, evolution? Of course this starts with the Soul. The Soul in astrology, at least in our astrology, correlates with Pluto. Most of us have learned that Mars is a lower octave of Pluto. Why is this? If we look at it very, very deeply we will find that within the Soul there is a dynamic that correlates with the evolutionary progression of the Soul. That dynamic is based on a dual desire nature within the Soul itself. One desire is to separate away from that which creates us; we can possibly call this God. And the other desire is to return to the Source of that which creates us. Of course these desires are inherently antithetical, and they go in diametrically different directions. This simple dynamic is the basis of what psychologists call free choice, or free will.

Anything that you desire, at least 90% of it, will translate inevitably into an action, an action based on desire. *The very nature of that desire determines karma.* It is that simple. The evolution of the Soul, then, is simply based on the progressive elimination of all separating desires to the exclusion of only one remaining desire, and that is the desire to reunite with the Source of the Soul itself. That is clearly going to take a long time for most of us. My point, by breaking it down to Mars, is that Mars simply acts instinctively upon the desires emanating from the Soul – Pluto. Mars, of itself, does not have conscious forethought. There is no pre-plan. It is simply instinctual action. An instinct means just that: without forethought, without conception. It is an impulse. A lower octave is a denser vibration of something else. In this case, a denser vibration of Pluto. Mars allows us to be conscious on a subjective, personality level of the desires emanating from the unconscious: the Soul.

Again, all of us are in a continuous state of becoming. A state of becoming simply means to act upon desires; grand ones and not so grand ones. The knowledge that we seek by way of Mars is gained through the reaction to the initiated action. It is very analogous to a baby touching a hot stove; the baby did not know the thing was hot until it touched it. The reaction to the initiated action thus produces knowledge. Similarly, we all carry on our lives in this way. We act upon desire in order to gain, through reaction, a progressive body of knowledge about ourselves, and the universe in which we live on an ongoing and continuous basis.

Let us remember that even though Mars as a planetary archetype embodies and reflects these desires emanating from Pluto, you are also going to have the sign Aries in your chart somewhere. You are going to have a sign on your Ascendant, i.e. the natural archetype of Mars and Aries. You are also going to have a planetary ruler ruling that Ascendant. All of these factors are probably forming aspects to other planetary energies and archetypes. My point in illustrating all of this is that the entire dynamic in total operates at once in your life in such a way that we instinctually act it out. To act upon the core desires emanating from Pluto thus correlates with personal evolution which is experienced on an ongoing and continuous basis.

The point is that the desires that emanate from Pluto by way of Mars, etc, more often than not correlate with the need to separate yourself from everything that you are not. By separating yourself from everything that you are not, this progressively gains to yourself everything about the distinctiveness and uniqueness of your existing personality, so much so that most people overly identify with their current personality and the egocentric structure which defines it. Most people, believe it or not, live in such a consciousness. For those who have studied esoteric and metaphysical things you may have come across the Vedantic notion of maya, i.e. the illusion of separateness. How many have had no familiarity with such a thought? Some of you? Well, guess what: it exists. What this means is that from an egocentric point of view many people feel that they are in fact quite distinct and separate from the cosmos or universe that they live within. This is typically linked with people who are living in a state of separateness. They can not see the interrelatedness of themselves to the rest of life around them: the over-identification with the ego.

How many are familiar with the word ego? How many know what it is? Here is a classic example of words that fly around in this kind of culture in which most people don't really know what it means. Most of you, especially those who have studied spiritual things, have probably been subjected to the thought that somehow to spiritualize you have to get rid of your ego. How many have heard such an insane consideration? Quite a few, eh!! The fact is that you can not do such a thing. If you look at the essence of the ego, its actual phenomenon, its actual structure, it is non-material in nature. It is not like you can open the brain and find an ego. You can't open the brain and find thought or ideas either, and yet they obviously exist. So what is an ego? An ego very simply is a vortex of energy, a concentrated vortex of energy. It is very analogous to the lens in a movie projector. You can have a movie projector with the film on the back reel, and a screen in front of the projector. But unless you have a lens in the projector you will have no defined images on the screen. Similarly, the ego in consciousness generates an image of self which correlates to this sense of individuality, this sense of separateness, personal identity, a necessary dynamic in consciousness which generates a distinct self-image of your current subjective identity. Even the great teachers of all time had to have an ego in order to be able to even utter their own names. So it is not a matter of getting rid of the ego, it is a matter of re-identifying the ego with a larger ego, and we can call that the ego of God. Water moving through the faucet, so to speak.

It can be illustrated this way. If I draw a wave on this blackboard which originates from the ocean most of us would agree that the wave has not generated itself. Most of us would probably see that of course the wave is emanating from the ocean. My point is that through the sheer law of physics the wave which is emanating from the ocean will have an upward momentum for a while. This upward momentum creates a natural resistance to returning to the sea in which it emanated. From the point of view of the wave, subjective egocentric identity, the appearance or illusion of separateness from the Ocean, God, can exist. Most egocentric beings get used to this momentum, become overly identified with it, and thus resist returning or identifying with the Source of that which created them. Yet, by the same law of physics, the wave must move, dissolve, back and into the ocean which created it. Similarly, the individualized ego must realign itself, identify itself, merge with the Source of itself: the immutable Soul which itself has been generated or created by the Ultimate Source – God. In the end, for most, this occurs at the time of physical death of the body.

The issue here is that when you look at the nature of evolutionary development, at some juncture for all human Souls this point is arrived at. This admittedly is a long journey for most people. Would it not seem clear that if my consciousness and sense of identity is centered in the ocean I can now simultaneously and consciously participate in my state of existence as a separate entity? Yes, but whose consciousness is defined by and linked to that which has created us? So I have a simultaneous experience, don't I? The deeper issue, for those who are concerned about emotional stability, is that if I am centered in the wave I can be buffeted this way and that by all the crosscurrents called life. This can create periodic states of clarity, confusion, feeling good, depression and the rest of it. On the other hand, if I am centered with the Ocean I can not be disturbed by anything, can I? I in fact am calm. Centered in the Soul. So the point of view taken, the interpretation made, the reaction based because of, are entirely different than if in fact I am centered in the ocean versus the wave. So the nature of personal evolution, in the last analysis, is based on this simple analogy. So this is what the nature of personal evolution is from life to life; in that at some point we arrive in the center of that ocean.

When we break this down to Mars and Pluto, you will have Pluto in a house somewhere, and it will be in a sign, and you will have Mars somewhere, and it will be in a house and sign. My point is that, again, these evolutionary desires are emanating from Pluto and become instinctively acted out through the Mars placement by house and sign. What this means is that if you look at where your Mars is – house, sign, and the potential aspects that it is making – this can now actually be linked to the leading edge, in every single moment, of your evolutionary development. The desires you are acting out, what types of desires, and the kinds of experiences they generate, and what kinds of reaction occur in order for you to learn from them. Now let us make an example. Let's put Pluto in Virgo in the 1st house, and Mars in Taurus in the 10th house. I would like some free flow here. I am tired of just being a lecturer, a completely boring role believe me. So if you have a core complex of desires symbolized by Pluto in Virgo with the 1st house, how are they going to be instinctively acted upon by way of Mars in Taurus in the 10th house? Who can make an analysis here?

Audience: Workaholic, driven by money.

Jeffrey: Let's make a very simple analysis. Let us agree that typically 1st house Pluto people instinctively feel that they have a special destiny to fulfill, something out of the ordinary, something other than just a mundane task. And let's say that this particular instinctual feeling is incredibly intense within their Soul which thus requires, at least cyclically, periods of independence and/or freedom in order to find out about this special destiny. This creates a subconscious fear – Pluto – of becoming overly involved with somebody else's need patterns, i.e. the polarity point of the 7th house. The need patterns of another are perceived – Pluto – as potential detours and/or weights that undermine this person's sense of special destiny. So you have an inbuilt emotional conflict right away between the need for independence and relationship: an emotional paradox. Let's say we just isolate on the simple desire for a special destiny, and how this desire instinctively manifests through the 10th house Mars in Taurus. How are these desires, by way of Pluto, going to be instinctively acted out through the egocentric personality of the incarnating entity? The pointer in now the 10th house and Mars and Taurus. What is a potential signature wherein this special destiny could be fulfilled?

Audience: They will want to be their own boss, to carve out a special role within society.

Jeffrey: So you are saying that these instinctive desires will manifest through their Mars function in such a way as to figure they have a special social role – 10th house – career/position to fulfill within society. OK, let's agree that that is a Mars in the 10th house statement. Now where does the Taurus come in? And the fact that Pluto is in Virgo? It means that the Mars in Taurus must learn how to identify inwardly its own intrinsic resources – Taurus; that which is already within them from birth, and once that identification is made then they can instinctively act upon those resources in order to define – 10th house – the specific form or role that reflects their sense of special destiny. In order for this identification of inner resources to occur the individual must cyclically withdraw from his or her external commitments, duties, and obligations. This type of withdrawal through the 10th house equals reflection and/or depression. Reflection or depression creates an inverted state of consciousness in which the person can focus upon, and become progressively aware of, the intrinsic resources that he or she possesses so that the evolution of the social role, career, that reflects the sense of special destiny can occur over time: the 10th house equals the phenomena of time and space: the finite. The problem now becomes, ultimately, Pluto in Virgo.

The structure of the Soul with Pluto in Virgo can be self-critical, too self-analytical, too aware of its imperfections, lacks, too aware of that which it is not, and by way of Mars in Taurus in the 10th house can unnecessarily compare itself to external authorities – 10th house – for which it would have an instinctive respect. This comparison reinforces the state of inner inferiority, generating the inner feeling and/or thought of never feeling quite ready and/or good enough to do what it instinctively senses that it could do, or become. The point is that this kind of self-critical, self-analytical focus within the Soul can generate crisis – Virgo; a crisis based on not actualizing into concrete form the sense of special destiny or purpose. Pluto in Virgo Souls have a compulsion to create crisis. One form of this crisis is self-denial, or self-undermining activity. Why is this?

The reason for this, in the largest possible sense, is that Pluto in Virgo focuses upon the archetype of atonement or perfection. This focus is based upon the evolutionary need to adjust or realign the egocentric structure of personality, to readjust how the ego is defined by linking it to ultimate principles, values, ultimate rights and wrongs, to what we call God itself: the polarity point of Virgo being Pisces. This Soul focus infers a deep sense of guilt based upon the ego acting out of itself, of overly identifying with itself: egocentricity. Thus to evolve from this egocentric focus the Soul creates a crisis of egocentric self-denial, or self-sacrifice, based upon the awareness of lack, imperfections, etc. The resulting crisis that is created produces, and is the source of, the compulsive self-analysis that is the signature of this generation; each person within the generation included. The dynamic of crisis linked with self-analysis thus produces self-knowledge. Is it not true that when we are in a crisis state that some degree of self-knowledge results as we attempt to figure out what the crisis is about, why it is happening, and to become aware of some sort of strategy to deal with it? And does it not seem that when a personal or collective crisis is occurring that 'larger forces' are operating that are beyond the control of the individual or collective ego? It is this sensing of larger forces – Pisces – that reflects the evolutionary need of Pluto in Virgo to identify with those forces in such a way that the individual or collective ego is in alignment with those forces. It is the Virgo/Pisces archetype that also correlates to masochism for the reasons just mentioned. There are two types of masochism. One type can be called religious masochism, and the other type can be termed psychopathologic masochism. In both types the core dynamic is to experience humiliation, self-sacrifice, annihilation, atonement, and the hoped for purification of the ego as a result of these orientations. The ultimate symbol or religious masochism is Christ on the Cross. The ultimate form of psychopathologic masochism is reflected in extreme sadomasochistic sexual acts.

Linking this to our example of Pluto in Virgo in the 1st house, and Mars in Taurus in the 10th house, we can now see where this sense of guilt/ atonement is occurring for the individual. We can see where the experience of crisis and self-denial could occur. We can see where and how, and for what reasons, the necessary realignment of ego must occur. In essence we would have a person at birth who would have unconscious guilt patterns based upon a misuse or misapplication of power and ambition linked with the Soul's desire for positions of social stature, and the means used to obtain these desired ends. Because there is a need to atone for this guilt coming into this life the individual would typically undermine itself from achieving these ends in this life until the necessary egocentric adjustments occurred.

Audience: The image that you are pointing out is that, in this case, Pluto has a generational effect which can be like the slow hand on the clock, and Mars is like the fast hand on the clock moving through the twelve different positions that are expressing the evolutionary impulse. Wouldn't that be a little bit general; that all people born in that large time frame who all have picked Pluto in Virgo to work out these same things? Or could you be more specific about that?

Jeffrey: To answer your question, it is true that all Pluto in Virgo people have this guilt, and a simultaneous need to atone for it. The reasons or causes of the guilt are specific to each person. As in this case that we are using as an example, with Mars in the 10th house, it is a guilt based on the misapplication of ambition via the desire for a special social role or work. This is my point. You can make it very specific by locating the planet Mars, in this case. Combined with Pluto in the 1st house this also creates a guilt based on not meeting others' needs, others' needs perceived to be undermining their own sense of individual purpose. Thus, a person who has placed career and social position above the needs of those closest to them. And beyond this, there are twelve houses, yes, but also twelve signs, and many possible aspect combinations that could occur relative to both Pluto and Mars, i.e. Pluto in Virgo in the 1st house in opposition to Venus in Pisces in the 7th house, or Mars in Taurus in the 10th house inconjunct Jupiter in Sagittarius in the 5th house, and so on. The various combinations/possibilities are almost endless. The point is by having these linkages through aspects you also have other dynamics that contribute to the very specific nature of the underlying archetype that would be true for all people with Pluto in Virgo, or Pluto in any sign or house.

Audience: The point I would just like to make is that I don't view Virgo, or Pluto in Virgo, necessarily as only a function of inferiority. It may be that those same individuals have come in, in fact, to bring an experience of the etheric Christ through Virgo which is another more positive experience of that which then leads to their Mars function for them to externalize that in what field of activity that they choose.

Jeffrey: First, I did not say that Virgo is *only* a function of inferiority. Second, your understanding of Christ may need to be examined. The fact is Jesus himself felt inferior: simply remember the words he himself spoke while hanging on the Cross: "Father, take this cup from me." What do these words suggest to you? They suggest a man who was not perfect, despite Christian revisionism to the contrary, a man who felt he was not totally equal to the task given to him by the Father. I would also suggest that as a generation the majority of such people are not manifesting the etheric Christ in a conscious, conceptual way. A very small percentage would be based on their own evolutionary development. I would say in a more pragmatic, realistic, and practical way that for the majority of the generation – because as we project into the future this generation will be in positions of social power maybe twenty years from now – this group of people will have a major role in the proper use of all kinds of technology in order to purify its application. They will also have an incredibly important role in health technologies, and medicine because the nature of the Earth upon which we live will become progressively more contaminated including the mutation of viruses and bacterias in which three or four will become life threatening to the species once they mutate and become airborne. In a de facto sense this might be the etheric Christ, but I would doubt that the majority would be conceptualizing themselves, at an egocentric level, in this way. And what about the millions of Souls who have Pluto in Virgo who live in other cultures that have no connection to Christianity, or Christ? You may wish to reexamine your question/statement, yes?

Another way of looking at this, using our own example of Pluto in Virgo, is that at the time that Christ was on the planet, whatever birth chart you might agree or disagree with, all charts will have Pluto in Virgo for him. Now he himself said that he was here to usher in a new age which is called the Piscean Age. So you see the polarity point for this generation, including himself as an individual within the generation, as Pisces. Is this coincidence or synchronicity? Or take the Pluto in Leo generation. Most of us would agree that somehow we are moving toward the Aquarian Age, or have already just moved into it. Progressively, the Pluto in Leo generation is going to have positions of social power as we already begin to see in our time. The polarity point for the generation is Aquarius. So, sure, we have this generational application, but we also have each person as an individual living in that generation: generations are comprised of individuals. Each individual has their individual framework within that generation in order to, as an individual, develop, to cooperate with and/or resist their own evolutionary requirements.

My point is that if every individual in their generation simply cooperated with their own individual lessons, then that generation would be in a state of harmony, and the evolutionary requirements of the planet would operate in a uniform way versus cataclysmic ways. But I think most of us would agree that most individuals do not consciously cooperate in total with their evolutionary requirements. The fact is that most people react to their evolutionary requirements in a very minimal way. We do a little bit each time. If you read metaphysics, this is why the story of incarnation seems to be so tragically long, i.e. the typical statement that we incarnate millions of times. This is because most of us do a little bit each time versus the whole ball of wax, so to speak.

Coming back to this example, can you now see through the illustration how this mechanism works? Pluto/Virgo/1st house and how it was manifested through the Mars in Taurus in the 10th house? Do you see this linkage? Was it clear to you? My point is that you can take this method and apply it to any chart. All of you are going to have Pluto in a house and sign somewhere, and it is going to have a generational and individual application. And you are going to have Mars somewhere; by house, sign, and aspects to other planets and the signs and houses that they are in. This is the leading edge of your own individual evolution on a day-to-day, minute-to-minute basis. How you by the way of Mars instinctively act out the evolutionary desires and requirements emanating from your Soul. The natal signature and requirements operate throughout life. The transiting movements of Mars, progressed planets forming aspects to natal Mars, Mars through progression forming aspects to other planets, and Pluto's movement through transits, and other planets forming aspects to Pluto through transits or progressions all correlate to the evolutionary development and requirements through Time in this life. These developments through time are referred to, and understood in the context of the intent reflected in the natal signature of Mars and Pluto.

Thanks for coming this early.

3

The Role of Mercury in Evolutionary Astrology

Jeffrey: The first way we are going to be talking about Mercury and its role in evolutionary astrology, and in our consciousness, may sound somewhat abstract We are going to be talking about the nature of consciousness, but then we will apply it specifically to birth charts, i.e. putting Mercury in various signs, houses, and aspects to make it as concrete as possible.

The very first thing to understand about the necessary role of Mercury is that it correlates in the human consciousness to the need to give order and linear structure to the nature of phenomenal reality. Now what this means is that what we call reality or creation of itself is phenomenal. In other words, this blackboard that is next to me does not call itself a blackboard. I do, you do. What this means is that the nature of existence is inherently phenomenal, simply the creation of appearances. Now for the human consciousness to feel secure, emotionally secure, it has to give names to all the phenomenal forms and images in order to create a linear structure of reality. One name, blackboard, connects to another name, floor, wall, room, building, parking lot, the city of Tukwila which we are now in, the Northwest, and, of course the planet, then the solar system, etc. My point is that of itself these things don't call themselves these names. We do. So Mercury provides this role of intellectually ordering the phenomenal nature of existence. Now we can ask the question: "How does it know what to call anything?" One of the reasons is to he able to communicate with each other through a consensus agreement of what is called what. If most people agree to call this phenomenal object a paper, instead of a sink, then there is a basis to communicate with each other. The bottom line is that we have, as part of consciousness, senses. Consciousness actually creates the phenomena of what you call senses: tactile, hearing, and so on. These are extensions of consciousness. In other words, if we approach a corpse, that is to say a physical body that is dead, it is no longer sensing. I can not walk up to a corpse and somehow put bread in its mouth and expect it to chew and/or taste the bread. There has to be consciousness to make that body sense, to be in motion. So what 1 am suggesting is that what we call senses are an extension of consciousness into the physical body. Now this is necessary because it is through the vehicles of senses that thought and perceptions are ignited in consciousness.

Now thought is a Mercury function. There are two types of thought. There is linear and rational thought, or what we could call deductive thought which is specifically linked with the left brain and Mercury. And there is intuitive thought, non-rational, non-linear, which is of course the right brain which correlates with Jupiter. My point is that based on sensory stimulus the very nature of this stimulus will actually induce or ignite thought. The bottom line is that that which is ignited, thought through senses, induces ideas: this is a blackboard next to me. Through senses I perceive form and function which allows for the idea to occur in consciousness. This very same mechanism, this dynamic, is that which ultimately orders all phenomenal reality. The point is that as we move through life, in any given life, we continue to have experience, meaning we continue to collect information and data from our external and internal environment. This ongoing collection of information and data continuously ignites more thought and perceptions which ultimately leads to the creation of whole thought, and how whole thoughts are ultimately connected to other thoughts to create an intellectual whole, an organized mental whole that generates our mental understanding of our experience called life.

These thoughts are of course linear and deductive by nature. The very essence of Mercury via the left brain correlates to deductive logic, not inductive logic. Deductive logic simply means one phenomenon linked to the very next phenomenon and so on to build a whole. An example would be analogous to taking a jigsaw puzzle out of a box and throwing it randomly on the floor. Of itself it is not now organized and yet has inherent organization within it. Sitting there it is a mess. As we begin to make connections (Mercury), i.e. this piece fits this piece, we enter into a deductive logic process in which we finally get the whole picture. All the parts finally are connected. This is a simple example of how Mercury works, and through the process of deductive logic we generate intellectual systems that help us organize as whole thoughts our experience of phenomenal reality. This is very important for those interested in human history for example. The very nature of thought/perceptions which are based on inner and external stimulus is the very basis of what we call language. The question is, since the human species happens to have been on the planet a whole long time all over the earth, why is there not just one language? We are all human beings, same species. Why not just one language? Why has there been this incredible diversity (Mercury) of language systems on the planet? Why? Anybody ever asked this question? Too boring to ponder? Very simply it reflects the evolutionary condition of the Soul, and is ultimately linked to the geographical locality of a people and the evolution taking place there. In other words, if you found yourself in aboriginal Australia, an aboriginal Soul, that is now living in the Outback of Australia, your experience of phenomenal reality in that type of organized ecosystem would he fundamentally different than if you found yourself in the late Renaissance of Western Europe.

The very nature of your perceptions and resultant thoughts would be different, and as a result your language would be different.

Audience: Where does invention come in, like say the light bulb? Before it existed there was no thought, no experience.

Jeffrey: Well, ultimately you are asking a Uranian question, and the basic issues here, and this is probably a matter of debate for some: can anything really be invented, or can it simply be attuned to and, thus, create the appearance of an invention. My point is that in my opinion all that is called Creation in totality, and in potential, was manifested at the same moment, and yet through the process of evolution, which is a non-debatable issue when linked with time and space, the evolutionary requirements of the species on any given planet determines that which it is attuned to in order to advance the development of the species at that time. So this to me is a Uranian principle, or what is called in the astrology books the 'higher mind'.

So the nature of language then is very important to understand. How many of you have studied different languages? For those that have studied different languages, is it not true that by absorbing yourself into the language framework that you are studying that it alters your perceptions of reality?

This is my point. Mercury provides this function, and it is totally based on the evolutionary requirements at hand. So language becomes a vehicle, obviously through which we communicate (Gemini, Mercury, Virgo) that which is the basis of our perceptions, the basis of our intellectual thought process. The very nature of communication itself is an ongoing learning experience. When you communicate with someone else more often than not you are going to hear something that you had not thought about.

That is why people talk in essence. And so here you are collecting yet more information. So it is an interesting process because as we generate experience of external phenomena stimulus it ignites internal stimulus manifesting as perceptions and thoughts; and vice versa which becomes perpetual. This is the essence of the learning process. Stimulus, again, is the very basis of thought and perceptions in consciousness. And consciousness evolves according to the requirements of time, space and geographic locality. Mercury thoughts are linked to perceptions and how we perceive, which in turn becomes the basis, as this progresses, of our intellectual framework. Rational, deductive, linear thought: sequential thought.

This is very different than Jupiter and the right brain. Again, the right brain is non-linear, non-deductive, non-rational. Jupiter's function is to provide an abstract or conceptual basis for that which we perceive and think about. If I find myself in aboriginal Australia and I am dealing with the nature of my phenomenal experience there, and I am generating language and perceptions and thought processes, at some point I am going to have to wonder, "What does this mean? What are the larger connections?". Right when I ask such a question this ignites the right brain. The point is that the right brain supplies conceptions or abstract principles to the linear and deductive thoughts of Mercury. This becomes the basis of what we call beliefs. The point is that Jupiter is the archetype in consciousness that makes us aware as a species, and as individuals, that we are connected to much more than just the immediacy of our physical environment; our eyes can perceive that there is a sky, stars, and planets around us. This gives rise to the larger questions of consciousness. How am I connected to this part of the universe, which becomes the basis of belief or religion or philosophy or metaphysics. All of us do this. If you examine the nature of civilizations East and West through time, you will find in every single one of them mythologies or religions that correlate to the individual's and the species' connection to the cosmos throughout time. This is a Jupiter function.

Now here comes the big issue. Who is right and who is wrong? Whose perceptions/beliefs are right? Whose are wrong? Are they all right, or are they all wrong? Are the exceptions/beliefs/ideas of Roman Catholicism somehow more relevant and right than the perceptions/thoughts and beliefs of a Tibetan Buddhist? Is my version right? Who is wrong? Who decides these things? The obvious issues – and here it comes – is that whatever your evolutionary condition is, i.e. what your Soul needs in each life to facilitate its ongoing growth, will determine the nature of your perceptions, which in turn determines the nature of your beliefs. If you have evolved and find yourself in a consensus state it simply means that your perceptions and ideas (opinions) are determined by your Soul's need to be in a consensus state, and as a result you will simply become a vicarious extension of the consensus beliefs of your particular culture. Do you understand this point? If, on the other hand, you are trying to be free from the consensus, to individuate and think for yourself, then your perceptions/thoughts and beliefs will simply equate to individuated thinking. Your thinking process will primarily be based on rejection and rebellion of consensus held beliefs as you seek to determine an intellectual/philosophical way of understanding the nature of your individuality as linked with the cosmos. If you find yourself in a spiritual state, which is very different than religion in the sense that religion is for the consensus, then you will ultimately realize that all perceptions, all beliefs, all paths lead to the same point of Creation. It is the ultimate Piscean symbol of unity in diversity.

This is a graphic point because if you will examine the nature of Mercury and Gemini you will find that it is connected in the natural zodiac to a mutable cross: 3rd/Gemini, 6th/Virgo, 9th/Sagittarius, and the 12th/Pisces. This mutable cross creates a natural state of dynamic tension within consciousness. Why is this and what does it represent, symbolize, in the area of consciousness? We have a natural conflict here between deductive and inductive logic. A natural conflict between singular and sectarian points of the view, and universal points of view which are not sectarian based. The tension of inductive and deductive logic is a quite dramatic issue, particularly in this type of culture. Most of you, at least in this room, have grown up in an educational system that places a premium on left brain, linear deductive processes. When you go to school you are basically asked to memorize what you are being taught, not the conceptual basis of what you are being taught. Most of you have been exposed to these systems in your early educational environments, and even in your parental environments, and have not found, as an example, meditation as part of the educational curriculum.

Audience: Why do you think that is? Do you think that the US and Canada are – I don't mean to generalize – in a lower evolutionary state than, say, the East?

Jeffrey: It is not a matter of judging at all. It is simply a matter of observing the phenomenon itself. Because when you break down the nature of existence by way of the human species, it ultimately comes down to each individual. I mean, why is it that the Soul decides to be born in the US versus Zaire or Tibet or New Caledonia? That reflects the individual Soul's requirements karmically and evolutionarily speaking. So to answer your question specifically, it was based on the developments of Renaissance Europe and the transference between natural science, which is based upon observation and correlation, to deductive and empirical science, i.e. the effort to prove empirically that which is perceived as phenomenal. So, whereas those of the East do the very same proving through the inner microscope so to speak, those of the West try to prove it through the external microscope. My point is that neither one is better or worse, it just is and, in fact, can be quite complementary to each other if one's philosophy is universal in nature versus sectarian and dogmatic. So you have this dynamic tension between deductive and inductive logic. The point here is that inductive logic, the very essence of the thing, is to grasp the whole first in such a way that the parts reveal themselves in their own natural order.

Whereas the deductive approach, again, attempts to build the whole out of the parts. In this type of culture this becomes a major conflict. Why? Because no matter what culture you find yourself in, East or West, you still have a right and left brain. You still have an intuition and deductive intellect. You still ponder and ask the big questions. You still have spontaneous realizations which are not products of deductive analysis. Yet, because you have been conditioned by this culture to empirically prove everything that you think that you know, this creates a conflict between the right and left brain. As a result many people in these types of cultures tend to doubt (Virgo, 6th house) what in fact they are intuiting (Jupiter, 9th house), and through the Pisces and the 12th house symbol confusion results. My point is that Pisces and the 12th house archetype linked with this type of issue will cyclically or perpetually dissolve any thought/perception/idea/opinion that is limiting the necessary growth of the Soul. How many here have not experienced intellectual confusion?

This is the experience of Pisces coming through Gemini, Virgo, and Sagittarius. Even if you find yourself right brain based and have these magnificent philosophical structures to explain yourself to yourself and others, if those belief systems or philosophic structures themselves are only a version of the whole truth then, at some point, those very happy beliefs will not be so happy any more. They won't work. The whole point of Pisces linked with this dynamic is ultimately to embrace the whole truth, not a version of it, not a limited understanding of it: all of it, Unity in diversity, all paths leading to the same point Now believe me, the left brain can not prove any of this. Of itself it is limited. So at some point in order for such a truth to be grasped there has to be a transference in consciousness from the left to right brains as your primary guide in your consciousness. That is to say, allowing Jupiter to lead Mercury, not Mercury leading Jupiter. Now when we link this with astrology you can put Mercury in various houses and signs and aspects. What is this going to tell us? If you have Mercury in Scorpio, or in Virgo, or in Pisces – amazing position for the thing – or Mercury in whatever sign, is this at all suggestive of what kinds of perceptions and thought processes you are going to have? Is it at all suggestive of how your intellect – left brain – is of itself naturally oriented to the phenomenal existence?

Is it suggestive of how you are going to intellectually put together and then communicate the nature of your phenomenal experience and existence? Is the Mercury in Scorpio going to be different than the Mercury function in Taurus? Are the very nature of its thoughts, how it arrives at those thoughts, how it puts together one thought with another thought, and how it communicates such thoughts, going to be different? And then the question becomes: why is it that your Soul would choose to have Mercury in whatever sign, in whatever house and with whatever aspects? Clearly the ultimate answer is to facilitate the very next step in your evolutionary development. If we look at it this way, is one Mercury in whatever sign better or worse than Mercury in another sign? Why judge it at all? Why not see it as necessary?

If we illustrate some of this stuff, if you find yourself with Mercury, say in Scorpio in the 1st house, what kinds of thoughts and perceptions do you feel such an individual may have? How are they going to be intellectually putting together their reality? How would you anticipate such an individual would communicate? Who has an idea here? Let me ask a rhetorical question first: do you think the person is going to be intellectually interested in superficial conversation? Do you think such a person would indiscriminately read any book? Why not? If you answer no – you are all shaking your heads – why not? Is it just possible that this signature is looking for very specialized information that reflects the general and overall sense of purpose in life? And is it also possible that by narrowing upon specialized information relative to the implied purpose, whatever that may be, that this narrowing could produce intellectual limitations that would be reflected through resistance to other sources or forms of information? If so, how would this impact on the individual's way of communicating, and how he or she listened to or received communicated information from other people?

Audience: I know an individual with Mercury in Scorpio in the 1st house and it would appear that his mental nature, the nature of his Mercury, penetrates down to the Soul level, always recapitulating knowledge and going deeper and deeper, stirring it up and transforming and evolving it.

Jeffrey: OK – Is it also possible for a Mercury in Scorpio individual to experience within itself, as a consequence external to itself, periodic limitations in its thought process; that they have reached some sort of limit?

Audience: By the nature of Scorpio going deeper and deeper, there would always be boundaries that had to be gone through and penetrated at deeper and deeper levels. One would assume that it would be a frustrating and liberating position. Frustration when they reached that boundary, and then liberating in terms of a great inductive breakthrough, i.e. Jupiter seeing the bigger picture, going to a deeper level.

Jeffrey: OK. It we put this very same Mercury in Scorpio in the 1st house it is like a de facto Mercury in Aries. Are we going to be looking for a person who is wanting to do independent thinking, to at least challenge (Aries archetype) the pre-existing opinions of many other people? Is it basically going to want to be a free thinker? If these are related archetypes, is it not going to have the ability (Mercury in Scorpio) to penetrate to the intellectual limitations or weak link in somebody else's argument? By being able to penetrate to somebody else's weak link, is it not in a de facto sense attempting to prove the worthiness in its own thought process? At minimum we would say such a person is an intense thinker looking for bottom line information that correlates to its life experience, and its requirements. Those very over-all life requirements are the determining or causal factor in the information that it selects to bring in. This is why it would have no tolerance for superficial, indiscriminate information. The Mercury in Scorpio within consciousness would instinctively operate in this way. If we contrast this Mercury with Mercury in Libra, and put the Mercury in Libra in the 11th house, now what kinds of thought processes, perceptions, communications, information gathering would we anticipate?

Audience: International mediator.

Jeffrey: Let's remember this very deep issue about Libra. You have to remember its natural polarity is Aries. In order for a Libra archetype to understand its individuality, i.e. the Libra/Aries polarity, it must initiate a diversity of relationships with a diversity of types, with a diversity of opinions, a diversity of value systems, and a diversity of belief patterns in order to evaluate its own individuality through comparison and contrast. If you have this as a Mercury function within the 11th house, have we not potentially magnified the potential volume of relationships and information necessary? In this initiation is it not possible for a Mercury in Libra person at some point to lose sight of its own individuality, what itself thinks, what its own mental process is, its own ideas and opinions? Is this not possible? If this occurs could we not anticipate the Mercury in Libra person running about trying to validate itself through the opinions of other people? "What do you think about this?" would be a typical Mercury in Libra statement. Could we not say in general terms that the Mercury in Libra person is intellectually oriented, is going to have a primary focus, to understand the nature of human dynamics and human relationships, and, more broadly, the inter-relationship of everything within Creation? And this being the very basis of its need to communicate and initiate with so many. Does this make logical sense to you?

What if you have Mercury in Pisces? Let us put it in the 3rd house, the natural Gemini house. If you have Mercury in its natural archetype, i.e. the 3rd house which is linear, sequential, deductive thinking and yet the very essence of Pisces is the antithesis of this archetype, is there not a natural internal conflict within this person's mental process? Is it not logically seen in this way? Is not the Mercury in Pisces of itself going to naturally think in metaphorical terms or parables or analogy: poetic? Our fellow friend Jesus had six planets in Pisces in the 3rd house. How did we experience his communication? Still trying to figure it out, eh? Pisces!

Audience: How do we know he had six planets in Pisces in the 3rd house?

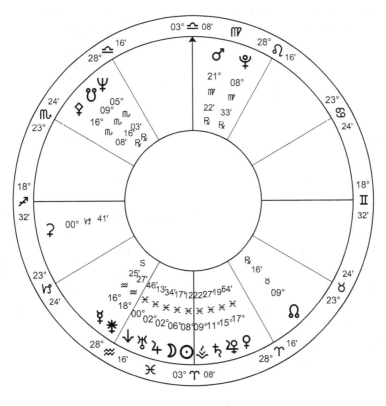

Jesus
1 Mar 0007 BC 01:47 LMT -2:20:48
Bethlehem 31N43 035E12
Geocentric, Porphyry house system

Jeffrey: It was a chart rectified by a theologian named Moby Dick. Funny name. His real name was Donald Jacobs. He is the father of Jayj Jacobs. He bases it on the Bible and rectifying. I mean, he was a theologian so he studied Biblical history obviously. Of course there are many charts created for Jesus by astrologers, but you know if you study Biblical themes yourself and read what he researched it would in all probability make intuitive sense to you. As an example: all those Pisces planets in the 3rd house are opposed by Pluto and Mars retrograde in Virgo within the 9th house. Is that possibly a symbol for crucifixion based on beliefs? It has Mercury in Aquarius: the unexpected message. It has the South Node in Scorpio conjunct Neptune – the son of God. Sagittarius rising – all the traveling that he did in his early life, let alone within Judea itself. And why is it that so many of his analogies are linked with fish and fishing; the 'miracle' of walking on water; the emphasis on healing, and the one God which is the essence of all gods and goddesses which were so prevalent in those pantheistic times. My point is that here is a man who clearly spoke in parable, metaphor, and analogy. It is one of the very reasons that Christians have been confused ever since. It becomes the breeding ground of sectarian points of view. This is the problem with Mercury in Pisces, that the Mercury part of this individual can sense, perceive, much larger wholes, much larger frames of reference than the Mercury function itself can logically order. As a result it must speak in metaphor, parable, allusion; to allude to something much larger, higher and grander.

This of course is problematic for many people who find themselves in modern societies. How many current modern societies in the West honor such an intellectual function? What happens to such a person when they are exposed to public education in 1989 in America? So typically this particular symbol learns (Mercury) to adopt (mutable archetype) the language systems of the culture that it is exposed to. Therein lies the origin of the conflict. Do you understand? We can also link Mercury to various planetary aspects as conditioning this function. As an example, what if we had somebody with Mercury inconjunct Uranus? What kind of thinking process, perceptual process, intellectual organization process, and communication process would we anticipate in such an individual? Let us remember that the essence of the Uranian archetype is to liberate from any pre-existing condition which is limiting growth, and as a result sets up the need to rebel. Let us agree, if we can accept any form of metaphysics, that Uranus at this level can correlate with the Universal Mind, the archetype that has been in place since the beginning, the blueprint which we only have to attune ourselves to somewhat like the radio dial. The signal exists. You just have to tune into it.

Audience: That linear thought becomes non-linear on occasion.

Jeffrey: Let me ask a rhetorical question now. Is it not possible in that person's consciousness that their radio dial, i.e. their inner Mercury process, is attuned to a signal (Uranus) that they find great difficulty (inconjunct) in finding the specific words (Mercury) to communicate through?

Audience: Would you then say that the individual is unable to explain the notions and concepts that he or she has of the greater?

Jeffrey: Yes, he or she would find very deep difficulty in finding the specific language or word sequence.

Audience: That Mercury by its nature moves an individual toward liberation and so in that moving toward liberation you have a rhythm and a build-up, and then every once in a while it will trip, you know, spontaneous Uranus, and it will get like a spark, liberation. Then, it is like a radio tuning out as soon as it gets strongest.

Jeffrey: That is right because one of the very deepest experiences of an inconjunct is inadequacy; less than perfect. So if you have got this mental process that is attuned to something higher than itself, and it is now trying to find a word to explain it, it is simultaneously aware of its inadequacy. This creates frustration in the communication. It can paralyze the individuals' mental process. This is analogous to the centipede that has a thousand legs. The thing is fine as long as it keeps walking, but as soon as it tries to figure out how, say, leg 46 works, it is over: paralyzed. So the whole challenge of the Uranus/Mercury inconjunct is to speak as it comes, not to (inconjunct) analyze as it is coming. If that happens you have leg 46 in operation.

Even if you look at it at a brain level, you know, Uranus happens to correlate with dendrites in the brain. Dendrites are responsible for the evolution of the brain. It also correlates with synapses and all the wiring of the brain as does Mercury. Well, if you have Uranus linked with Mercury it is like 10,000 watts coming through a 5 watt bulb. It tends to blow itself out. It can create a tremendous excitation in the brain. When you see that particular signature all that you have to read yourself is that that is a Soul that is planning to rapidly evolve its brain in this life, to create all kinds of new dendrites, all kinds of new realizations. Any time you have an 'aha', or a new realization, or a new thought you have never had that spontaneously occurs, that is a dendrite being made in your brain. You are experiencing within yourself Uranus. And, of course Mercury kicks in and tries to find the linear word sequence, logical sequence, to explain what it just spontaneously got. That is when frustration can occur.

These are typically people who have obviously unique and original thoughts. Yet those very thoughts can be so far ahead of their time (Uranus) that it creates crisis (inconjunct) with many others who attempt to hear it, or listen to it. Keeping in mind that Mercury correlates with the anatomy of hearing. It can overload the nerves that allow us to hear. People tend to – Mercury – tune out or externally rebel against this person's communications. Why? They are challenging the existing status quo of mental consensus; thus the emotional security dynamic in consensus type people. Guess who had Uranus in the 3rd house Retrograde in Virgo? That's right: Einstein. Most of us remember the little slogan he made for us: when genius interfaces with mediocre minds you should expect violent opposition. The essence of this interface is resistance because of the challenge to the existing status quo mind-set.

Audience: Immanuel Velikovsky had Mercury conjunct Uranus, and he came out with his book way ahead of his time, and was ostracized by the scientific community as a result.

Jeffrey: That is very true. In fact if we carry that particular example forward he postulated, based on his theories in the 1950s, that if his theories were right they would find a certain type of climate on Venus. This was before they sent any spaceship up to Venus. At that time the prevailing scientific community had a completely and altogether opposite view of what that atmosphere would be. Of course he was roundly criticized, blackballed from university speaking and so on for 20 odd years. And then when they sent the space probe up to Venus guess who was right? So now he is revered. His ideas were ahead of their time.

The last thing to grasp is that we are going to have transits of Mercury. Also we are going to have a sign on the 3rd house cusp, and it is going to be ruled by a planet which also then directly correlates to this mental function of organizing the phenomenal nature of reality. There will be a sign on the 6th house, and a planetary ruler which will correlate with the analytical function of rational intellect. There will be a sign on the 9th house, and its planetary ruler, and, of course, a sign on the 12th house with its planetary ruler which all contribute to this left brain/right brain function of consciousness in a total sense: from ideas and perceptions to a philosophical belief system dynamic that allows any individual to understand the nature of his or her existence. And yes, we must consider the specific nature of the houses and signs that Jupiter, Mercury and Neptune manifest through. This may sound like a lot to understand, but this total dynamic is the basis of understanding how all of these signatures, these planets are always transiting through the birth chart all the time. If you just key in on those particular transits, and particularly Mercury since that is what we have focused on today, you will find exactly where you are seeking new information at any point in time, and how this new information either supports or conflicts, obliquely or directly, your pre-existing intellectual apparatus, your pre-existing opinions, your pre-existing beliefs at all times.

If you have a transiting Mercury moving through the 3rd house for example, what would be a simple analysis here? Is it not a simple statement that that person's consciousness is looking for new ways to understand the nature of their life at that point? And that the sign that it is transiting through will determine the quality and type of that information? Let's say you have Cancer on your 3rd house and let us assume that maybe you have had some difficulties in your biological family. Now let's say that the transit of Mercury moving through the 3rd house correlates to a period of time in which the person naturally reflects on that early environmental experience, and as a result seeks new ways of understanding (Mercury) that experience in his or her life. Is it not possibly a time in which the person may attempt to initiate conversation with those parents, maybe a time in which a new book on the psychological dynamics between children and parents was read, or maybe going to a seminar, workshop or class for this purpose?

Audience: I see the impulse to gather more information and churn it around to communicate more, but isn't that focus of understanding going to be based upon a Jupiter transit?

Jeffrey: The connection to a larger understanding would be. The collection of information is Mercury.

Audience: In the case of a Mercury transit as to the 3rd house or anywhere else, is there really any desire for understanding attached to it?

Jeffrey: Of course. I mean that is the very nature of going back to where we started. Why would I call this a blackboard? For me to feel secure I have to intellectually organize my reality, to give it names. Then later on Jupiter kicks in and simultaneously links it with abstract concepts and beliefs. Another example: what if we transit Mercury in Scorpio through the 12th house. What would we anticipate? And let us say that it is going to be there at least a month. And what would happen if it went retrograde there?

Audience: Intellectual chaos, but eventual transformation. That could be a tremendously evolutionary leap depending on how you dealt with it. If you go inward it would kind of be like a sifting through, a travel through space, but eventually when the transit leaves then the person is going to come back out having better knowledge.

Jeffrey: Yes, but it presumes that the person allows for a metamorphosis of pre-existing intellectual structures that are limited to be dissolved. If there is an allowance of that dissolution then it can translate into inspiration, new inspired thought. On the other hand, the person may experience within him/herself all kinds of thought demons in their consciousness which they can not trace the origin of. They might at that point feel like they are a prisoner (12th house) of their own mind. Or, depending on how it is handled, it might be a time frame in which the individual attracts to him/herself people, based on their own inner need, who have all kinds of highfalutin 12th house way of explaining reality (Mercury) that now confronts the person's existing intellectual structure. Of course, in typically Scorpio language, the person may say "Why is this happening?"

How many of you have Mercury retrograde in your chart? Some of you probably do and don't know it. How many have a retrograde planet forming an aspect to your Mercury, your Mercury itself not being retrograde? Almost all of you now have Mercury retrograde! These are called oblique retrogrades. Now when you have Mercury retrograde at birth just think of the retrogrades as an arrow, an arrow that is pointing to Jupiter. In other words, it is attempting, through its left brain function, to make it 'non-rational'. Evolutionary speaking, this particular symbol means to intellectually/ philosophically simplify. It means evolutionary that there have probably been some prior lives in which the person has not been intellectually discriminate, and has collected at random too much information and data to the point where the intellect has been overwhelmed and confused. As a result the individual comes into life into which he or she must exercise extreme discrimination in terms of what information it allows itself to bring in that is specific to the person's evolutionary purposes. This is why typically, not always, but typically retrograde people, when they go through a learning experience, if that information is not pertinent to their personal purpose they are going to have a very hard time taking it in. They just tune out.

Audience: Why is that?

Jeffrey: Why? Because they are trying to only select information that is pertinent to their personal purpose.

Audience: Where does that come from – connected to your own personal purpose?

Jeffrey: Well, I just gave the answer a moment ago, that in most cases …

Audience: I need to hear that again, I have Mercury retrograde!

Jeffrey: That typically these people, prior to this life, have indiscriminately selected and collected too much information and data to the point where the mental apparatus is overloaded. Confusion, too many competing perspectives, intellectual doubt. As a result they come into a life in which they must exercise extreme discrimination in terms of what information they take in which is now specific to their personal purpose. This is why we have advocated for many years that, at least in this type of society, there should be schools for Mercury retrograde people, taught by Mercury retrograde teachers! It makes logical sense. Where is the school? You start one. Somebody has to. We'll call it Mercury retrograde school.

Audience: To help people discriminate, is that what you are saying?

Jeffrey: No. It simply requires very personal attention in education; to teach the child or the adult what they are interested in at the time they are interested in it. Then they will take in what is being taught wholesale. It is almost like a photographic memory at that level. But you have to remember that you have a natural dynamic of Gemini/Sagittarius/Virgo and Pisces. If the person is in fact not interested in what they are hearing they tune out. They kick in Pisces/Neptune. They space out and they have fantasies or imaginations that are more interesting than what they are being exposed to. Any more questions?

Audience: Yes, I would like to know what is your idea, what do you think about the idea of Pluto being exalted in Gemini?

Jeffrey: You want my opinion? Bullshit. To me there are no such things as falls and exaltations. It is just what it is. This is old time astrology. Well, we must conclude this lecture now. I hope you have all found something interesting here today, and thanks for coming.

God Bless.

4

The Planetary Nodes and
Evolutionary Astrology

Jeffrey: What we're talking about today is the nature of the geocentric planetary Nodes. Why should we work with them? Most of you who have been doing astrology are already used to working with the North and South Nodes of the Moon, yes? If we go ahead and utilize the nature of the North and South Nodes of the Moon in our work, why not also use the Nodes of the planets? When we deal with the North and South Nodes in relationship to their natal planet, we're in essence working with the evolutionary notion called the trinity. Even if you look at it from a non-metaphysical point of view, you still have three points to consider: a planet's South Node, the planet itself, and its North Node. They are like its past, present and future. For evolutionary purposes, as I suggested Friday night, if we are reading one particular chapter of a book, in order to have an understanding of that chapter, we probably should have read the ones that came before.

Any natal planet will have its own North and South nodes. The natal planets correlate to the current life of course. Yet each one of these planets has a past that has brought it to the current life. And that past is defined not only by the actual house and sign of the natal planet, but also its own South Node. Thus, the relationship between the natal planet by house, sign, and aspects correlates to the totality of its past that directly correlates to how and why it has come into the current life: the past that has lead to the current moment, one's current life. So, in essence, the natal planet by house, sign, and aspect, relative to its South Node, is the totality of that past that has lead to the current moment, the current life. This is no different that the South Node of the Moon, and the current natal Moon in one's birth chart. All the prior life egocentric structures created by the Soul that have correlated to prior life evolutionary dynamics that have lead to the current life, the current egocentric structure that has been created because of the totality of the past. The current life Moon sign is the bridge between the past and the future, its North Node, as integrated and lived on a moment to moment basis in the context of the current life. Thus, the current life Moon by house, sign, and aspects, relative to its Nodes, and the planetary ruler of those Nodes by their own house and sign locations, the aspects to them, is the constant that evolves within itself as a reflection of this dynamic tension between the past and the future as integrated in each moment of our life.

This is exactly the same for all of our planets. They are in their own houses and signs, making whatever aspects to other planets, that have all contributed to the past life development of those planets that constitute the existing reality for any of us at the moment of birth. The South Nodes of these planets, like the South Node of the Moon, correlates to the history of those planets at different points in time. This correlates to the inner memories in any of our Souls that have all lead to the orientation of our Souls to the current life that we are living, the very reasons for the current life in all of its dimensions that must keep evolving, keep moving towards a future that is reflected in the ongoing evolutionary intentions for our Souls.

All planets have their North Nodes, just as the Moon does. The North Node of these planets, like the Moon, correlates to the evolutionary progression and development of those planets. The natal position of the whatever planet, like the Moon, correlates to how the dynamic tension of our past and future is lived and integrated in each moment of our life. In essence, our past leads to the current moment, and that current moment is always moving towards a future. We can only know that there is in fact a future because we have had a past. The past leading to the moment is that which serves as the way any of us integrate, and move forwards into our future, where that future is the evolutionary intentions for our current life. Thus, the North Nodes of the planets serve as the vehicles for the evolutionary future to manifest which is integrated in each moment by natal position of those planets.

The Nodes of Jupiter, Saturn, Uranus, Neptune, and Pluto move very, very slowly over great lengths of time. Thus, they have a generational as well as an individual application. Individual because they will be in each person's natal chart somewhere that is unique to that person. Yet generational because they are in the same sign for all of us. The South Nodes of Pluto, Jupiter, and Saturn are in Capricorn for all of us. The North Node's in

Cancer for all of us. Historically speaking, the South Nodes of these planets are in Capricorn, and that is the time frame in which the transition between the Matriarchy and the Patriarchy occurred. All Souls on Earth as a result are linked to that time whether they actually lived at that time or not. It is the *collective memory* of that time that all Souls will draw upon as reflected in the current life they are living. So too with the South Node of Uranus which will be in Sagittarius for all of us, its North Node in Gemini. And the South Node of Neptune is in Aquarius for all of us, and its North Node in Leo. The North Nodes of all of these planets thus correlate to all peoples living on the planet now. They correlate to the evolutionary intentions for the entire species as that species, human beings, continue to evolve as a species. And, of course, the ongoing evolutionary intentions and necessities of the species can only be understood in direct relationship to the past of that species: the South Nodes.

It is, to me, incredible to also realize that the South and North Nodes of Pluto take one astrological age, 24,000 years, to move through the entire zodiac. Within this are the South and North Nodes of Mars, the lower octave of Pluto of course. The Nodes of Mars also take 24,000 years to move through all the signs of the zodiac. In any given year the South and North Nodes of Mars will be in three signs for the South Node, and, of course the natural three polarity signs for the North Node. For example, right now the South Nodes of Mars range from Libra, Scorpio, and Sagittarius, with the resulting North Nodes in their opposite signs. And this has been true since 500 AD. When we step back and look at this from an evolutionary point of view it becomes truly incredible as we contemplate the ongoing evolutionary intentions for the species, and each person in that species, not to mention all the other forms of life relative to their own evolution.

Mercury and Venus, and their Nodes, move through the signs much more quickly that the outer planets do. And these planets all correlate to that which is highly personal and unique to each Soul, its own individual reality that exists within the context of living with all the other humans that are living at the same time. The same principles of the past leading to the moment, and how that moment moves to the future applies in these Nodes as well of course. The natal sign of these planets is that which is the constant, that which integrates the dynamic tension between the past and the future that is experienced in each moment. This then allows for an evolution to take place within the natal sign and house of these planets. Nothing is ever static. Everything evolves.

In doing Evolutionary Astrology, as we can see, it is essential that we are able to see and deal with the various dimensions of time, and how those various dimensions of time, specific time frames, that correlate to specific lifetimes and the reasons for those lifetimes, interface and interact within themselves. It is this that correlates in each Soul's inner reality about the nature of its own evolution through time. It is this that correlates to the specific nature of each Soul: its own unique prior lifetimes, and the reasons for them that have been created through the vehicle of desires. It is this that allows us to understand the nature of the *current life, and why the current life.* And, it is this that allows us to understand the evolutionary intentions for any Soul, it own next steps as reflected in the North Nodes of the planets. When all of this is understood through the core evolutionary paradigm for all charts, the natal Pluto, its polarity point, the North and South Nodes of the Moon, the location of its planetary rulers, then a total understanding of any Soul's evolutionary journey can be understood.

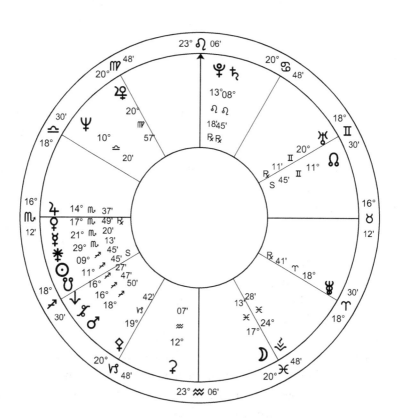

On the chart in back of me, you can see marks correlating with the Nodal axes of various planets. Here are the Planetary Nodes for this birth chart.

Ascending Nodes	Descending Nodes
Mercury: 19/24 Sagittarius	02/59 Sagittarius
Venus: 23/05 Scorpio	12/29 Sagittarius
Mars: 16/54 Aries	27/08 Scorpio
Jupiter: 16/27 Cancer	05/15 Capricorn
Saturn: 27/51 Cancer	19/36 Capricorn
Uranus: 13/31 Gemini	13/31 Sagittarius
Neptune: 12/52 Leo	09/35 Aquarius
Pluto: 20/52 Cancer	18/32 Capricorn

By putting in these Nodal axes, you can find themes and emphases in the birth chart that you would not see otherwise. Look at the nature of that 2nd house/8th house axis, now that we've put in the planetary Nodes. Do you see that emphasis on that axis? If you can observe what is emphasized in a birth chart, you see the foundations upon which the structure rests. Each planet is an archetype that correlates with a component in your overall consciousness.

There are so many ways to illustrate this, but the most dramatic case in all the counseling work I've done was a boy six years old who was still wearing diapers. He simply refused to go to the bathroom in a normal fashion, and his parents had taken him to all the doctors and a psychiatrist. They didn't know what the heck was going on. So finally the parents went to the counselor of last resort, who is typically an astrologer. The end of the line. (laughter) It was a very clear case, because with the nodal axes put in, the emphasis in his 8th house was simply overwhelming. In prior lives, that little boy had experienced so much emotional betrayal, violation of trust, abandonment and emotional loss that the compensation for his fear that it would happen again was to keep that diaper on. He just wasn't going to grow up and get back into all that again.

First, I suggested to the parents that the underlying issue was linked with this sort of psychology. It was very easy to figure out the antidote. I said to them, "Wait until your son is asleep, then get very close to his right ear and whisper the following words: 'You will always be loved; we will

always take care of you and we'll never abandon you.'" Within two weeks
the problem was resolved. That's how dramatic this stuff can be. Imagine
it from the parents' point of view: they had spent thousands of dollars with
no results; they finally come in and see that counselor of last resort, pay out
their hundred bucks or whatever and the problem is solved in two weeks.
Imagine what they thought. And these were traditional parents!

From Jupiter on out, the Nodes shift very slowly and therefore have
more of an application to what we can call generational waves, which I'll
illustrate for you in a moment. From Mars on in, they tend to have a much
more personal application. The inner planets move pretty quickly and
therefore their Nodes tend to shift fairly quickly too.

Everybody born in the twentieth century will have the South Nodes of
Jupiter, Saturn, and Pluto in Capricorn, with the resulting North Nodes in
Cancer. When you deal with the Moon's Nodes, that axis is always an actual
one-hundred-eighty degree opposition. If you have the South Node of the
Moon at eighteen degrees Pisces, your North Node of the Moon is at eighteen
degrees Virgo. That's because the Moon's motion relative to the Earth's
ecliptic is constant. But the motion of the outer planets is not constant, and
therefore the degrees, most of the time, are not directly opposed. When you
start looking at this from a generational view, the evolutionary purpose of
the generational wave or pattern is simple: it takes more than one person to
accomplish the evolutionary intentions of the planet. Why does this whole
group of folks in this century all have the South Nodes of Jupiter, Saturn,
Pluto in Capricorn and the North Nodes in Cancer? This entire group also
has the South Node of Uranus in Sagittarius and its North Node in Gemini.
We all have the South Node of Neptune in Aquarius and the North Node
in Leo.

When you look into the history of astrological Ages and sub-ages,
you discover that the unfortunate Patriarchal transition began during the
Capricorn sub-age of the Cancer Age. Lo and behold, everybody in this
century has the South Nodes of Jupiter, Saturn, and Pluto directly linked
with that transition. From your life experience, you can realize that we're in
the beginning of a time in which the feminine principle is resurrecting itself
and throwing off the shackles created by the Patriarchy. So we can clearly
see a link. Here we are at the beginning of the Aquarian Age again. Five
hundred years prior to the manifestation of Christ was the beginning of the
Essene community, whose own stated purpose was to lay the foundations for

the expected Messiah. Similarly, we are in a five hundred year time frame in which a certain percentage of people, clearly not the entire population, are beginning to lay the foundation for the Aquarian Age.

The last Aquarian Age was twenty-five thousand years ago. Men want to call that time the fruition of the Matriarchy. Which itself is erroneous, because what they call 'the Matriarchy' in so many ways is simply a metaphor for how we've lived the majority of our time on this planet, meaning under natural law, by the principles of nature. If one is living in harmony with natural law, one realizes that it is in fact the feminine principle which manifested the male principle. All forms of life when originally conceived are feminine. This must mean something. For those who want to objectify things, the penis is like an extended clitoris. The feminine creates the masculine. It's men who want to think in terms of hierarchy and would call the social system of the last Aquarian Age a Matriarchy. In natural law, natural living, there are no hierarchies. Even though the woman was the ultimate authority, that was not lived out in the way that men in the Patriarchal sense would live it. Things were simply lived as they naturally are. For example, if you live with an Indian tribe, which I have done, the corn picker and the shaman are co-equal. It's not a matter of who's better or worse; it's a matter of what role has to be fulfilled to sustain the whole. It's a natural order and natural law.

Here we sit with all of our South Nodes of Neptune in roughly eight to nine degrees of Aquarius. And guess where the Uranian transit is right now? This would tend to suggest that the original spiritual roots of the people on the planet today lie in those distant times called the last Aquarian Age, and that they are now beginning to be re-energized, relative to this transit of Uranus. And guess what else is behind this? Neptune. Neptune is very shortly going to be transiting over its own South Node. Now let's throw in the South Node of Uranus, which is between fourteen and seventeen degrees of Sagittarius for most of us. Here again we see what principle? The archetype of Sagittarius, meaning the ultimate archetype of natural law. And what transit is getting pretty close to this South Node? Pluto! Remember years ago where Pluto was supposed to 'just be a generational thing?' What comprises a generation? Is it not people? (laughter) In any case, yes, we have generational waves or patterns, but of course there are people in that generation. So we also have to look at this on a personal level: where is the South Node of Neptune in your personal chart? Where is the South Node of Uranus in your chart? Where are the South Nodes of Jupiter, Saturn and Pluto in your chart? Saturn has a direct correlation with the intrinsic structure of consciousness.

From the point of view of Neptune, consciousness is analogous to water. Water has no specific form. But if I put water in a cup, then the water can only assume that form, the cup. Yes? Similarly, if I put consciousness in the human form, it can only assume the function of that form. Is that consciousness in human form naturally structured by way of natural laws and natural principles; or is that consciousness going to be conditioned, Saturn, by the nature of whatever society or time in which that particular human being is born? You understand what I'm getting at? We all have Saturn's South Node in Capricorn, directly connected to this transitional period from the Matriarchy to the Patriarchy. That transition set in roughly around 6,500 BCE. It took about one thousand years actually, although after that there were two thousand years of residual transition.

In that one thousand years of transition, right around 6,500 BCE to maybe 5,600 BCE, there was a small period of time in a Patriarchal context in which men and women were in fact totally equal. In a Patriarchal context. Why? Let's say a man wanted to be a priest. In that time frame, he would then have to marry and/or form an allegiance with an existing female priest, in order to have any sense of authority. That's actually historically accurate. So there is this small period of time, even in a Patriarchal framework, when men were trying to gain power. But to gain that power, they had to form alliances with the existing female powers. The point is that we all have these memories, in terms of the structural nature of our consciousness, that are being drawn upon now. The very same thing applies to Jupiter and our pre-existing belief systems. Belief systems determine how you interpret the nature of phenomenal reality. How does this possibly link with the small points in time when men and women were in fact equal?

Don't all of us tend to agree that this seems to be a model that most of us want to move towards? Is this coincidence or synchronicity? How about the very structure of the collective Soul here? That's also in this time frame, is it not? So why would then the North Nodes of these planets be in Cancer? Cancer has a lot to do with one's self-image, does it not? Your self-image implies what? An ego. Yes? So with these three planetary North Nodes in Cancer, what does this tend to suggest in terms of the evolutionary direction of the entire species? With respect to ego structure equaling self-image?

The original human self-image was fused with nature. Animal and plant life were equal to human consciousness. What would these North Nodes of these planets in Cancer then mean? Is this going to be a new self-image of some sort that is still linked with original principles, and if so, what would that self-image be? Not only for each person, but for the entire collective? What would it look like? Who would have some Neptunian thoughts on that?

Audience: Androgynous?

Jeffrey: Androgynous would certainly apply. For example, on the island of Crete, the Matriarchy, the original one, was sustained until the fourth century AD. That's because it was disconnected from the mainland. When you study their history, you will find that in the first, second and third centuries, men and women looked identical. They wore the same clothes, they wore the same jewelry and hairstyles. Everything was an absolute state of balance. An amazing culture. By the way, do any of you know the sign that connects to androgyny in astrology? Libra. For example, in ancient Greece and Rome, they had the concept of the hermaphrodite that was held in a state of high honor. Ancient Rome connects with Libra. Androgyny is clearly a symbol here. Would it mean that more of us look like the men and women of Crete? Why is it that in recent times, more and more men have pierced ears with earrings in them? And that men, since the late 1960s, progressively began to rebel against the shackles of their own conditioning? Men started growing their hair long then, did they not? And women also began to rebel against the shackles imposed on them by men. We had the beginning of the women's movement and so on. Women who had desires to succeed in a man's world, the corporate world, even began to wear the clothes that men did: suits and ties for example. And these are the very people who all have natal Neptune in Libra!

We have to consider all of these planetary Nodes from all of these angles. With the South Node of Uranus in Sagittarius, what are you looking at? You're looking at every human being on the planet having some sort of natural linkage to the idea of nature and natural law. That's why more and more people are becoming increasingly interested in what we need to do to get nature back in its place of balance, to restore its integrity. Is this happening on the planet? Yes or no? With this Uranus in Sagittarius symbol in mind, we also see a connection to a time in history when the population was essentially nomadic. A lot of living on horseback, or marching great distances to go someplace else. See how graphic this becomes? So many people currently alive never have the feeling of really being at home. And there's some sort of subconscious impulse to find home which is never discovered unless they're alone in nature. You would not know why unless you threw in these Nodes. That's my point. Take the imagery of Sagittarius: the Centaur.

The way the Patriarchy wants you to interpret it is the human trying to be free of the animal. This is the typical interpretation. But if you interpret it from the point of view of natural law, it simply means the human trying to fuse with, not only the principles of nature in general, but specifically the worlds of animals and plants. There is a Latin word pronounced 'day-mon'. Daemon. The Christian perversion of this word is 'demon'. But another definition is: A human soul that has fused itself with the totality of nature and specifically the world of animals and plants. When this is accomplished, this soul becomes – 'listen carefully' – a messenger of God. Since we all have the South Node of Uranus in Sagittarius, we can all connect to the archetypal idea of the daemon. Meaning that most of us have an incredible sympathy for nature and an incredible sympathy for animals and plants. Yes or no? Which is why so many of us are beginning to rebel against the rape of the Earth itself. How many of you in this room accept this raping of the Earth?

Audience: (comments indicating massive rejection) No... I don't...

Jeffrey: We just had a Uranian response, didn't we? No one accepts it. That means we're rebelling against what? A pre-existing phenomenon. See how it's working? This is called astrology in your face. It's not happy words in the wind someplace, this is where we are living. This is living, breathing astrology. Yes? Good. Before we continue, are there questions?

Audience: I wanted to ask you to say more about this Cancer archetype that we're all supposed to be working toward.

Jeffrey: There are a lot of applications. One of the deepest lessons of Cancer is to learn the difference between security of a dependent or external nature versus developing a state of inner security. When you link this back to its natural triad with Scorpio and Pisces, this is why you have one of the buzzwords in current therapeutic circles, 'self-empowerment'. Self-empowerment is a Scorpio-Taurus phenomenon. You cannot become self-empowered until you develop a state of relative internal security. So why do we all have, at a minimum, three symbols in Cancer? Do you see what I'm getting at? This refers back to Capricorn. In other words, despite the fact that there was the very small period in Patriarchal history in which men and women were essentially equal, the Patriarchal transition didn't stop there. Despite the New Age woo-woo of why the Patriarchal transition happened, the actual historical fact was that up until around 6,500 BCE, men and women simply did not have the knowledge that man contributed equally to making a baby. When women conceived, they were thought to have done something like what we would call making love with God. Which is also why sexuality was intrinsically spiritual then. You see how that's linked?

But around 6,500 BCE, suddenly this new knowledge created a weird sense of power in men. And for men to have increasing power in that time really came down to position and land. Owning land. For men to have increasing power, they had to have some sort of vehicle by which they could pass down their holdings. Up until then, only rarely did we know whose children were fathered by whom. It didn't matter. Children were raised communally. That's why there was no monogamy as we now know it. There were no possessions other than personal possessions. Land was communal, etc. But suddenly a man wanted to know who his kids were, which became the origin of the institution of marriage, and paternity.

Put this back in the context of belief systems, the structural nature of consciousness, and the collective soul that we still drawn upon. Progressively, what occurred is that women were given two choices. They could either make the choice of being, in quotes, a 'good woman', which meant becoming married and having an incredibly restricted and powerless life. Essentially they were required to live in a hovel, not allowed out of that hovel, not allowed to be educated or have possessions, and their only real function was to produce babies, which were hopefully male. Or legally they could declare themselves prostitutes.

Which then meant they could be educated, own possessions and in fact operate like a man. You see these two institutions coming all the way up into our time, don't you? It connects with our South Nodes of Saturn,

Jupiter and Pluto in Capricorn, directly linked with that era. Even down to the murder of female babies that's happening in China as we speak. Do you understand my point? Is this synchronicity or coincidence? God is in a continuous state of evolution relative to God's own quest for perfection. The natural law behind this is the contracting and expanding nature of the universe over great lengths of time. We have two natural principles throughout Creation called male and female. The Matriarchy was also not a perfect time. People were not perfect then. So what you have here is God alternating between the inner principles of male and female over great lengths of time, and manifesting what we want to call, from the human point of view, Matriarchy or Patriarchy. Check out the last twenty or thirty years of history. How many women from this time would accept the traditional Patriarchal model of raising a family like Betty Crocker and the Marlboro Man? Most women in our age group want to rebel against this. Their rebellion refers to what? To the need for equality. Not a hierarchical reality in which the man is in control.

Pluto's moved into Sagittarius, and Neptune and Uranus into Aquarius; Pluto's coming up on the South Node of Uranus, and Neptune's coming to its own South Node. This is clearly a time frame in which the nature of any belief system assumed to be true will be challenged. The extension of all this stuff becomes incredibly fascinating, because the last time in modern history that Pluto was moving through Sagittarius, and Neptune and Uranus through Aquarius, though not necessarily all three at once, was the Renaissance, i.e. 'humanism'. Which was a rebellion against what? The pre-existing reality of that time: the church as the ultimate authority. The paradigm was God-centered; we had a Renaissance and it became human-centered. But in that time we also, from the white European's point of view, discovered the New World. That was the intent of that symbolism then: to expand beyond the existing boundaries of reality as they knew it. Thus, all the sailing boats that were built in order to expand beyond the existing boundaries in order to discover new realities all over the planet. Now we have the same symbolism. In our time and context, it means that the human species has once again reached a time to expand beyond the existing boundaries of known reality. In our time, it will mean detaching ourselves, Aquarius, from the planet itself. And progressively colonizing this solar system: the Moon and Mars.

For those who really get into metaphysical speculation about the potential origins of life on Earth, is it possible that such life originated from Mars? Do you remember when Clinton got so excited talking about this rock from Mars? And that there might be life there, and NASA got all excited and the rest of it? Remember that Mars at one time had an atmosphere similar to the Earth's. A lot of folks want to speculate that the origin of life on Earth came from Mars, when Mars had a lot of the stuff ejected off its surface. During all the hoopla around that Mars rock, the transiting South Node of the Moon was in Aries! Coincidence or synchronicity? If in fact there was some sort of evolved life form on Mars, and Mars had an Earth-type atmosphere and it's not there anymore, how come? Suddenly we're exploring those ideas when the Moon's South Node is in Aries? Think about it.

Let's talk about the end of the next millennium, i.e. the end of the Aquarian Age. Two hundred years before its final culmination, Pluto will stand at twenty-eight degrees of Sagittarius, at the center of the galaxy, and the transiting South Nodes of Saturn and Pluto will go into Aquarius. When you study Nostradamus' predictions, he had one for exactly that time frame. He said that humanity would enter what he called a hecatombe and would then become members of a galactic community. Put this in the context of the South Nodes of Saturn and Pluto shifting to Aquarius and Pluto being at the center of the galaxy. Pretty interesting symbolism to fit his prediction.

Let's get back to the planetary Nodes in individual charts. A couple comes to the astrologer. They want a synastry chart done. Typically the modern, traditional astrologer is going to be looking for Mars/Venus stuff and so forth. You're doing your traditional synastry stuff, and you find no specific connections between Mars and Venus or Venus to Venus or Mars to Mars. The traditional astrologer is going to stand there utterly stumped. "This doesn't fit the rules that I've learned." But let's say we employ the nodal axes of all their planets, and we find that one person's South Node of Mars is in nine degrees Sagittarius, and the other person has natal Venus there. Or maybe one's South Node of Mars is conjuncting the other's South Node of Venus. Got it?

What we're going to do now is go through an individual analysis of the chart behind me.

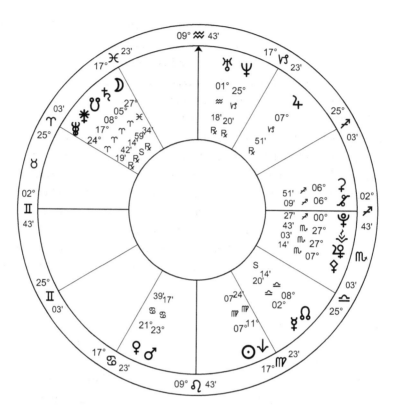

North Nodes	South Nodes
Mercury: 18 Leo	27 Virgo
Venus: 4 Leo	15 Libra
Mars: 29 Gemini	22 Libra
Jupiter: 18 Cancer	0 Capricorn
Saturn: 27 Cancer	19 Capricorn
Uranus: 16 Gemini	10 Sagittarius
Neptune: 12 Leo	10 Aquarius
Pluto: 21 Cancer	19 Capricorn

Again, astrology only operates relative to the observed context. From the point of view of evolution, you have four natural states to consider. Seventy percent of any collective mass is in a consensus state. Twenty percent are, in a Jungian sense, in an individuated consciousness from another form of life. Three to four percent are in a spiritual state, which does not mean religion. Religion is for the consensus state.

Our subject's evolutionary condition is the spiritual state. She's had many prior lifetimes supporting and teaching a variety of philosophical, religious and spiritual systems. First we have the natal planets involved, and hopefully we can make some sort of sense or meaning of that natal signature. What I want to focus on now are specifically the South Nodes of these various planets, to try to develop pre-existing chapters in her particular book, so we can understand what the book is for her in this life. Let's start with the dominant emphasis in the 9th house, where we see the South Node of Saturn as well as the South Node of Pluto. And we see the Moon's South Node in Aries here, don't we? We see a Saturn structure in the 11th house, and a Moon structure in the 11th house. We have the planetary ruler of that South Node opposing Uranus, and in opposition to Neptune in Capricorn. You're looking at a Soul who will accept no repression of herself, or have any external authority attempt to repress whatever it is that she has to say or wishes to do. Because of that fact, she has gotten herself into tremendous trouble with the system: the powers that be. Just by seeing the Soul structure in the 9th house here, i.e. the South Node of Pluto in Capricorn in the 9th house, minimally we could say that the essence of this being is intuitive, yes? That she naturally thinks in conceptual or abstract terms; that she has the kind of consciousness that is trying to figure out the nature of phenomenal reality. Does that not breed an intrinsic alienation from normal reality?

I'm going to give you a story so you can understand the type of Soul that you're trying to evaluate here. Her parents often took her and their dog on a walk to the local park. One day, before she was two years old, she put the collar on the dog and slipped out and walked to the park by herself! When she got there she realized she was lost. And when she realized she was lost, this was a two-year-old: she took herself to a house and knocked on the door. She knew she was lost. And of course the people called 911, and the parents got her back. She was two years old! What kind of intelligence are you looking at there? Just deal with 9th house terminology to answer the question, Pluto's South Node in the Ninth. Is it a restless Soul? Is it a Soul defined by nature? Yes or no? In this context, would we say that, because of this overall signature, she was a wild child? Is that a leap of logic? As it turns out, this little girl never even wants to be in the house; she wants to be outside all the time. She gets extremely angry about even having to wear clothes, (laughter).

The story I'm about to tell you does not mean to imply that she was actually the historical figure I'm about to name; only that it provides a way of understanding her. Are all of you familiar with the story of John the Baptist? And how he was standing there always doing what? Think Aries, for this kid's South Node of the Moon. John the Baptist was screaming, yes? About baptism and the expected messiah, yes? What happened when he was rounded up? Was he not put in the dungeon? What ultimately happened to his head? And why was that? With the message being delivered, yes?

Can you apply that story to this chart? Something about a detached head with the Moon's South Node in Aries in the 11th, yes? And angering the existing system. Look at this 3rd house-9th house interaction. And being persecuted for what he was saying, yes? We are looking at the karma of a martyr. Any time you have the karma of a martyr, you are dealing with, from a psychological point of view, an abnormal life that became larger than life itself, and assumed almost supernatural dimensions. There is clearly the karma of a martyr here, meaning this soul has had a very specific mission, so to speak, a mission from on high. Yes? Moon in Pisces, 9th house stuff, that she had no choice but to play out. You can see many lifetimes of violence triggered by that which was spoken through her. You can see violence coming at her through, not only the nature of the existing system, but from people who have been powerful. One of the signs that connects to ancient Rome is Libra. Now look at the nature of the Libra symbol standing in her 5th house, and Mercury and Chiron there. The signs Pisces and Aries correlate to the transition, in the West, between the new and old testaments. Both have a direct correlation to Judea. That was why I used the John the Baptist story. And you can see, in that signature in this chart, a person living in that time and place who had interaction with the Roman culture. And that it was a time of collective rebellion against the powers that be: Rome. And a time in which the expected messiah was at hand.

Look at the dramatic statement of having the South Node of Neptune in Aquarius essentially conjunct her Midheaven. Is that not a signature like the story of John the Baptist? You see what I am getting at? Even the ruler of that Node would be Uranus, would it not? Where does it stand, in what house? And retrograde? You see what I'm trying to suggest that you learn to see here, how to interact with the symbols? At a minimum, you know the 9th house rulership of religion, yes? And if we relate that to the South Node of Neptune on the Midheaven, is that a stretch of logic? Because the symbol is retrograde, conjunct Neptune retrograde, was the message that she was delivering part of the existing system or something against the existing system? Against it! Now put that in the context of these oppositions to the Mars-Venus conjunction. You now have the obvious signature of violence. Yes? Of trying to kill the messenger because of the message. Is that a leap in logic? You can clearly see the incredible power of oratory, can you not? You have a signature here of a Soul's lifetimes, of even writing those messages, of using whatever vehicle was available in order to teach. You already see, by the sheer fact of Mercury standing on the North Node, that this is something also connected to the past; it's existed prior to the current life.

So you can also see the possibility of this person being well known in former times. A planet that is conjunct the North Node of the Moon means that that planetary function has already been developed, or has been in the stages of development, prior to the current life. What in the world would this South Node of Uranus be doing standing with the natal Pluto? The North Node of Mars is also linked with Pluto. There's something about a wound there, isn't there? What is it?

Audience: A wound relating to the collective?

Jeffrey: This would be a Soul always working on behalf of the collective. But how would the wound manifest on a personal basis, beyond the collective? The actual wound is based on a Libra phenomenon, a Soul that is defined by fair play and justice. When you link this back to a dominant 9th house, by that which is naturally right and wrong. The key words are naturally right and wrong. For example, I don't need the Bible or the Torah to tell me its wrong to put my baby out on the highway. It's just naturally wrong. I don't need these books to tell me not to go kill somebody on the street for my own amusement; it's just naturally wrong. So you have a Soul that is defined by a lot of natural rights and wrongs, linked with equality, justice and fair play. So what is her personal wound here? Is it going to be linked with her own Soul sense of disillusionment, Neptune on the Midheaven? Disillusionment with what? With 10th house garbage. With Patriarchal systems which are hierarchical in nature and create suffering because of the hierarchy. Are you getting it? So we have a deep wound there.

Audience: I can't see what's in the 4th house with all the.........

Jeffrey: The North Node of Neptune at twelve Leo, the North Node of Mercury at eighteen Leo. The South Node of Mercury stands at twenty-seven Virgo. You can already see now, just with this symbol, other lifetimes of being persecuted, Virgo, for the very nature of what, Mercury? Ideas. The whole solution is not for her to change what she is here to do. The issue is how it is communicated. If you use the allegory of John the Baptist, you could say that the problem wasn't the message; it was how it was delivered. Because of his intensity, it created an instinctively defensive posture in those in power.

So the issue is not the message as such, whatever she's going to say, but how it's specifically communicated. And this is why, if you had such a Soul in a counseling scenario, you would tell her to learn to use other people's linguistic structures and characteristic turns of speech to talk to them and with them, not at them or above them.

Audience: But with that North Node in Aquarius, using dramatic language...?

Jeffrey: If I'm with this client who has her reality and talks about it in her own terminology, I must learn to use that terminology for the client to have to accept what I have to say. That will be an ongoing personal issue for her. Because she would come in with a pre-existing attitude of, "Why are all these people so stupid? Why don't they intuitively understand what seems to me so simple?" And because of this attitude, she has a tendency to get angry and talk at people, not with them. Do you see? So the whole solution is taking in how to connect to people, so that the message can be. Libra, well received. Because we have Jupiter T-squaring these Nodes, not eliciting an instinctually defensive reaction in which other people's authority comes down on her. Does that make sense?

The whole point, again, is to understand that we have pre-existing chapters in a birth chart. Perhaps you can see, from this sort of workshop, that the more you allow yourself to move beyond the boundaries of the technical world of astrology, the better. Don't limit yourself just to reading astrology, but expand your brains. One of the most useful things to read is not this New Age woo-woo, but history. The more you learn about the nature of actual history, time frames, historical context, while employing the use of planetary Nodes, the more dimensions you've added not only for your own understanding of a chart, but for the perspective you can offer the client.

Audience: We've done past and present... so then the North Nodes, they're the future?

Jeffrey: Yes. That's what you're evolving towards. Have you all got a little something you can work with? That's all I can do today, give you something to work with.

Thanks for coming this morning.

The Ages and their Sub-Ages

LEO AGE 10,900 BC - 9,820 BC

10,900 - 10,810 - Leo
10,810 - 10,720 - Virgo
10,720 - 10,630 - Libra
10,630 - 10,540 - Scorpio
10,540 - 10,450 - Sagittarius
10,450 - 10,360 - Capricorn
10,360 - 10,270 - Aquarius
10,270 - 10,180 - Pisces
10,180 - 10,090 - Aries
10,090 - 10,000 - Taurus
10,000 - 9,910 - Gemini
9,910 - 9,820 - Cancer

AQUARIUS SUB-AGE 9,820 - 8,740 BC

9,820 - 9,730 - Aquarius
9,730 - 9,640 - Pisces
9,640 - 9,550 - Aries
9,550 - 9,460 - Taurus
9,460 - 9,370 - Gemini
9,370 - 9,280 - Cancer
9,280 - 9,190 - Leo
9,190 - 9,100 - Virgo
9,100 - 9,010 - Libra
9,010 - 8,920 - Scorpio
8,920 - 8,830 - Sagittarius
8,330 - 8,740 - Capricorn

CANCER AGE 8,740 - 7,660

8,740 - 8,650 - Cancer
8,650 - 8,560 - Leo
8,560 - 8,470 - Virgo
8,470 - 8,380 - Libra
8,380 - 8,290 - Scorpio
8,290 - 8,,200 - Sagittarius
8,200 - 8,110 - Capricorn
8,110 - 8,020 - Aquarius
8,020 - 7,930 - Pisces
7,930 - 7,840 - Aries
7,840 - 7,750 - Taurus
7,750 - 7,660 - Gemini

CAPRICORN SUB-AGE 7,660-6,580 BC

7,660 - 7,570 - Capricorn
7,570 - 7,480 - Aquarius
7,480 - 7,390 - Pisces
7,390 - 7,300 - Aries
7,300 - 7,210 - Taurus
7,210 - 7,120 - Gemini
7,120 - 7,030 - Cancer
7,030 - 6,940 - Leo
6,940 - 6,850 - Virgo
6,850 - 6,760 - Libra
6,760 - 6,670 - Scorpio
6,670 - 6,580 - Sagittarius

GEMINI AGE 6,580 - 5500 BC

6,580 - 6,490 - Gemini
6,490 - 6,400 - Cancer
61400 - 6,310 - Leo
6,310 - 6,220 - Virgo
6,220 - 6,130 - Libra
6,130 - 6,040 - Scorpio
6,040 - 5,950 - Sagittarius
5,950 - 5,860 - Capricorn
5,860 - 5,770 - Aquarius
5,770 - 5,680 - Pisces
5,680 - 5,590 - Aries
5,590 - 5,500 - Taurus

SAGITTARIUS SUB-AGE 5,500 - 4,420 BC

5,500 - 5,410 - Sagittarius
5,410 - 5,320 - Capricorn
5,320 - 5,230 - Aquarius
5,230 - 5,140 - Pisces
5,140 - 5,050 - Aries
5,050 - 4,960 - Taurus
4,960 - 4,870 - Gemini
4,870 - 4,780 - Cancer
4,780 - 4,690 - Leo
4,690 - 4,600 - Virgo
4,600 - 4,510 - Libra
4,510 - 4,420 - Scorpio

TAURUS AGE 4,420 - 3,340 BC

4,420 - 4,330 - Taurus
4,330 - 4,240 - Gemini
4,240 - 4,150 - Cancer
4,150 - 4,060 - Leo
4,060 - 3,970 - Virgo
3,970 - 3,880 - Libra
3,880 - 3,790 - Scorpio
3,790 - 3,700 - Sagittarius
3,700 - 3,610 - Capricorn
3,610 - 3,520 - Aquarius
3,520 - 3,430 - Pisces
3,430 - 3,340 - Aries

SCORPIO SUB-AGE 3,340 - 2,260 BC

3,340 - 3,250 - Scorpio
3,250 - 3,160 - Sagittarius
3,160 - 3,070 - Capricorn
3,070 - 2,980 - Aquarius
2,980 - 2,890 - Pisces
2,890 - 2,800 - Aries
2,800 - 2,710 - Taurus
2,710 - 2,620 - Gemini
2,620 - 2,530 - Cancer
2,530 - 2,440 - Leo
2,440 - 2,350 - Virgo
2,350 - 2,260 - Libra

ARIES AGE 21260 - 1,180 BC

2,260 - 2,170 - Aries
2,170 - 2,080 - Taurus
2,080 - 1,990 - Gemini
1,990 - 1,900 - Cancer
1,900 - 1,810 - Leo
1,810 - 1,720 - Virgo
1,720 - 1,630 - Libra
1,630 - 1,540 - Scorpio
1,340 - 1,450 - Sagittarius
1,450 - 1,360 - Capricorn
1,360 - 1,270 - Aquarius
1,270 - 1,180 - Pisces

LIBRA SUB-AGE 1,180 - 100 BC

1,180 - 1,090 - Libra
1,090 - 1,000 - Scorpio
1,000 - 910 - Sagittarius
910 - 320 - Capricorn
820 - 730 - Aquarius
730 - 640 - Pisces
640 - 550 - Aries
550 - 460 - Taurus
460 - 370 - Gemini
370 - 280 - Cancer
280 - 190 - Leo
190 - 100 - Virgo

PISCES AGE 100 BC - 980 AD

100 BC - 0010 BC - Pisces
10 BC - 80 AD - Aries
80 AD - 170 - Taurus
170 - 260 - Gemini
260 - 350 - Cancer
350 - 440 - Leo
440 - 530 - Virgo
330 - 620 - Libra
620 - 710 - Scorpio
710 - 300 - Sagittarius
300 - 390 - Capricorn
390 - 980 - Aquarius

VIRGO SUB-AGE 980 - 2060 AD

980 - 1070 - Virgo
1070 - 1160 - Libra
1160 - 1250 - Scorpio
1250 - 1340 - Sagittarius
1340 - 1430 - Capricorn
1430 - 1520 - Aquarius
1520 - 1610 - Pisces
1610 - 1700 - Aries
1700 - 1790 - Taurus
1790 - 1380 - Gemini
1880 - 1970 - Cancer
1970 - 2060 - Leo

5

Understanding the Sexual Archetypes and Evolutionary Astrology

Jeffrey: My name is Jeffrey Green and this is the Astro2000 Conference.

First, I really want to thank all of you for making the effort to come to this particular conference. It is, as most of you will find out, a little bit different than most conferences, as we try to create a family type of atmosphere and, of course, bring in truly qualified speakers. So both Noel Tyl and I do thank all of you for making an effort to come.

Now, today's topic is, of course, on Evolutionary Astrology and Sexuality. The way I like to approach this is that when a question comes into you ask your question at the moment that you have it. The reason I like to do that is to keep us clear as we are moving along. What tends to happen is if you are sitting with a question, and you don't ask it, you keep thinking about that question and don't follow the lecture; so if you have that question, go ahead and ask it. Any questions? (Laughter). Good. That's the end of that.

The first question really is this. Why should we ever look at the nature of sexuality and link it with astrology? And the answer should be clear: that the whole issue of sexuality is that it is obviously a part of our lives. Everybody has their own unique orientation to it, their own reason for that orientation, and the point is that unless you have skills and understanding of the actual sexual archetypes from the point of view of astrology, what use can you really be to such a client who is having specifically sexual questions? Clearly, you can be of no service. So, what we will be doing today is going through the archetypes, the sexuality of each sign, Aries through Pisces. And you can translate that into the relative, relevant planetary ruler of that sign. So if we are describing Aries, we will also be describing Mars and the 1st house. Yes? So we are just going to go through and put the sexuality through the signs and then as we have questions, ask!

Now, the first thing we should probably embrace and try to understand is as long as we have this manifested Creation here and are living on the planet called Earth, there is going to be a whole set of natural laws or natural principles responsible for the Creation itself, and how that Creation is manifesting itself in a time/space reality that we call Earth. This is going to be a whole set of natural laws, including natural sexual laws. The key word here is natural, which is vastly different – in fact, it is different now – when you start suppressing natural law, whatever the reasons may be.

So what we are describing here is that up until 6500 BCE all human people on this planet were defined by living true to natural laws, not only in general, but as far as natural sexual laws, and up into right around 6500 BCE this set in motion the famous transition that we call the Patriarchal Transition. And this actually occurred from an astrological point of view in the Capricorn sub-age of the Cancer Age. And for those of us who have been doing research or understanding in terms of gender issues, sexuality issues linked with astrology, Cancer and Capricorn both correlate to what is called gender assignment as defined by the nature of the consensus reality of whatever society you find yourself in, and whatever century: gender assignment. And when we come into this Capricorn sub-age of the Cancer Age, we can then see the perfect symbolism for the flip-flopping between what is called the Matriarchy and the Patriarchy. Please understand that the Matriarchy, in so many ways is really a metaphor for how the human person lived on the planet for the majority of its time, which means again living through, and being defined by Natural Law, and this again includes natural sexual laws.

Again, starting around 6500 BCE we had this transition to what we now call the Patriarchy and, progressing within the Patriarchy, were the inventions of its religions that had the effect of progressively suppressing roughly ninety percent of all natural sexual laws.

Now the key point to understand within that is that whatever is natural – whatever it may be, including something sexual – if it is repressed, for whatever the reasons (in this case, Patriarchal transitioning), whatever is naturally suppressed becomes a causative factor of distortion and rage. So, humanity started off living in and defined by natural sexual laws which began to be repressed when the Patriarchy began its transition.

These natural sexual laws progressively began to become repressed, and anything we repress becomes distorted, so with the repression of those natural laws we set into motion the distortion, and then the rage that occurred, because of that distortion. And the reason I am pointing this out is that as we go through our happy definitions of the sexuality of each sign, we are going to be describing the Patriarchal sexual reality because that is where we are still living, and that is where 99.9 percent of your clients are still living. So to deal with actual reality, whether it is distorted reality or not, it is in fact that reality; and you had better have some sort of equipment or ability to understand just what the sexuality is of each sign, from a historic point of view. Do you see what I am getting at?

We don't have to like it. But in fact, that is the reality we are living. I will give you just one simple example, and what I am going to share may offend some, but that is the nature of current conditioning. So, what I am going to describe to you here is in fact a natural sexual law which prevailed for the majority of time that human people lived here. And I'll show you then how this natural thing got repressed and show you the application of that repression by its distorted manifestation. So, for example, for the balance of human history it was custom all over this particular planet – keeping in mind natural living – that there was no such thing as monogamy as it is defined by the Patriarchy. People lived communally. And even children were raised communally. There was no monogamy as you know it. In fact, monogamy is not even natural to the human species. It is not yet genetically programmed. The reason for that is the ongoing need for diversity within the gene pool.

Now, when we start approaching this sort of work, i.e., astrological, sexual analysis, and you are dealing with a client, the thing that all of us need to understand, from the point of view of evolution, is that the Soul will create the life it needs in whatever century in whatever country. And that whatever life it's designing for its own evolutionary reasons also includes the specific sexual orientation of that life. The reason that we need to look at it this way is that as we are making an analysis of the birth chart or working with a client, we need to look at this, and analyze this, and judge it from the point of view of what they themselves naturally need to do, from the point of view of their own evolutionary necessity. It is not your job to stand there in moral righteousness and issue your judgments, relative to who they are sexually, and if you feel you have the need to do that, you should probably get out of counseling work. So let's try to understand and approach it from that point of view, yes? At least for this hour. You can hurl your tomatoes later. (Laughter).

We will start with Aries. Aries from an evolutionary point of view correlates with Mars in Aries or Mars in the 1st house, for example, and this will always correlate with the beginning of a brand new cycle in evolutionary terms in terms of that person's sexual discovery of themselves – a brand new cycle; something brand new is under way. And, because it is brand new, then it is going to operating instinctually, not conceptually. That is to say that when Aries is sexualized it is operating instinctually, not conceptually. And this then means that as the Aries sexualizes in the early part of its life, all that it is inwardly aware of is various sorts of sexual instincts equaling specific kinds of sexual desires. When Aries is left to itself, obviously it is going to require the Arian freedom to initiate whatever experiences that it deems necessary. Because the way that Aries learns in general and sexually is in the reaction to the initiated experience. Instinct implies no foreknowledge; no prior plan is operating instinctually; and, therefore, the desires that emanate through Aries, sexually speaking, are just that – instincts without prior knowledge. This is why the Aries requires the necessary freedom to instinctually act upon the instinctual desires themselves.

By creating actual experiences that reflect that desire or desires, the reaction occurs relative to the experience itself. It is in the reaction that the individual understands ever more – through Aries – about itself. It is a process of perpetual becoming in Aries. All of us have Aries in our charts anyway, and it is a universal experience. I don't care what your belief systems are, and I don't care what country you live in, it is a universal experience that we all share called a continuous state of becoming. That is the Aries, Mars, 1st house in your chart.

And so when Aries is sexualized, the person is in a perpetual state of becoming. There is no real limit to the nature of the desires that can manifest instinctually through Aries. There used to be a euphemism in this country: I will try anything once. Well, guess what? That is Aries. The only kind of sexual experience that Aries, of itself, will preclude is any kind of sexual experience that correlates with being degraded, or humiliated, or power-over type sex. That is the one thing that Aries will instinctually rebel against or reject. But anything else to Aries is fair game.

And, remember that Mars is a lower octave of Pluto, yes? And a lower octave simply means a denser vibration of something. So in the end, all sexual desire emanates from the Soul. So here we have the lower octave manifesting through Aries. You can then see that directly linked with the Soul we are beginning a brand new evolutionary cycle requiring total freedom. Now Aries clearly is intrinsically an initiatory energy. It is cardinal in nature; it is fire. It is energy moving out from the center, yes? And, therefore it wants to act; it wants to initiate. It is not in a situation of reception; it is in a situation of action.

Now because of this and its natural link through Mars to Pluto, Aries then carries or reflects (and maybe is still called) animal magnetism. It simply radiates from an instinctual point of view its sexuality. It is quite magnetic relative to other people. Aries in and of itself doesn't know what's happening; that's just what it is. How many of you guys have Scorpio rising here? That is pretty exceptional. For the few that are here, you have probably heard throughout your life, the following words, 'You are intense'. But the ascendant is an instinctual phenomenon. The Scorpio ascendant does not know itself to be intense; it is just what it is. And it hears that it is intense from its environment.

And it's no different with Aries sexualized. It may reflect this very strong animal magnetism, but it doesn't know it. No different than the Scorpio rising not knowing that it is intense. It is just what it is. But this instinctually radiating energy can be highly attractive to other people, is the point. Meaning Aries sexualized, whether it is male or female – what is your euphemism – they get 'hit on' a lot, just because of this instinctual magnetism. Do you see what I am getting at? And that can be quite surprising to Aries; why is this person being attracted to me? "I don't feel that energy myself", would be the typical complaint or statement. And it is just a reflection of this instinctual energy.

Now think about this in the context of partnerships. What if you happen to be with a partner who is an Arian type sexually? And let's say you're an insecure woman, and now you're out at a restaurant with your man. And then all of a sudden – because of this man reflecting this Arian type of sexuality, and he is just sitting there being him – and yet all various people in that immediate environment seem to be looking at this fellow because they are interested sexually. They don't know why, they are responding instinctually too. Now what happens to this insecure woman who is now perpetually bombarded every time they go out? Now what if they came to you as a couple to be counseled, and here is her complaint: "It seems like all these people are attracted to him, and he is doing this." No, he isn't doing this. Do you see what I am getting at? That's what you tell this insecure woman,

"He is just being who he is." There is no intent here. Now, the worst part of Aries here is that sometimes they learn that this is, in fact, happening, (audience is laughing) and now they begin to use it – consciously use it to manipulate – and that is the difference. Do you see what I am getting at? Now that is a different scenario.

Now again Aries sexually is open to almost any sort of experience, and also understand that from the Arian point of view, that Aries does not care how long the specific sexual act lasts. Aries, obviously, relative to fire, is just concerned with the quality of that experience. If it happens to be one minute of intense passion, Aries is fine. But what if they are with a Capricorn? (Much laughter) They just barely got their pants off and Aries is done! Sorry for Capricorn! Aries is really concerned with the passion and the sweat of it, so to speak – the bodies that are really together and groovy and sweaty and all this stuff – the intensity of it all. It's concerned with the sheer intense passion of it all and however long that duration is, so be it. Similarly, Aries could care less where the sexual act takes place. It is just as happy in the back of a car as it is in some nice bed. It doesn't care. It is concerned with what's going on between those two people.

Now, it can also be quite true that Aries does have a problem in the Patriarchal reality, relative to the Patriarchal definition of monogamy. Aries does not want a constraint. Aries discovers itself through ongoing experience. And after all, sexuality is just another kind of experience, in the end, in which it produces its own kind of self knowledge. So the point here is that Aries is not that comfortable fitting into a monogamous scenario. It's not that it can't be monogamous, obviously it can be. But it is always going to experience these instinctual attractions, even if they have made the decision to be monogamous. And, if you find yourself in counseling work, one of the better things you can do for that Arian type – if in fact, they are in a monogamous relationship – is to suggest to that person that as these attractions instinctually occur, that they relate via the Libra polarity (these attractions) to their partner. In other words, to always keep it out of them, not to not keep it in. If they keep it in, it creates its own kind of inner compression, and if the compression intensifies to a point they are going to rebel against the limitations of monogamy, then they are going to go out and do their own thing. So the point is, if they include their partner in this sort of process, it has a way of diffusing – diffusing –- the build up of that sort of intensity. Do you understand this plan? Now, the sexual energy within

Aries is constant. It has a perpetual heat on the nerves which correlate with the genital area.

Are there any questions on Aries, because I am going to abbreviate some of this stuff, due to time constraints?

We get into Taurus then, and Taurus is a naturally yin energy and naturally feminine energy. It is earth. It is energy moving back toward the center; whereas Aries is energy moving out from the center. Taurus wants to consolidate. The very first thing to know about Taurus sexualized is that Taurus, in fact, directly correlates to the instinct in all forms of life – including human – of surviving. It is the survival instinct itself. In order for a species to survive, it obviously has to be able to procreate itself. Therefore the pro-creational instinct is right in your 2nd house, Taurus and/or the inner side of Venus. One of the other direct archetypes that connect with Taurus is the entire archetype called self-reliance; that is to say, your capacity to sustain your own life. When the necessity of self-reliance is linked with the procreation instinct, and you sexualize this, this becomes a causative factor for masturbation. Now, this itself becomes its own issue.

Let's say you are looking at client x, and let's say they have four to five planets in the 2nd house. Right away you know, in general, that the person has the evolutionary intention to learn self-reliance and self-empowerment. But that also includes sexual self-reliance and sexual self-empowerment, equaling a very dominant sexual nature in that signature. We can look at this, we can see it, we can objectify it, yes this is what is happening, and yet what if that person finds himself, say, growing up in Montreal (Quebec) and they are growing up in a very strict Roman Catholic family in which they are being progressively exposed to the Bible and the taboo of touching oneself? And yet they are sitting here with a dominant 2nd house. Do you see what I am getting at in terms of cultural problems relative to who a person naturally is? In fact I had a client like that in Montreal, and she was literally sitting on her energy, and because she was sitting on it, she was compressing it, and therefore creating all manner of emotional and psychological distortions just based on trying to unnecessarily contain this energy that she had. And here comes this hippy astrologer from the States. It was a very clear case. I just validated the woman. This is your nature, this is why it is happening, and this is what it means in evolutionary terms. All she needed was one person, particularly a man, to give her permission to be herself. Her only other complaint was, "Well, I am married; what would my husband think?"

Now here comes a piece of advice for when you run into these clients. Say you are dealing with a couple and say one of the people in that couple does, in fact, have this strong 2nd house emphasis, or another way of looking at it a very strong nature of strong self-sexual activity. All too often in such relationships, the other partner can interpret that as threatening. That somehow it is taking away from the relationship. So what would you do as a counselor? Obviously the suggested adjustment would simply be something like, learn how to include this activity within your sexual relationship, as you are being sexual together. Do you see what I am getting at? A simple adjustment that would immediately improve that relationship. Do you see what I am getting at?

So in any case, 2nd house /Taurus has a direct link with the phenomenon of masturbation. The 2nd house, in and by itself, Taurus, the inner side of Venus could care less with what we would call sexual experimentation. That would be linked with Aquarius and some other signs. All Taurus is concerned with is what I call meat and potatoes type sexuality, just basic positions. They don't want the arm over here… (Laughter). The point and the reason for that is that Taurus, the inner side of Venus, 2nd house, does in fact have a natural orientation to what we call durational sexuality, sustained sexuality. Aries was happy with the quickie. Taurus does not like quickies. They want durational sexuality, and the reason is that the longer the sexual act goes on, it induces an increasing sense of inner compression via the intensity. This is how Taurus and also Capricorn, I might add, becomes unlocked. Capricorn and Taurus have naturally inwardly compressive, locked up within themselves, type of archetypes that have occurred because of Patriarchal conditioning. There is a need to consolidate in Taurus. There is a resistance to growth.

You know, a perfect picture for Taurus is the picture of the frog standing in the bottom of the well. It looks out and sees that much sky and thinks it is the whole universe. They can control that space. It is secure there. Then you can also see there the resistance to growth. That's why there is the Scorpio polarity, so it can induce necessary confrontation via existing limitation. But because the frog is sitting in the bottom of the well, its resistance to growth and the energy moving back to the center create a naturally compressive inner state. This then becomes a causative factor for the need for durational sexuality. The increasing intensity of unlocking that compression creates a sense of emotional freedom; the psychological freedom is the point. So there is this need for durational sexuality linked with meat and potatoes orientation to sex.

Now, Taurus becomes actually the first archetype in which the Soul has the opportunity to realize the difference between what could be called profane sexuality vs. sacred or spiritual sexuality. Now, how can we see this in this particular archetype? The reason is, as we have all learned, the higher octave of Venus is Neptune. And therefore, we have a natural implication (Neptune), within Venus, within Taurus. And you can see from a Soul's point of view, evolving through time and space, that there always comes a moment in one's evolution which one must transfer or shift or evolve beyond these base forms of sexuality – no matter how intense that may be – to remembering or learning how to use the sexual vehicle as a way of contacting inner Divinity. Knowing Divinity within oneself, the Divinity in one's partner and ultimately Divinity together. This is why we have the natural polarity to Taurus called Scorpio, and one of the applications to Scorpio is ritual. And one of the applications of ritual can be called sexual ritual. The common word in the culture now for this phenomenon is called Tantra. So we have this initial archetype of Taurus in which this lesson or remembrance involving the difference between base or profane sexuality, and sexuality used to contact God, occurs. The reason for this is that in natural law God is always teaching us that we are co-creator with it, and the teaching occurs through one's sexuality. Think about it – co-creating – that's what this teaching is. An initial part of this teaching occurs through Taurus. Any questions on that part?

Audience: Inaudible

Jeffrey: What you just asked is pretty much underway all over the planet already anyway, i.e. questioning, not just one's sexuality, but reality in general. The super conjunct that you are describing is really going to serve to accelerate the survival instinct on our planet. One thing you can anticipate is an acceleration of earth type events, as in earthquakes, volcanoes, extremely accelerated weather pattern changes, the contagion of disease. The mutation of viruses and bacteria is linked to the polarity of Taurus, and all of this is square to Aquarius, and you have an acceleration of such mutation, which have now become airborne and spread through contagion in such a way that the very survival of the species progressively is on the line. And, what you really have here is a situation where – because of the current rate of evolution and where the collective finds itself – what you are going to have here is change through necessity, not change due to this new age rule of some instant collective enlightenment. It is just not going to happen. It is going to occur through circumstance and necessity. If your life is on the line, you will change or do what you need to do to survive. That is what is in the wind. It will certainly have an effect in terms of trying to curb the birth control rate all over the planet through circumstantial necessity.

Now because Taurus is Venus ruled, we have a receptive aspect of sexuality here. Taurus is not initiatory, sexually. Aries goes out and gets what it wanted; Taurus waits for things to happen. Think about that. One of the applications of Venus is called expectations. What happens if you are in a yin consciousness, sitting there with certain sexual expectations that you are not enunciating to your partner and yet, in a Neptunian fashion, silently expecting that somehow they are going to know what you need sexually, and yet you are not really in there communicating what you are needing and communicating? And then all of a sudden a person is not performing to your expectation and then you are blaming him or her. So what is the message here of Taurus? Relating what you need to relate, not just silently expecting the other person to somehow understand and silently know. Again, we have to abbreviate a lot of this stuff, any questions on the Taurus? Good.

When we get into Gemini we have a natural yang thing, masculine, mutable. It is air; it is energy moving out from the center and, of course, following Taurus, necessarily so; it gets pretty boring at the bottom of the well. The well might go dry. There are problems that cause the frog to jump out of that well, and expose itself to the diversity of the environment. That is the intent of Gemini – to move out of the environment in the full blown sense in order to attempt to know the very nature of that phenomenal environment they are involved with; that's why the intrinsic restlessness of Gemini. So what happens in Gemini when it is sexualized – first keep in mind that it is Mercury ruled – is that Gemini to become sexualized, or to have sexual interest or desire, there has to be some sort of mental stimulation first. Let's say they find someone in a café somewhere, and there is this great mental exchange of like-minded ideas that can arouse Gemini.

In other words, unless there is this mental arousal or attunement, the sexual thing isn't going to kick in, so to speak.

Now one of the problems in this is that, because it is mental overlay, when Gemini is engaged sexually, because of the Mercury overlay, from the point of view of Gemini within itself, it feels like it is not fully physically engaged. There is a form of what we can call mental voyeurism, as it is observing itself being sexual, in such a way that part of its sexual excitement or satisfaction is based on observing itself doing whatever it is doing sexually. It is like a mental amusement: Look mom, no hands! But in the very same way, there is a frustration because they are not fully engaged.

And what can happen in certain cases dependant on other factors. Gemini and/or Virgo in this case, can progressively orientate to various kinds of sexual methodologies or techniques whose intentions are to engage the body in an ever more physical way in order to remove that frustration. That is why when you link it to Virgo for example, an application of that level would correlate with S&M type of sexuality, just for that reason. But, another application – because here we have to be blunt – one of the domains of Gemini sexualized is the orientation to what we call sexual devices or sexual aides, (not AIDS as a disease) as in sexual toys of one sort or the other, particularly when they involve the use of electricity. (Laughter) Let's leave it right there. I am a Pisces Moon sitting here doing this stuff; this can be embarrassing. (Lots of laughter) Anyway, there can be this fascination with that which involves electricity linked with sexual devices. And let's leave it right there.

Sexually, of course, Gemini can get bored very easily. And typical with Gemini, they are always interested in the newest idea, the newest thing to do, and therefore, there can be a direct fascination with whatever the current culture is, and the current cultural sexual fads. For example, for us who survived the late 60s (you all did, you are sitting here) we all remember from the late sixties, the slogan, 'Free Love', and all this experimentation of different ways of being in relationship, different ways of being sexual, and, of course, this correlated astrologically when Uranus was transiting through Libra: 'free love', and all the experimentation therein. And of course, Neptune was in Scorpio, and as a result of all that experimentation we got sexual diseases. That is when Herpes started, believe it or not. There was Neptune transiting Scorpio! The point I am making here is for us who came through these 'hippy' times, and we had all this freedom, apparently, and all this experimentation, and all the current cultural clichés amongst that group.

Now what if you were strongly Gemini? You would find yourself very susceptible to simply acting out whatever the current cultural groovy thing was to do. Now the question becomes, what if that wasn't actually part of your natural nature or need? The point is that Gemini can violate itself by simply orientating to whatever the current cultural fad is, sexually speaking. Do you understand the point I am getting at? Because when you are dealing with these types, and you are dealing with them sexually, you want to make sure, and you can even suggest to them, to always try and honor whatever their natural truth is and just not follow whatever the current cultural deal is, because in most cases, they are going to be in violations of themselves. That is what will happen.

Now, again, Gemini sexually is very, very restless. They can get very sexually bored. And if you are with a Gemini type sexually, you had better have some sort of capacity to adapt. Because for a Gemini to remain faithful and/or monogamous to you, you have better have some degree of adapting to whatever their newest need is. Gemini will not preclude any kind of sexual experience, in and of itself. It is another possible form of knowledge. With Gemini (you have all seen the glyph, the twins), we have a natural square to Pisces and a natural trine to Aquarius. What does the square to Pisces mean? It creates a direct correlation to bi-sexuality. The point is that Neptune tries to dissolve unnecessary boundaries between people. And ultimately to realize that every human Soul is simultaneously male and female – simultaneously. And when Uranus (Gemini) makes this square to Neptune (Pisces), one of the intentions there in evolutionary terms is to make the consciousness aware of that fact; and when that fact becomes aware within consciousness and you sexualize it, it can then translate into a bi-sexual orientation.

You see, when people lived in natural law, nobody had all this morality judgment about when a woman made love to a woman or a man to a man. There were none of these judgments. Because in natural law the issue was that they are making love to the other person's Soul, not just a physical body kind of thing, which so much prevails in cultures like this. Do you see the difference there? So in many cases, the phenomenon you call bi-sexuality initially occurs in the archetype of Gemini.

This can also correlate with sibling sexuality. Now we have all learned that Gemini has a direct correlation to siblings. When siblings become intimate, it is not Gemini any more, it becomes Libra. Remember that you have a natural triad between Gemini and Libra and Aquarius. And when it becomes intimate (Venus) you then go into the next sign in that triad, Libra. And the whole phenomenon of siblings being intimate occurs much more than most people want to recognize, believe me. When you have done this counseling work for this long, you have heard every story.

When Cancer is sexualized it will be born with fundamental fears of insecurity linked with the act of birth itself. The anxiety of separation from the womb of the mother is symbolized by not only the birth moment, but also by the cutting of the umbilical cord. As a result of the separation anxiety experienced at birth, Cancer exhibits a deep fear of sexual vulnerability which mirrors the fear of emotional vulnerability relative to trust. The emotional and psychological compensation for these fears is to create situations in which Cancer attempts to totally control its emotional and sexual life. As a result, Cancer can be very sexually and emotionally possessive, domineering, and irrationally jealous. Hypocritically, Cancer can demand that their partner be absolutely faithful while at the same time giving themselves the right to have sex with someone else.

Cancer's sexual energy and needs are directly linked with their existing emotional dynamics. Because the emotional dynamics can be so complex in Cancer the nature of its sexual dynamics can be just as complex. The root issue, again, is linked with the original anxiety of separation from the womb at birth, and, through extension, with the various causal factors of emotional problems from childhood. As a result, the male application of Cancer can manifest as a strong preoccupation with the breasts of women, and a strong oral orientation to the woman's vagina. The female application of the Cancer archetype can a have a strong oral orientation to the mouth of the man, and to the male sexual organ. This orientation reflects the child's need to bond with the mother at birth through breast feeding, and the security that this creates in the child. In essence, it also reflects the Cancer desire for the original security of the womb.

When Cancer is sexualized it can also manifest as various forms of sexual violence or dominance as a reflection of their unresolved anger. In women this can manifest as psychologically, emotionally, and sexually 'castrating' the man in some way, and in men it can manifest as sexual power over women. Such men use women as sexual objects in order to build up an otherwise weak male self-image. Some will remain sexually arrested or immature, which will also cause various forms of sexual dysfunction. Sexual distortions can be focused on children or on people who are very much younger or older.

Once Cancer realizes the evolutionary intention of inner security, their emotional and sexual orientation to life will change. Instead of being controlling, domineering, and possessive they will become supportive, nurturing, and display an incredible emotional empathy that can truly heal the emotions of others. They will reflect a deep emotional wisdom that is offered in non-manipulative ways. They will be self-empowered, and seek to empower others. Sexually, they will be secure from within themselves, and will no longer fear being sexually or emotionally vulnerable. They will encourage and support the emotional and sexual vulnerability of others. They will desire to emotionally and sexually unite with another so that the sexual experience becomes a source of emotional and psychic renewal. When this occurs, Cancer has realized the evolutionary intention of their Soul.

As their lives evolve, these individuals must embrace the Capricorn polarity. Essentially, this will mean learning how to accept responsibility in their own actions, to become totally self-determined, to become emotionally and sexually mature, and to access the causative factors for their various emotional states, along with the sexual desires that manifest from them.

We now go to Leo which is ruled by Fire, it is fixed, and it is energy moving out from the center. Leo sexualized can be very, very passionate, very ardent; can make you feel that you are the best lover they have ever had. Leo wants to be considered as the most special lover of all, and this can be specific also to the Pluto in Leo as a generation; it is a unique thing to this generation. There is this need to be special and this can also apply to the sexual dimension. Am I your most special lover? Tell me that. And what if they are not? What are you going to do? What is that woman going to do with this compulsive Leo man: Am I their best love? Typically they want to keep the peace and say, "Yes, you are the best", and get out of my face now. But of course the Leo is compulsive, and they want to hear it almost every single day. And, that gets pretty darn tiresome.

When Leo is sexualized it will be pretty darn creative sexually, like Aries, but will preclude any sexuality which is degrading, and linked with humiliation. And when Leo is in love with you, sexually speaking and otherwise, again, they can make you feel like you are the only person in the universe. But on the other hand, once they lose interest in you, then you are simply the object of disdain – psychological disdain. How many of you have experienced disdain from a partner? That wasn't very enjoyable, was it? And unfortunately, Leo can do that. Just the opposite of how they had appeared otherwise, "You are the one for me", and the rest of it. And the reason for this is that Leo has this ongoing compulsive need to be told how wonderful it is, whatever it is doing. And let's say it has been with a partner for ten years; it doesn't want to hear that feedback from that partner anymore. They have already assumed that to be true. And so now it needs another partner to recreate that hit. It is like getting a fix, so to speak. And this is why you read in the traditional books, that Leo is somehow linked with love affairs, and this is why. It is this ongoing compulsive need for the feedback to tell the Leo just how wonderful it is. And once you take away whatever that quotient is about, then you have just opened the door to that Leo to be elsewhere.

Leo will manifest an intense, deep, passionate, assertive, and narcissistic orientation to the sexual experience. There is a high degree of focus on self-pleasure. In men, this can correlate to the 'Adonis complex', where they expect to be sexually worshipped. In women, this manifests as the 'Cleopatra complex', where they also expect to be sexually worshipped. In both men and women there will be a strong focus on using their own bodies as temples of creative self discovery through autoerotic practices. In men, there is a glorification of the phallus as a symbol of metamorphic power. In women, there is a glorification of the vagina as a temple of birth and regeneration. Many will be highly creative in designing masturbatory practices that allow for a deep intensity of psychological, emotional, and physical sensation, the intensity of which serves to renew and release the Soul simultaneously.

In their sexual relationships Leo is focused on experiencing their own intense stimulation through their partner. The partner serves as a vehicle through which this stimulation occurs. Through increasing the degree of stimulation and sensation in this way, Leo thus stimulates the partner because of the inner intensity of their own sensations. The specific nature of the types of sexual desires that Leo desires to creatively actualize can be determined by the actual house the Sun is in, the aspects that it is making to other planets, and the houses that those planets are in.

As Leo evolves sexually, it means to learn how to objectify and embrace the sexual desires and needs of their partner: listen and learn how to satisfy their partner's needs and not just their own.

When Virgo is sexualized it will express itself through the pathology of sadomasochism. The range of expression can be from an absolute denial of anything sexual, to a total absorption into sexuality as a primary focus in life: sexual addiction. These forms can range from overt masochistic practices, to overt sadistic practices, with all combinations therein. A common application of the masochistic archetype in women and men is to focus on sexual methods and techniques that serve to stimulate and please the partner to the exclusion of themselves: a form of masochistic self-sacrifice. The pleasure that is experienced by the Mars in Virgo person is the vicarious pleasure that is experienced through the partner. A common application of the sadistic archetype in women and men occurs through 'sexual games' in which the partner is physically restrained in some way. Because Mars in Virgo creates a personal energy system that is focused upon what it lacks, a deep inner energy of emptiness, the temptation is to fill up this emptiness with something of an external nature. Linked with sexual dynamics, this can lead to sexual addiction, or the 'always keeping busy' syndrome as a way of diffusing such energy: this becomes a de facto sexual act.

This dynamic can also exist when the Virgo experiences an almost absolute lack of sexual life with another person. Even 'normal' sex can be experienced as lacking from the point of view. As a result, Virgo will typically create sexual imagery that excites their mind and Soul. Instinctively, they will then desire to make real the inner imagery relative to sexual situations with a partner and/or to visit sexual environments in which such imagery is acted out; this can include sexual magazines. During sexual intercourse, Virgo is then 'making love' to the imagery because of the excitation this produces, instead of 'making love' to the actual person that they are having intercourse with. When this occurs, this is actually a form of sexual sadism because it is a way of humiliating the partner. To the extent that such a partner conforms to these types of sexual desires, Virgo can be quite satisfied. When the partner does not or will not conform to these types of the desires, this becomes a potential ignition point of physical, psychological, or sexual abuse by Virgo: an anger fueled by frustration dictating such behavior.

And because of the inner sense of lack or emptiness, Virgo can compensate through manifesting an extreme sexual/physical intensity that attempts to consume and overwhelm the partner; a form of sadistic dominance. Conversely, Virgo can desire to be consumed through physical/ sexual intensity on a repetitive, compulsive basis as a way of feeling full in order to replace the sense in inner emptiness; a form of masochistic surrender.

Let me dismiss something about Virgo. A lot of times you've read that Virgo is somehow linked with the Virgin and the virginity issue, and the purity therein. In most cases, within Virgo you will find a great inner existential void, psychologically speaking, and when that is sexualized in many of the Virgo cases, they go out and initiate sexuality just to fill in the inner existential void, not exercising discrimination. This is why Virgo has a direct correlation with Bulimia and Anorexia. These are actual de facto sexual events that displace an inner void, especially Bulimia. Think about it: a person is filling themselves up and having an orgasm through vomit. That is what it is about. In another case, Virgo can be absolutely asexual because there is such an underlying fear of sexuality, equaling being contaminated. And, when this is the case, literally sitting on their sexuality, then they make this list of things to do. Just one thing after the other as a way of avoiding what is actually going on.

As Virgo evolves it must embrace Pisces. Sexually, this will allow for these individuals to accept their sexual natures and desires as they are. No longer will there be any guilt association with those desires, thus removing the causal factor in any form or manifestation of sadomasochistic sexual practices. They will now learn that it is just fine to have their own sexual needs fulfilled versus always trying to please the partner first and experiencing fulfillment through their satisfaction. By removing Patriarchal beliefs, men will no longer feel sexually inadequate relative to gender assignments manifesting from the Patriarchy (performance expectations). Women will no longer feel that sexually that they must submit or surrender to a man's will (masochistic expectations). As a result, both men and women will feel the freedom to just be who they naturally are.

When Libra becomes sexualized it reflects a Soul that desires to inwardly unite the inner male and female through sexual role equality. Within this, there is a keen instinctual nature that is able to harmonize with the sexual energy of the partner. This instinctual harmonization reflects the Libra desire to give. In this way, a mutual harmonization takes place wherein the partner gives back, producing a mutually deep and permeating sexual response. Mars in Libra contains a unique gift to unlock and set free the sexual energy in a partner who has been 'locked up'. Typically, Mars in Libra is very sexually refined with a keen sense of touch and sexual grace.

The neat thing about Libra is that it has a tremendous capacity to tune into the sexuality or needs of its partner and then to literally give to that partner exactly what it needs, based on that tuning in. Now what Libra is doing, unconsciously, is creating a dependency on that partner for them. Keeping in mind that Cancer squares Libra, there is an underlying insecurity in Libra; therefore, it is an unconscious investment in trying to make their partner feel that they are their very best sexual partner and they can do that due to the attunement. Please understand the underlying cause. They need to feel secure with that partner, and that is why they need to tune in and to give, and to give in that way does not necessarily mean that their own need is being met – other than their need for security.

Libra does not like dirty sex. They want their fingernails to be clean. They like the ambiance. They like the little incense flying around. They like the glass of wine. Remember, Aries couldn't care less. But you better have clean fingernails if you want to be with Libra sexually. Also Libra is one of the archetypes which correlates with homosexuality – same sex. And because of the need to inwardly unite the inner male and female principle Libra sexualized can also be sexually androgynous: bisexual. Libra is the archetype, as well, of the hermaphrodite. Libra can be also very sexually versatile. They won't preclude any experience except that which degrades. Unfortunately, Virgo in many cases is orientated to sex that degrades, humiliates; it is part of their own native compulsive crises.

The Libra sexualized is also learning about sexual karma. This is reflected in the desire to initiate a diversity of relationships with many types of people, stimulating Libra's desire to continually expand its conscious horizons. Many of these connections, again, will have sexual overtones. Because Libra is a Cardinal archetype, many of these connections can be initiated on a relatively brief basis without any real follow-through or completion. Once the sexual fluids are exchanged through any form of sexual contact, a mutual exchange of karma occurs. As a result, a karmic link is established. The key for Libra is to complete each connection it has with another, even if such a connection is the famous 'one night stand'. They must enter each connection with conscious awareness and intention that is mutually understood instead of a 'love them and leave them' attitude. When Libra is sexualized and becomes attracted to someone, but is already in an existing relationship, it is karmically necessary to be honest with the existing partner and not to enter into such a connection without honestly communicating and informing the partner about such a connection. When this does not occur, additional karma is created with that partner.

As their life evolves, Libra meets its polarity: Aries. The Mars in Libra person is often so instinctively aware it creates a state of ongoing balance, versus extremes. Sexually, this means for them to honor their own needs, not just the needs of the partner. Mars in Libra can become so involved in the sexual needs and responses of a partner that they lose touch with their own needs and desires. Sexual equality means for them to attract partners who are just as sensitive to them. Equally aware, both become more than satisfied.

Scorpio is the archetype in which we are literally learning through the Piscean triad, linked with the Taurus polarity, to where we can utilize rituals, very specific sexual rituals, so we can remember or relearn how to become incorporated with God and reality in general through the vehicle of sexuality, therefore sexual ritual. Sexuality in Scorpio is intrinsically compulsive. The sexual energy in Scorpio is consistent or constant. It never goes away. There is a need for perpetual, psychic release. Scorpio can have a direct correlation to what we call rape, by using sex as power, the sexual predator, with sexual dominance as the result. And the converse to this, sex used as metamorphic transformation of one's psychological and emotional reality because the underlying purpose of Scorpio is to merge: to merge with a partner, merging back with the Source, and we call this God. In terms of sexual energy, this is the most intense level, Scorpio. In Germany, it is called a hammer. Boom, boom, the most intense of all is Scorpio.

Karmically, Scorpio desires to learn the value of emotional/sexual commitment versus following every compulsive attraction. Within this, Mars in Scorpio desires to learn about its sexual compulsions, its attraction to sexual taboos, the nature of sexual possession and the jealousy that follows, the nature of its projected sexual fears linked with a partner's potential infidelities, and the nature of its sexual desires that are linked with the archetype of the sex as power.

In evolutionary terms, Scorpio must learn, and desires to learn, that karma is directly osmosed and exchanged through sexual union with others. Sexual discrimination becomes a key lesson. In addition, it must learn the difference between sexual intensity used as domination, possession, and as a potential vehicle to work out its built-up anger and rage: sex as power versus the need to use such intensity as a vehicle to unite the Soul and Divinity from within itself, and with another.

As their life evolves, Scorpio must embrace their polarity: Taurus. Scorpio's emotional and sexual addictions, and fears linked with loss, betrayal, and abandonment that can create a fundamental fear of real intimacy can be overcome, and evolved beyond, by embracing the Taurus lessons of self-fulfillment, self-reliance, and self-sustainment. In so doing, an evolution in attitude and inner orientation has been accomplished that produces a state of self-empowerment. These individuals have learned to use themselves as their own vehicle of metamorphic change.

When Sagittarius is sexualized the Soul intuitively understands that sexuality is a natural part of Life: that it is an inherent principle within Nature. As such, there is a desire for sexual adventures of all kinds, and a desire for partners who are just as free to explore sexuality in this way. Sexuality in all its various expressions becomes a vehicle in which these Souls understand the larger connections to life itself. As such, many of these Souls are natural sexual teachers in the sense of helping others understand the deeper issues within themselves that are linked with their specific sexual behavioral patterns.

Within this, there is a desire for sexual honesty, and a desire to expose sexual dishonesty within itself and/or the partner. As a result, it is not uncommon for the sexualized Sagittarius to attract partners who are not honest about their sexual history. Sagittarius also desires to know how the partner is feeling, or has felt, relative to sexual experience through conversations and discussions that follow the sexual act. This will also include discussions with the partner about the individual sexual histories. This desire again reflects the need to connect the sexual experience to the larger elements of life. In this way, deeper personal truths are revealed to the partner as well as to Sagittarius itself. Sagittarius can be natural sexual healers.

There is a strong and constant sexual nature. They bring the spirit of adventure to the sexual experience, and are instinctively passionate and intense. The passion that fuels their intensity is the passion of spirit focused within the physical body, and the desire to consciously experience the descent of spirit within the physical body. Instinctively, Sagittarius understands the right use of sexual energy as a vehicle for personal renewal and as a positive outlet that allows other areas of life to be maintained in their proper perspective.

Sagittarius involves the entire phenomenon of Natural Law in general, which we want to call Gaia, and therefore the issue of natural sexual law. But, again these things can change during different times. And we have all heard that Sagittarius interacts with religion. So, how can religion have an impact on Natural Sexual law? Let's make a funny stupid example. In the late 1890s in this country, there was a bizarre religion called 'Calvinism'. Their method involved living in a community, and the way they would make these people reproduce, make babies, was the man would stand here, there now is a hole in the wall, and now here is the woman, and they would make babies this way. Now does that sound natural do you? And, does that not sound like a religion doing something funny within natural sexual law?

The point is that we have the actual archetype of religion and how religion creates moralities, relative to its conceptions and how this affects and impacts what is assumed to be correct moral behavior, including correct sexual behavior. Remembering if a majority of people assume or agree that something is real, then that assumption is called reality. It doesn't mean it is actually real in terms of ultimate reality.

Now Sagittarius at best can operate as a sexual healer for other people. It is a fire sign and one of the problems in the male sexual application of Sagittarius, and this can also happen to Aries in a male, is called the pre-ejaculation syndrome. Why? Because the nerves in the genital area become overly stimulated prior to the sexual event. They are thinking about it. And, they over stimulate their nerves therein, so when it comes time to be sexual, they become pre-ejaculatory and in certain cases, impotent, linked now with the fear of failure.

Sagittarius, sexualized, of course, always wants to sexually grow. It wants to have ongoing experience, ongoing discovery. It does not like tedium or boredom, like Aries or Leo, and although Leo does concern itself more than Aries with the duration of sex because of it being fixed: Sagittarius and Aries do not. They care about the quality of the exchange. And just like Aries, Sagittarius is just as happy making love out in the cornfield as it is in some neat canopied bed. Sagittarius, in and of themselves are not monogamous. They want sexual freedom and adventure therein. It doesn't mean they can't be monogamous; they just need a partner who can participate with them in whatever experiences they need. And they can be very passionate.

One of the great things that Sagittarius brings to sexuality – listen carefully – is levity. (Lots of laughter). Does sex always have to be so serious? Ask Capricorn. (More laughter!) They bring humor to the darn thing. They bring levity, lightness. It can be a fun thing to do! Capricorn is saying "What? You are telling me this?" So that is a great element they bring. Also they reflect what would be called a sexual sincerity.

Generally speaking, the Sagittarius must learn to sexually slow down, as their sexual instinct can become overly stimulated. This creates a high degree of arousal and stimulation that can lead to quick and intense physical orgasms. In women, this leads to a multi-orgasmic energy system, and in men it can create premature ejaculation, causing frustration for the partner.

When Capricorn is sexualized it desires to break free from all sexual inhibitions and sexual constraints. The repression of natural sexual desires over many lifetimes has created a deep sexual/emotional anger. The anger linked with repression has also created deep distortions of the sexual/emotional desires and needs. Because of the desire to unlock these distortions, and the closed doors that repress their natural sexual/emotional desires and needs.

Capricorn, of itself, will have a very high sexual energy, yet this energy can be suppressed is life. The first lesson for such Souls is to accept themselves as sexual beings. When this occurs, the psychology of concealment will be purged, and the fear of inner and outer judgment will cease to exist. As a result of the current life intention, the Capricorn will typically attract partners who are also quite emotionally and sexually fractured, repressed, or crippled in some way.

These types of partners, of course, mirror Capricorn itself. Because of the intention and instinct to break free, to learn to accept themselves as emotional and sexual beings, Capricorn can then attract partners who mirror their own sexual/emotional distortion. The manifestations of this can range from sexual violence, which can include being forced to have sex, to various forms of sexual domination and control, to sexual humiliation in which the Capricorn ends up feeling cheap or dirty in some way because of the nature of the sexual event or dynamics, to being attracted to certain kinds of environments: disco clubs, for example in which sexual possibilities exist. And the pretense of the disco club serving as the rationale that masks the actual intent.

All too often, Capricorn must rely on some intoxicant (wine, for example) to unlock and relax its instinctual inhibitions. Once unlocked in this way, the normal 'boundaries of propriety' are dissolved. Now disarmed, the sexual energy reflected in the Dark Eros of distortions caused by previous repression is unleashed. Unleashed, Capricorn learns and discovers that they are intense sexual beings who have a deep and unresolved emotional need to be nurtured and healed. Sexuality becomes a vehicle through which these emotional needs are accessed. Through the intensity of the sexual exchange, an intensity based on duration and/or sexual frequency, the emotions come to the surface. Once the intensity is released through the act of physical orgasms, the harbor of emotional safety and need is found in each others' arms; at least for a while. Above all else, Capricorn desires to be emotionally healed and can truly bring the gift of emotional healing to another. They can bring the gift of making their partners feel worthy, and important. They can help their partners define their own life goals and objectives, and help their partners actualize such goals through the psychology of self-determination.

When personal integrity and honesty permeate the relationship dynamic, Capricorn desires to sustain the relationship over the long haul: for life. As the Mars in Capricorn Soul grows older, their life force and their sexual energy become stronger. This occurs as the 'doors of the inner prison' are progressively unlocked.

Capricorn evolves through the Cancer polarity which will allow these individuals to access their greatest sexual need: to lose total control of themselves. Safe and sustained sexual intercourse of an increasingly intense nature will be the means to accomplish this.

When Aquarius is sexualized it desires to experiment with all possible ways of being sexual. This includes the possibility of detaching from the sexual instinct itself: to be asexual or celibate. The instinct to rebel from current cultural social customs or morals leads such Souls into considering different ways of being sexual that many others would judge as kinky, weird, or bizarre. These 'sexual deviations' can include group sex, group marriage, 'open' marriage arrangements in which one or both partners are allowed to have sex with other partners, observational sex of a vicarious nature reflected in sex magazines, clubs, or theaters, experimenting with all kinds of sexual devices, restraint of the physical body that is then intensely stimulated in a variety of ways, many different forms of autoeroticism, and/or embracing spiritual sexual methods that allow for a transformation of sexual energy from the primal to the sacred.

Because of the core detachment of Aquarius the sexual act is similar to a scientific experiment in which an observation is made of the specific effect of various methods of sexual stimulation on the subject. This detached observation (cause and effect) produces psychological/sexual knowledge for Aquarius. This detachment can also cause frustration for such Souls, because it does not allow for full engagement with the physical body. The mental dynamic in consciousness is always energized and observing. This frustration can cause a psychological anger to occur, in which Aquarius desires to fully engage their body in such a way that their mind becomes obliterated. This desire then leads into discovering ways to be sexual that are so physically intense or all consuming that the mind can no longer observe the body. The unique gift that Aquarius has is to simulate and encourage the desire for sexual creativity in their partners, to stimulate desires buried within the unconscious of their partners. As a result, Aquarius desires partners that manifest the courage to be different in all kinds of ways, including the courage to sexually experiment.

When Pisces is sexualized it desires to experience a descent of spirit into flesh; to experience the power of the divine or God through the energy of sexuality. For some, this will lead to thoughts/desires to transmute gross sexual/physical expression into harnessing and focusing the sexual energy through various forms of spiritual practice. For others, this will lead to the employment of specific sacred sexual practices that are aimed at using the sexual energy to transfigure consciousness itself. For still others, this will lead to a necessary acting out of all the residual sexual desires of lifetimes that have not been acted on; that which initially appears as sexual fantasies within the interior of their consciousness. Through the necessary acting out of these desires, a process of elimination occurs that then allows for the core sexual desire to experience the descent of spirit into flesh relative to sacred sexual practices.

The nature of these fantasies can be anything, depending on the specific nature of each individual. For still others, this can manifest as a cyclic immersion into many forms of gross or primary sexuality, and cycles of enforced celibacy reflecting the guilt associated with the cycle of gross immersion. For still others, this can manifest as a total immersion into acting out all kinds of sexual fantasies of a primary nature throughout life: an unconscious rejection of the desire to evolve into sacred sexuality. When this is the operational dynamic, Pisces desire to be consumed, or to consume another, during the sexual act. And for still others, this will manifest as a conscious rejection of divinity outright: an unconscious anger at God.

These types will typically desire perverse forms of sexuality defined by masochism or sadism. When that is the operational dynamic, sex as punishment becomes the primary orientation. Additionally, Pisces can have irrational sexual fears, or fears that have been caused by actual sexual events. When this is the case, the evolutionary intention is to examine the nature of these fears, and to heal these fears as a result. Specific sexual methods must be employed for this to occur. An example of such a method would be learning non-sexual touch. Through non-sexual touch, Pisces can learn psycho/emotional safety and trust. Once learned, sexual healing can follow.

The core intention with Pisces is to understand the difference between profane and sacred sexuality. Because of this, Pisces, especially in men relative to the times that we are living in, desire that their partner be 'pure': Angel Mary types who reflect the innocent qualities of the 'virgin archetype'. Yet, because of their own inner struggles over many lifetimes defined by the cycles of guilt/atonement, and guilt/anger, that have manifested as cycles of celibacy and immersion into many forms of primary sexuality, they attract partners who vibrate in exactly the same way. Thus, they are initially attracted to people who appear innocent, sensitive, and 'pure'. Then, when they discover that these types of partners have had a sexual history that is very much like their own, they feel disillusioned and angry.

This disillusionment and anger is projected on the partner in a variety of ways, which can include a total withholding of their emotional/sexual self. It can include verbal abuse in the form of projected judgments of a moralistic nature. It can include unconsciously wanting to hurt such a partner through intense sexual practices of a dominating nature; to overwhelm and make the partner helpless through intense sexual stimulation. It can include becoming sexual with other people thus creating humility: to humiliate the partner. And it can include becoming sexually or physically violent to the partner.

Again, the key is for such Souls to realize the connection between what emanates from their own Souls, and the circumstantial realities that are created as a reflection of those emanations: desires. Once the Pisces makes the conscious connection to their own inner duality, that what they are attracting is but a reflection of their own inner self, then compassion, nurturing, forgiveness, and a real healing of these wounds will occur: for both people. Once the transference is made between man-made religions to natural law, an acceptance of that which is natural will occur. Once this occurs, a healing and dissolving of the guilt leading to anger and atonement will also take place. When this takes place, Pisces has realized its karmic and evolutionary intentions in this way.

I am sorry that we had to abbreviate this. You can probably see the depth that could be included if we had more time. So I guess we can just wet the whistle today. But a lot of this information is in my Pluto Two book, so if you want to get into it, read it there.

Thanks for coming.

6

Saturn, Capricorn and the 10th House:
Chaos and Dark Eros

Jeffrey: The topic today is the nature of dark Eros and chaos, linked with the archetype of Capricorn. Now, most of the time when we think of Capricorn, we're not going to be thinking generally in terms of chaos and dark Eros. (laughter). But it's an incredibly important part of the archetype to understand because, as we go through it, you will see that in its own way, it's a very specific cause of all kinds of psychological disturbances and distortions of one sort or another in our present culture. Let's first explore Capricorn from the largest point of view, then come down the ladder to specifics. I want to do it that way so you can truly understand where this issue that we're going to call dark Eros and chaos originates.

If we look at Capricorn from the largest possible view, which is the perspective of creation itself, we have to start by remembering that the nature of creation in the beginning is simply energy, energy projected out from some sort of center. When you project energy outward, you set in motion a dual electrical charge, positive and negative, which then sets in motion the natural laws of duality and of cause and effect. Via this projection of energy, a third natural law is created that we call gravity. And gravity is very specific to the archetype of Capricorn. So when you apply gravity to energy, then you have a condensation of energy into specific form, which is the real function of Capricorn. From this point of view, and specific to the time/space reality called Earth, we are then observing the inherent natural laws that are responsible for the manifested phenomenal creation, including the phenomena of consciousness. Now, consciousness itself is very similar to water. Water in itself has no form. But if I put water in a cup, it assumes the function of that form. Phenomena, or phenomenal, simply means the world of appearances. When consciousness manifests in the human form, it can only assume the function of that form. So if we reason from the point of view of phenomenal reality, the only way consciousness in human form can truly know the nature of phenomenal reality is in fact through the vehicle of the senses. Everything in your nature in the human form is about sensing. And it is the interaction of the senses with consciousness that generates thought.

We're going to look at consciousness from two different viewpoints. We can look at consciousness from the point of view of its natural structure, the natural structure of human consciousness. And then we can look at it from the point of view of socially conditioned consciousness, which correlates with the archetype of Saturn. This distinction is very, very important, because for a group of people to have any degree of stability, and for that group to live and work together, they have to create what are called 'social contracts'. They're also called social norms, customs, taboos, laws, regulations and so on. We need to do that. If we didn't have social contracts and social rules, the consequence would be a literally Uranian reality: anarchy.

How many of you in this room would like to live in an anarchistic society? Most of you would not enjoy the experience. The human being essentially is a social organism, so we had to create social contracts, agreements in effect, about how we're going to live together. It's essential. But as we evolved, there came a point in human history at roughly 6500 BCE, when the transition between the Matriarchy, or what is now called the Matriarchy, and the Patriarchy began. In many ways, the word 'Matriarchy' is a metaphor for how human beings have lived for the majority of our time on this planet. This means human beings defined by natural law, the principles of nature which are self-evident, and which exist whether human beings are here or not. For the majority of human history, that's exactly how we lived. So by the time we hit 6500 BCE, the Patriarchal transition began. Amazingly enough, when you look at it astrologically, that transition occurred during the, guess what, Capricorn sub-age of the Cancer age. Look at it in terms of gender transference. Capricorn and Cancer have a lot to do with gender assignment relative to cultural definitions of roles. So we see this classic transition reflected in that time. What progressively began to occur during this Patriarchal transition was that all kinds of projected thoughts, called beliefs, were created in order to enforce a specific view or conception about the nature of the phenomenal creation.

The point here is that there was a progressive movement away from natural law defining the human organism, a movement away from direct perception or experience which is how all humans came to understand the phenomenal nature of anything. Direct experience was replaced with beliefs. There are things, for example, called natural sexual laws which are vastly different than what is now considered to be 'correct' sexuality from the point of view of the Patriarchy. We'll be looking at that in a lot of detail today.

Question: how many of you have tried to live to some degree a spiritual life? Including meditation and yoga and the rest of it. Or orientations to some sort of guru? Now check this out: how many of you realize that up until, say, 7000 BCE, there was not even an idea of what we would call God? There was not even a conception for it. Up until around that time, God was considered to be what we call Gaia. Earth.

Around 7000 BCE, there was the very first conception in human consciousness of what we now call God. Amazingly enough from the Patriarchal perspective, the very first concept for God was a woman. The original name for God in history was Namu, which was a woman. Even in that cosmology, it was vastly different than how we picture God now. In this Patriarchal reality, when men started to invent a Patriarchal God, the invention started with the conception of a God that was perfect. Perfect. Now let's just ask one simple Pisces question: how can a perfect anything create an imperfect anything? It's not possible. Within this conception of a 'perfect' God, we had the invention of all the 'spiritual should be's'. *Should be's*. This is why none of you have been successful in your Patriarchal spiritual life, because all these famous Patriarchal 'should-be's' are in violation of natural law. (laughter).

Going further, the Patriarchal view included this preposterous notion that tells you that to know God, you have to suppress your senses. Let's go back to where we started. When you put consciousness in human form, it can only assume the function of that form. And that means consciousness in human form can only know the nature of phenomenal reality via its senses. So we have to suppress our senses to know this perfect God, which doesn't exist! Do you understand what I'm getting at? Do you see how twisted this is? Then there's the incredible invention of the word transcendence. This word actually was born out of another delusional Patriarchal doctrine: the 'conflict between spirit and flesh'. Meaning, for one thing that sex is somehow antagonistic to or in conflict with spiritual life along with anything else you perceive through your senses. So for all those who are trying to live this happy Patriarchal spiritual life, you'll now probably begin to understand why you feel so crummy and guilty inside. Here you are meditating, and you get an erection or you feel a little aroused. Uh oh. (laughter) This doesn't fit the doctrine. So imagine the guilt trip you're doing on yourself. "There must be something wrong with me", and all the rest of it. And it's also, as an aside, why so many monks are smoking cigarettes. Why? Because in a Capricorn archetype they are suppressing natural law. And the psychological act of suppression generates a psychological and emotional compression and intensity. And so even a monk in many cases is reduced to smoking cigarettes because of this build-up of inner compression, stress and tension. I know this because I lived as a monk in various monasteries for years. It's all because of repressing that which is natural. This goes right to the heart of the matter in terms of the connection between Capricorn and dark Eros, because of the way it relates to the question of natural sexual law versus what modern humans have done with it. The history of sexuality will blow you away, in terms of what we've done with it. So first of all, let's agree that there's no intrinsic conflict between spirit and flesh. None whatsoever. If you agree with the notion, even the Patriarchal notion that God is 'the Origin of all things', then wherein lies the origin of sexuality? And, while we're at it, wherein lies the origin of imperfection? Wherein lies the origin of anger? Everything that you are is also what God is, and beyond. Think about it this way: you didn't create yourself; God created you. So the real issue becomes what is this thing we call God?

There are these standards that we can call natural sexual laws. For example, just to give you a peek into the majority of human history, in a Matriarchal reality there were no nuclear families, and nothing that we would now call monogamy. Children were raised communally. You were allowed to have personal possessions but that was it. The land was communal. And up until 6500 BCE or so, neither men or women knew that a man contributed equally to making a baby. That might sound shocking to us, but in fact it's historically true.

As a result when a woman conceived a child, this was considered to be a direct expression of what we would call God. Sexuality was considered to be naturally sacred in its own right. We also must understand, from the point of view of earthly reality, that the feminine is the origin of the masculine, not the other way around, as Patriarchal people would have you think. All you have to do is consider the nature of the genitalia, and you'll understand this primary truth. In fact there was an interesting book written in England about twenty years ago, by male scientists, called *The Redundant Male*. What this book postulated and then proved, keeping in mind they're scientists, is that a woman actually has the capacity of reproducing the species without the male. Just as a seahorse can, as well as other forms within the Creation.

Audience: How?

Jeffrey: They are simultaneously male and female, which relates to how you can also understand the phenomenon of the hermaphrodite. But given the fact that we lived on the Earth, the feminine principle 'realized' that there was in fact a need for the male because clearly the male form is a bit stronger, on a muscular level, than the feminine form. But the deeper reasons for this is the nature of the immune system. If asexual reproduction was the norm then the immune systems cold not evolve so as to protect the species from various diseases. So procreation with the male and female allowed the immune systems themselves to evolve so as to deal with the ongoing issue of the survival of the species itself. So the female had to create the male for this to occur. So it was a functional survival necessity that produced the male form.

Then around 6500 BCE, the Patriarchy started taking over. Why? Right then and there is the time frame in which the man and woman realized that a man had an equal role in making a baby. This is the actual historical cause for the beginning of the Patriarchal transition. And for reasons that nobody can really, truly explain, it created a bizarre, distorted sense of power in men. For a man to increase his power in those times, he had to be able to pass on his possessions, primarily land, to a succeeding generation. This became the causative factor, historically speaking, of the nuclear family and what we now call 'paternity'. Meaning the man had to know which woman he was with to know which baby he made, and that no other man had made that baby. That's the historical cause of paternity, and the beginnings of what we now call monogamy from a historical point of view.

This was the time frame in which all that which is natural, including natural sexual laws, were progressively suppressed. And whatever is natural, including sexuality, becomes the basis of distortion and rage when it is repressed.

Let's understand that the sexual instinct in all people emanates from what is called the primary brain. In astrology, this part of the brain directly correlates with the Moon, Pluto, and Mars. Now this is also where consciousness comes from, from your primary brain. Not your cerebral cortex. And the primary brain of itself is unconditioned. It is defined by natural law. It is utterly instinctual. There is no conceptualization within the primary brain. And it regulates all the instinctual functioning of your body: breathing, excreting, sexuality, etc. But when we pass through history and we subject this natural consciousness to social conditioning, social contracts, belief systems, and so on, and we have this progressive movement into the Patriarchy, there is a progressive repression of all that is natural. This distortion becomes the basis of rage.

Take another natural law, and for the women in the room, if you're truly inwardly honest, you will recognize the truth of what is about to be shared. All women, under natural law, have two sexual archetypes that are co-equal. One desire-archetype is to be with a man who is the primary partner. He is the kind of man who wants to be with the woman on a day to day basis. But a woman has, co-equally and just as strongly, a need and desire to be with a diversity of men. Now there are two reasons for that, and if you doubt this, just go visit an evolutionary biologist and he or she will prove it to you. One reason is strictly for survival purposes. The greatest danger to human life is the world of viruses, bacteria, parasites and fungi, which mutate much more quickly than we do. This is why the human organism oriented to sexual intercourse as a way of propagating the species, versus asexual reproduction. Why? Because if you have asexual reproduction, you have basically a static immune system, whereas with sexual intercourse, you are creating an evolving immune system, collectively speaking, by producing a third entity that is a synthesis of two others. This is why sexual intercourse was adopted. The stronger sperm are more likely to fertilize the egg, strengthening the species. You see the link to the immune system here? It's a biological reason. Now the other reason for this second, more experimental face of female sexuality is a metaphysical one. The key here is that all fluids on earth, including sexual fluids, contain memory. Keep in mind that we all carry our entire evolutionary and karmic background in our sexual fluids. This is actually, to my mind, the greater argument to exercise some judgment and discrimination in terms of our sexual expression: not on some artificial moral basis, but on the basis of what you want to happen in your consciousness.

Because we are osmosing, Pluto, the sexual fluids of our lover, and therefore bringing into ourselves that person's entire reality, past and present. And vice versa, of course, our lover is absorbing our own. So why, from a metaphysical point of view, would a woman want to expose herself to a diversity of sperm? Because it would also mean exposing herself to a diversity of human knowledge. And by bringing this into herself, the woman inherently has the capacity, physiologically speaking, of then alchemically changing the sexual fluid she's bringing in, mixing it with her own, so that by the time she sleeps with the next man she's imparting the first man's knowledge to the second man through the act of sexuality. This is how humans used to evolve in knowledge and understanding. It had nothing to do with blackboards and books and teachers and the rest of it. And they enjoyed it! (laughter)

Consciousness, naturally structured, is a consciousness defined by the principles of sharing, giving and inclusion. You shift to a Patriarchal reality, and you have consciousness defined by self-interest and exclusion. You see these two core differences? They are absolutely critical. In the collective sexual psychology that we have now, created by the Patriarchy, we see possession, jealousy, feeling threatened, trying to limit the partner's growth for one's personal self-interest and so on: all based on self-interest and exclusion. In a natural way of living, this psychology simply would not exist. It wouldn't occur in that kind of consciousness. Do you understand my point? It just would not occur in the context of sharing, giving and inclusion.

There are all kinds of natural sexual laws. The highest one embraces the intrinsic sacredness of sexuality in which one merges one's Soul with another Soul, and through that mutual merging, one contacts inner divinity. This is what men call tantra. Much of what flies under that banner is totally false, by the way. Those who have looked at these 'tantric' books in your bookstores, you've typically read the following: "it's the duty of the man to repress ejaculation." And then they invent all these groovy myths around it, it nitrates this and neutralizes that, and blah, blah, quack, quack, (laughter)

Sure, men can repress their orgasms, but in reality what actually occurs is that the sperm comes through the bladder and is simply urinated away. That's fact. Go ask a doctor. And the reason that men created this doctrine, around 5500 BCE, was to mimic women. From a man's point of view, the woman seems to have the capacity for 'unlimited sexual response'. Now, what does the man do when he has sex? He has his happy little orgasm, then he rolls over and goes to sleep. (laughter) Meanwhile the woman's going, "Huh?" (laughter) You women know the drill. The point here is that men were feeling threatened by the feminine principle, and as a result of feeling threatened, they invented these things that they want to call 'tantra' in essence to mimic the woman. Do you see the connection to repressing orgasm? So the astrological bottom line in all this stuff is that Capricorn, as an archetype progressively wrongly defined and distorted by the Patriarchy, then becomes an archetype of repression. Repressing what? All that which is natural. Further, if we understand the nature of the word repression, you can clearly see its extension to include the word 'control'. If something threatens us, we try to repress and control it. Yes? And if you are dependent on the happy astrology books out there, this is what you're going to read about Capricorn. They're 'control freaks'. Yes?

So herein lies the heart of the matter from an evolutionary point of view. We've all lived in Patriarchal times, in this lifetime and others, and so we've all been progressively conditioned. That is the functional nature of Saturn/Capricorn in a Patriarchal reality: to condition consciousness. Remember my earlier point about groups of people living together needing to make social contracts, laws and the rest? This is the very basis of social conformity. It's also the basis of the word 'reality', meaning that if we have enough people agreeing about social contracts, social belief systems, and so on, then all that starts to be called 'reality'. It is just assumed to be true, and actual sensory experience be damned. Assumption, in astrology, is symbolized by Capricorn. So in any country there's a collective myth called reality. But the real question becomes, is that an actual reality under natural law, or an invented reality, a reality invented through social contract? This second kind of 'reality' includes social laws, regulations, norms, and taboos that are agreed upon and assumed to be right and true. Based on the fact that the individual, the Soul, the human being is in fact essentially a social organism, in order for each person to feel secure within that group, he or she must conform to what the group has decided to call 'real'. And that then becomes the basis of 'morality'. And again, remember anything that is natural which is repressed or suppressed becomes the basis of distortion and rage.

Think about it, and you can now understand the causative factor of psychological, sexual and emotional abuse to women and children. You can understand the causative factor for sadomasochism. You can understand the cause or wanting to hurt somebody sexually, or to rape. Do you understand what I'm trying to get at here? It all comes down to rage. Something in us rages when natural law is repressed. The primary brain remembers the old ways, the natural ways. From the point of view of the Capricorn archetype in a Patriarchal reality, this is why you've read in astrology books about the supposed Capricornian need to control. And this is also, going back to the subject of the talk, you can begin to see why I've called this lecture, "Capricorn, Dark Eros and Chaos". At the deepest inner level of all Capricorn archetypes, beyond the apparent need to control all things, limit all things, define all things, and all the rest of it, is an absolute need to lose control. This is not something you're going to read in your typical astrology book about Capricorn. There's the deepest inner need to lose all control. And as a result of needing to lose all control, to access psychological chaos: that last part is only true in a Patriarchal reality. The need to lose control equaling chaos is a reflection of, and is caused by, the repression of natural law. You all have heard of a tremendous psychiatrist named Thomas Moore. Most of you are probably only familiar with his book *Care of the Soul*, but he wrote a book before that about which I'd like to say a few words. It will illustrate what I'm really trying to talk about here. *Care of the Soul* is a great book for middle class, consensus reality types, and of course it had wild success because of that need. But how many of you have heard of his first book, that had a circulation of maybe only eight thousand? It's called *Dark Eros*, and the subtitle is *The Sadian Imagination*. Now how come this book isn't in circulation by the millions? It's by the same man, written two years before the second one.

Audience: Dark Eros!

Jeffrey: *Dark Eros: The Sadian Imagination*. Thomas Moore. And he's not advocating S&M, this is not the point of his book. (laughter) By the way, Thomas Moore is very sympathetic to astrology. In fact even in his first book, *Dark Eros*, he employs the symbolism of astrology. What he's talking about is what I'm sharing today: that the repressive nature of Patriarchal reality, and the various sorts of religions that come out of those realities, are the causative factor for all 'modern ailments' such as neurosis, psychosis, schizophrenia, the serial killer, the child rapist. The point being just what we're sharing here, that the primary brain reflects natural sexual law, and that when you repress these natural laws via social conditioning you create distortion and rage, which then manifest in these very hideous ways of which we're unfortunately all too well aware. What he is promoting in the book is the idea that, to have not only a healthy person but a healthy society, we must return to a state of natural law. Take the issue of sexual fantasy, for example. If you're living in a state of natural law, you will not have sexual fantasy. Fantasy is a reflection of repression and is caused by it. When something natural is being repressed, it manifests as fantasy. This is how you can explain the entire pornography industry. You understand what I'm trying to get at here? Thomas Moore is arguing for a removal of these repressions by asking each person to examine honestly the nature of his or her own sexual fantasies. The very nature of the fantasies becomes a symbol for what is being repressed in that individual, indicating what he or she actually needs to do in order to be whole, integrated and healthy.

From a Patriarchal viewpoint, that would look like 'immorality', which is why we have the Capricorn connection to dark Eros and chaos. To let oneself lose control is viewed as wrong under that belief system. Any questions on this stuff? Comments you want to make? OK, let me ask you a question. How many of you ever thought about Capricorn in the sense of dark Eros and chaos? You have? Good for you.

If you start looking at this in historical perspective it becomes incredibly fascinating. For example, all of you know by way of the Bible, that the only correct sexual expression is to use sexuality to propagate the species. If you have any enjoyment at all, oh my god, you're guilty. Now let's take this one thought and run with it. I'll show you how ridiculous it becomes. There was a Christian sect in the 1890s here in this country, a variation of Calvinism, and their method of allowing sexual intercourse to occur is that they had a wall here, and the man's on this side, the woman's on that side, and they had a little hole in the wall... (laughter). This is how intercourse happened, and of course it was only for the propagation of the species. It's historically accurate. I mean... (laughter). It's not your method of choice?

Audience: I'm just trying to picture how the woman would line up there... (laughter)

Jeffrey: The point there is that history is full of this stuff and it blows your mind when you read it, but if you understand the archetypical basis of it, it makes absolute sense. If we understand these ideas then we understand why so many 'priests' get arrested for some degree of sexual molestation of, guess what, primarily children. Do you see the connection? I've had about 20,000 clients, so I've heard about every story you can imagine. One of the more difficult ones was a priest; a priest coming to see an astrologer. Think about that. Complete with his white collar on. (laughter) What?

Audience: You have all these strange people coming to see you.

Jeffrey: Yeah. Then you wonder why I want to retire, (laughter). And it was really sad, with this priest. If you can imagine first my shock seeing this guy walking into my office. Anyway he sits himself down, and he wouldn't even look into my eyes. He walked in with his head down. Apparently he had heard of me through one of his parish people. He heard I was really non-judgmental and all this stuff, because I just take each person as they are. You know, why judge anybody? Except for being true to who you are. So anyway he sat down and his confession to me was that, on the one hand, he's trying to live the life of the traditional Catholic priest and doing what they do and so on. And yet, on the other hand, he had this, in his words, "absolute compulsion" to be oriented to pornography, including visiting the pornographic theaters and the sex clubs and the magazines and all the rest of it. Beyond that, he was a compulsive masturbator which for a priest is of course a big no-no, because he's meant to be celibate. Of course he was in a great degree of psychological despair. Truly in despair he could not understand any of this, because his orientation to God from his religion was incredibly sincere. That was not the problem. He was really dedicated to the role that he was playing. And in fact he did great work as a priest, actually founded a shelter for abandoned children and so on. He was really well-known in his town. And so he was doing a great job as a priest and yet in his private life there was this altogether different reality and he just couldn't understand it for the life of him. He went through all kinds of soul-searching, asking God to take this away from him, this evil, this demon, all the Christian words. He was truly in despair. He was to the point of being suicidal.

And we had a long chat. I didn't even bother to do his chart; I was just sitting there talking to him. That's actually sometimes when the best work can get done. And I was talking to him as I'm talking to you, just sharing the historical basis of things. Thank God he had the awareness to really hear it and really accept it, and then I showed him why this was going on: again, how when that which is natural is repressed it becomes compressed, distorted and full of rage, and how this was the causative factor of the intensity of his addiction to pornography. It was in direct proportion to the Soul-intensity that he put into his work within the context of that distorted belief-system. And so I said, "Why don't you just accept yourself as you are? And understand these natural laws. And that God is the origin of your sexuality." And once I said those words, "God is the origin of your sexuality", you could just see the light bulbs going on. And this man was able to integrate himself. It was really a holy moment, literally.

Audience: When that took place, he was living in a context where he was supposed to be celibate, he's supposed to not have all this going on. Did he continue in that context with an understanding that now he could privately integrate his sexuality?

Jeffrey: Yes.

Audience: So he was able to maintain his priesthood but also then allow himself to have his sexuality...

Jeffrey: Yes, because he changed his inner orientation. He understood it.

Audience: But he still maintained his celibacy, he still maintained his...

Jeffrey: Oh sure. But his orientation to his other life is what changed.

Audience: Did he stop the pornography...?

Jeffrey: Yes, but with a new orientation, without shaming himself and trying to use that shame as a way of stopping. And he understood it as an expression of his own inner repression relative to his religion. You see? The point in all of this is that you're all subjected to these kind of conditioning patterns. Believe me, when you do a lot of counseling, you hear every kind of story. For me personally, some of the more important work I do is simply to validate people to themselves. For that kind of work, you have to suspend your conditional judgments. For example most of you would be shocked at how many women come into the counseling office who have a sexual fantasy about having sex with a group of men at the same time. Most of you in your conditional consciousness would be shocked to hear such a thing. Are you going to be able to help that person if you're sitting there being shocked because of your own conditioned reaction?

To be a really, truly effective counselor, you'd better have some historical awareness, so you can understand the origins of such things. And if you share the historical basis for something like that with the client, don't you see how that's going to help such a person accept what is going on within her? The reality here is that most people living in a Patriarchal reality have sexual fantasies.

Audience: Even if we were to remove the repression of natural law, it seems that there's a higher reality that somehow we can't have everything we want, though. I mean, say a woman has a fantasy about sleeping with a group of men, but does that mean she can automatically have that?

Jeffrey: When we lived within natural laws the women who desired to have sex with a group of men would simply do that. Thus, there would not be any need for such a fantasy.

Here's the big question with Capricorn: if I give myself the freedom to act upon my sexual impulses, keeping in mind the fear of social judgment, what does this mean about me? What does that tell me about myself, once I embrace the chaos? That is the operational psychology of Capricorn, the fear of negative judgment: internalized negative judgments based on conditioning. So Capricorn can inwardly feel this stuff, but that automatically gives rise to the question, what does this mean about me? When that question is answered relative to cultural conditioning, it will in most cases cause the repression of that impulse, and all the distortions that follow. Judgment is a function of the Capricorn archetype. And it's part of natural consciousness; it's how we learn. The issue is not judgment itself. The issue is what inner content or basis we're utilizing to make the judgments. And is that content a reflection of natural law? Or is that content a reflection of Patriarchal conditioning patterns? There are Capricorns who are angry at their bodies because their bodies feel pleasure. You know what it's like to be in a system where you're angry at your own body because it feels pleasure? How insane that is! Most of you intuitively understand the insanity of that. But you know how many people are running around with an emphasized Capricorn archetype who feel just that? What I wanted to share today was these core points about Capricorn and the nature of natural law versus conditional law, and what happens because of the conflict between them. You can see that these simple facts are implicated in the causes of the current Patriarchy's wars, violence, abuse, sadism and masochism. Up until around 6500 BCE, and this is historically accurate, there is simply no evidence from any source of any kind of wars or violence between people. None.

Audience: When was that?

Jeffrey: Before about 6500 BCE. In the old days, one of the reasons that women exposed themselves to a diversity of men was what they used to call 'mixing blood'. The woman would think that if she exposed herself to this man and then that man and then this man, then these men would not be violent towards one another. This is one of the ways that women used to maintain stability in the social order. This is radically different than how men want you to think, but it's historically accurate. If you doubt it, read history. You could start with *Whores in History* by Nikki Roberts, or *Sacred Pleasure* by Riane Eisler. The repression of natural law is the causative factor of the rage and violence we all experience, unfortunately, in today's Patriarchy.

Now we're at a five hundred year point in history prior to the beginning of the Aquarian Age. What's astounding is that the last Aquarian Age, twenty-five thousand years ago, was the fruition of what we now call the Matriarchy, which again is simply a metaphor for natural law. As we move towards this new Aquarian Age, there will be an essential change on our planet, through circumstantial necessity requiring human beings, heeding their survival instinct, to re-orient themselves to natural law. We don't have time to go into it all, but I will end this lecture with a comment about thee extraordinary relevance of the planetary nodes to this topic. Every person in this century has the South Node of Neptune, meaning their original, karmic spiritual roots, at roughly nine to ten degrees of Aquarius. The planetary Nodes of the outer planets move very slowly, so ours are all pretty close together, by the way.

Everybody in this century has three planetary Nodes in the same sign: the South Node of Jupiter, meaning their belief systems; Saturn, meaning the structure of their consciousness; and Pluto, meaning the collective soul in this case. Guess what sign those South Nodes are in? Capricorn. Pointing right back to our karmic roots in the original transition out from under natural law. What is this group of people doing on the planet at this time? What karma have we come here to release?

Think about it.

Thanks for listening.

7

Evolutionary Transitions

Jeffrey: This morning the topic is evolutionary transitions. We're going to focus on a number of archetypes, primarily the Pluto transit and/or progressions to Pluto. We'll be talking about the transiting lunar axis, and most of you will be hearing an idea or two that you probably haven't heard before. To illustrate these particular points, we'll be using the famous Clinton-Lewinsky routine. From there we'll talk about other kinds of transitional symbols, such as the Saturn and Jupiter cycles.

The first thing we want to talk about is the nature of evolution itself. Clearly evolution is a natural law; it is beyond debate, despite certain philosophical systems on our planet. There are really two kinds of evolution. There is the Darwinian system, called the theory of uniformity. Now think of the nature of these words: 'a theory of uniformity'. This theory followed the Napoleonic wars, when people were looking for simplicity as opposed to chaos. Here comes Darwin, and he creates this particular theory. What uniform evolution means is slow, progressive change. The other type of evolution is what we can call cataclysmic evolution. Obviously it implies major upheavals, as in volcanic eruptions. The sudden unexpected death of a loved one, or the lover coming home and making an announcement, "I have a new lover": these are cataclysmic events for most of us. Most people's lives are characterized by uniform evolution with a few cataclysmic events mixed in. That will be the norm. On the other hand, there are always exceptions to norms. Some folks' entire lives can be a series of cataclysmic events. Other people might have no cataclysmic events. It's clearly the symbolism and the extremity that are reflected in the I-Ching. The I-Ching is a reflection of natural law. So then we ask the question: what creates the evolutionary necessity for cataclysmic events? We will in fact find two causes for them. One cause is resisting, Pluto, necessary growth. When the needle reaches the red line on the tachometer, if you don't shift gears, you're going to blow the engine. When a fault line reaches a critical point of stress, it snaps; we have an earthquake. Similarly, some people will resist the need to grow. And it's the resistance itself that becomes the cause, the critical mass, that will suddenly generate what appears to be a cataclysmic event.

Why would we resist growth? The answer is rooted in an emotional issue: our need for security. And security is a function of consistency with our past. For most people to feel secure, they need consistency. Consistency comes from an extension of our past. The only way we can surmise there is a future is because we've already had a past, and because the present moment was the future of that past. The past is real. The present is real. But the future is an abstract and unknown, because we haven't lived it yet. What most of us tend to do is to project our past not only into the present moment, but also into the future, in order to avoid feeling insecure about the unknown. Therefore we tend to recreate our past. How many of you in this room today could safely and freely embrace the feeling of absolute insecurity, and feel fine? (Jeffrey looks around the room.) No takers! (laughter) Because of our need to feel secure, we tend to resist the need to grow beyond where we are in the present. When the need to grow reaches something like a critical mass state, we create a cataclysmic event to enforce the evolutionary necessity of growth.

Audience: Do you find that people with strong Scorpio or 8th house influences are able to roll with that better than, say, somebody with a strong Taurus or 2nd house influence?

Jeffrey: No, because in either case you're dealing with Fixed archetypes. If you've got a heavy-duty 8th house or Scorpio or Taurus type of nature, imagine your partner's coming home and saying, "Hey, let's go to a party". The typical automatic fixed response is "No". The reason is that they have to get used to the idea. And when they get used to it, they might say yes. But in terms of the instinctual reaction, it's "No", because that's the nature of fixity.

So we reach these critical mass moments, relative to the evolutionary need for the Soul's growth, when the growth will occur with or without the apparent cooperation of that Soul. How many of you have experienced this? All of a sudden this cataclysmic event appears. You weren't anticipating it. All of a sudden out of nowhere, like an earthquake.

Audience: You're saying that the Soul can resist the evolutionary intent, but I thought that the Soul took part in forming the evolutionary intent?

Jeffrey: The Soul does indeed create its evolutionary intent, from life to life. Even though within the Soul itself there can be an intent to do this or that for its ongoing evolutionary needs, it can, at the same time, resist that intent from within itself. This resistance, and the intent to evolve beyond that which is the cause of the resistance, can occur within the Soul. And this is then reflected through the ego that the Soul creates in whatever life. Most people do not have the consciousness's center of gravity located in the Soul. For most people, the center of gravity is in the ego. The ego then reflects this inner conflict and tension with the Soul. It is this very dynamic within the Soul that then is the causative factor in creating cataclysmic events so that the Soul's evolution can proceed.

How many of you have enjoyed your cataclysmic events? (laughter) No masochists, huh? In any case, we have these two types of evolution. When you look at a birth chart, you can actually deduct the Soul's intention for any given life, relative to what types of evolution it will experience in that given life. For example, let's say that you have one chart with Pluto aspecting all the other planets. Then in another chart, you see Pluto making only one or two aspects. Could we make a deduction that the person with Pluto aspecting all the other planets is probably going to have a life much more defined by the cataclysmic type of evolution than the person whose Pluto only makes one or two aspects? Would that be an unrealistic deduction? We can also consider the nature of the aspects. When you find stressful aspects to Pluto or to the ruler of your 8th house, or planets in Scorpio making stressful aspects, this will tend to correlate with cataclysmic types of evolution. Most of us, when we go through a difficult life experience from a Plutonian point of view, want to know why in order to have some degree of perspective on the experience, and therefore some ability to resolve it. One problem with cataclysmic events is that rarely does the understanding of them come while the events are occurring. Sometimes, even long afterwards, we may not be able to understand why they occurred.

How many of you have experienced this? And have you found it pleasant? Have you found it easy to move on from there? Some things in life are not resolvable. The sense of perspective won't come. Total understanding does not occur. What are you going to say to a client going through such events, or to yourself if you're going through them, when there's such an intense, driving need to resolve things, to bring them to closure, to gain perspective? The only thing you can say is, "Some things in our lives are not resolvable.

That's just the way it is, and you have to carry on anyway. In some other life, understanding may occur". That's what you want to tell yourself or to tell such a client, so they stop looking for resolution, so they can carry on instead of being stuck in that place. These are typically Plutonian phenomena related to stressful transits or progressions involving Pluto. Believe it or not, sometimes 'non-stressful aspects' can also produce cataclysmic events. But the difference is that with the less stressful aspect, the Soul tends to have much more ability to understand the event even while it's happening. The person may not like the event, but will understand it. Sometimes these non-stressful aspects bring to fruition what we could call a positive karma: certain opportunities for which that soul had been preparing.

Audience: Do you refer to conjunctions as stressful or non-stressful?

Jeffrey: Sometimes they can be extremely cataclysmic, and other times not. You have to understand the entire signature of that chart. When you have a balsamic type of conjunction, it will tend to generate cataclysmic events relative to an evolutionary need to culminate something, to bring it to closure.

Another example is a new phase conjunction. This can also create cataclysm in certain cases, because the impulse is to generate brand new life experiences. There are four ways that Pluto, which is the Soul, manifests its evolutionary intent. Two of them are non-cataclysmic and two are cataclysmic. The most common way is to form a relationship to something or someone, or to a symbol that represents something the Soul feels it needs, and does not yet have. By forming that relationship, a Plutonian sort of osmosis takes place, in which the Soul becomes that to which it is relating. That osmosis triggers evolution.

A simple example: at some point, all of you became interested in astrology and you formed a relationship to it. You studied it; you thought about it. And by a kind of 'osmosing' it into yourself, you evolved. You became something more than you had been because of your relationship to astrology. The most common way we do this is through human relationships. Most people form relationships because each person represents something that the other person feels he or she needs or wants but does not yet have. In the course of the relationship, Plutonian osmosis occurs. You see? This is why so many relationships in Patriarchal reality are based on use and need, and therefore we have manipulation, which then creates abandonment, betrayal and loss.

Another way that Pluto brings about its evolutionary intent is through another typically Plutonian experience: stagnation. Stagnation can be cataclysmic too. All of a sudden someone senses she's stopped growing. She might feel that her life is meaningless. This does not imply an awareness of why she feels that way. The Soul will typically withdraw from external life in order to figure out why, and the worst form of this withdrawal can lead to catatonia.

Audience: Is there actually evolution if there's not understanding?

Jeffrey: Sure. Because the understanding will occur at some later point.

Audience: So that's just a hang up, sort of, the need to understand?

Jeffrey: It's not a hang up; it's a perfectly natural human emotion. It's also linked with the sense of security and stability.

Another way that Pluto will manifest its evolutionary intent is when we become aware of a latent capacity or ability, take action upon it, and evolve. For most of us, this method will tend to be non-cataclysmic. For example, when Jimmy Carter decided to run for President, Pluto was transiting his Sun. "Oh, I could become President." It certainly generated evolution for him, did it not?

The last way that Pluto will carry out its evolutionary intent is when someone becomes so overly identified with, or attached to, a certain situation or person or thing that the degree of attachment is preventing growth. We're trying to hang on to something. When evolution comes along and change is required, if we continue to hang on to that thing, it will be removed with or without our cooperation. For most of us, that will tend to create a cataclysmic event. So we have these four natural ways. These are just natural laws, and they're universal life experiences. They have nothing to do with belief systems; they have everything to do with our life experiences.

We can also deal with the notion of fate here. A simple definition of fate is that when something is fated, no matter what you do, it will happen anyway. It's meant to happen. Fate clearly implies evolution. Now, a causative factor for 'fated' cataclysmic events can also be karmic issues. Let's say I go out in the street and kill somebody for my own amusement. Either I myself could be killed in the very next moment, or the karmic consequence may show up in another life. We don't always have instant karma. If it shows up in another life, maybe I'm walking down the street and somebody blows my brains out. From that next life's point of view, I don't have any perspective on it at all, do I? Because I probably don't have any memory of that other life. Do you see what I'm getting at? So an event with karmic causes can clearly be cataclysmic, especially when we don't understand the causes in the context of this lifetime. Sometimes you can also see this process in operation through a Pluto transit. Sometimes what's being brought to a head during those transits is an element of our own karma, based on our previous actions. In a moment, we'll see how it all connects to Judge Starr, Monica Lewinsky, and Bill Clinton.

This whole drama for Clinton has been connected to a Pluto transit on his natal South Node in the 3rd house – which is why we've had much more of a crisis in the media, versus a crisis in the actual Presidency. Clinton became a lightning rod that exposed the agendas and motives of the US media. Of course the media won t give you that perspective!

Our next step to look at is the transiting lunar nodal axis. I will illustrate for you how it works. We have a transiting North Node in whatever sign, and we have a collective application of it. But we also have a personal application. For example, right now the transiting Nodes are in Aquarius and Leo. So on the one hand we all have the transiting South Node in Aquarius. Look how that is reflected in the US elections, by the way. Didn't Gingrich just resign? Hallelujah!

Personally, we all have particular houses that the lunar Nodal axis is transiting. Let's say it's the 4th and the 10th houses. Now, this is going to correlate with what I call the apparent issue. If we locate the planetary rulers of these transiting Nodes, in this case, natal Uranus because the transiting South Node is in Aquarius, then wherever the natal Uranus is, that's going to be the actual issue. So, the transiting Nodes show the apparent issue, while the positions of the planetary rulers of those transiting Nodes in the natal chart show the actual issue. Do you understand the difference between apparent and actual here?

Let's say I had the transiting South Node in my 6th house, and the planetary ruler of that transiting South Node is in my natal 2nd house.

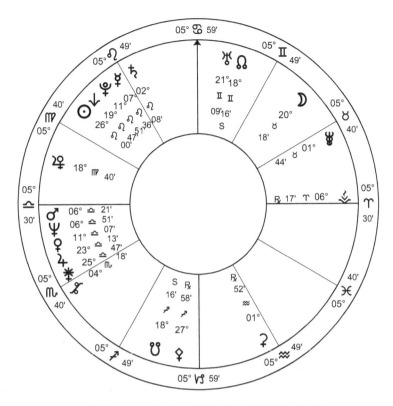

Bill Clinton 19 Aug 1946, 08:51 CST +6.00
Hope, Arkansas 33N40 93W35
Porphyry house system

On the one hand, we have an apparent issue, the South Node transiting the 6th, but the actual issue is shown by the natal house location of the transiting Node's planetary ruler, which in this illustration lies in the 2nd house. So if we make a simple deduction, what would be an apparent issue that we could identity with the transiting South Node in the 6th?

Audience: Work or health.

Jeffrey: Work or health. And what would be the actual issue, if the ruler of the transiting Node was in the natal 2nd house?

Audience: Meaning.

Audience: Security.

Audience: A lack of self-worth, because of the limits of the 6th?

Jeffrey: Maybe we should back up for a moment, because we always have to understand everything in context. Let's apply the archetypes involved here to an actual individual context. Let's say this person has the transiting South Node in Aries in the 6th house, and the Node's ruler, Mars, is in the natal 2nd house. And let's say that this person has been working for twenty years, and has been supporting the entire family for all that time. That's the actual context. What would the South Node, relative to its ruler, natal Mars in the 2nd, mean now?

Audience: She's tired.

Jeffrey: It would mean that this person is now becoming tired and angry about sacrificing himself or herself for twenty years: South Node transiting the 6th house, yes? And she's getting angry about it, relative to what? To Mars in the 2nd house. See what I'm getting at? And now the actual issue is what? Getting something for herself! Because we have to remember that Taurus or the 2nd house is a Venus-ruled archetype. So what does the actual issue become? This person wants to start receiving something, not just to be sacrificing and giving all the time. In this scenario, the transiting North Node would be in Libra in the 12th house, confirming everything we're seeing here. Do you see what I'm getting at? Suddenly she's reached a point where she's become so angry at this twenty years of sacrifice that now it's coming to a head, relative to that transiting South Node. She could make up all these apparent issues: make a lot of statements about being tired of working. If you actually saw that client, that's what you would probably hear. But if you can identity the actual issue, you can help that client own it. Then she could speak much more directly about it to her family members. You can't predict the choices of the other family members, but you can at least validate that client to herself.

Audience: How would that change if the Nodes were reversed, the North Node becoming 6th house Aries?

Jeffrey: First of all, we have to understand the difference between the transiting North and South Nodes. The South Node is bringing something in our past to a head.

Audience: So this dynamic of the actual and apparent issues only applies to the transiting South Node?

Jeffrey: In terms of bringing something from our past to a head, yes. The North Node demonstrates what the future can be, if the person allows the past to come to a head. In my example, with the transiting North Node in Libra, what is the underlying issue again? To receive. Understanding this issue can help this client make a brand new orientation to her life. That's the whole point.

Audience: If she's more conscious about it, then she could choose to leave and do something for herself, but if she was unconscious, might she get fired or something?

Jeffrey: If it was unconscious, there'd be a period of time in that scenario in which she would be having sudden outbursts of anger, complaining about everything and finding fault in everything. That'd be nice to live with, huh? (laughter)

Audience: If the transiting Nodes or their rulers are making major aspects to the birth chart, then all those aspects are ignited?

Jeffrey: Yes.

Audience: Relative to the house and sign of the Aquarius/Leo axis in someone's chart, for the current transiting Nodes?

Jeffrey: That's right. I'll just use my own chart to illustrate it for a moment. The transiting South Node is in Aquarius in my 4th house. The transiting North Node is in Leo in my 10th. I've just made a decision, yesterday in the airplane, to stop traveling so much. To totally change my orientation to my career, take total charge of it and focus primarily on writing. Do you see this sudden shift and/or liberation: South Node in Aquarius, liberation from something that's already been in place for a long time? It refers back to my natal Uranus in Gemini in the 8th. The actual issue is that I want to write about the Soul. The transiting North Node is in Leo opposing my 4th. The Sun rules Leo. I want more control over my career, and I'm tired of traveling, (laughter).

Audience: Well, just stay here, man. (laughter).

Jeffrey: And it's great. I feel liberated making that decision. I've been traveling and lecturing once a month for twenty years. I'm just simply tired of it. Look where I made the decision: in the airplane. In the atmosphere, right? Aquarius.

What we're looking at in the North Node are circumstances that reflect where we're trying to go in evolutionary terms. If we make choices that reflect the statement or archetype symbolized in that transiting North Node by house and sign, referring back to its planetary ruler, then we're growing. Do you see? (agreement) The transiting Nodal axis's house, sign and aspects tend to correlate with creating dynamics that reflect our past. We are then given a choice: do we continue to make choices that reflect our old choices, because old dynamics have been triggered, or can we make new choices in the face of those dynamics?

Audience: Are you saying that the transiting South Node brings up the past?

Jeffrey: Sure.

Audience: What if the transiting South Node is conjunct your North Node?

Jeffrey: That's virtually the same thing. You are creating circumstances reflecting past conditions, and you are given the choice either to make new choices in the face of those past issues, or the same old choices. And if you make the old choices, guess what? There's no growth.

When you have the transiting Nodes squaring the natal Nodal axis, these are what I call crossroads. The crossroads can correlate with a crisis in action, or with a crisis in belief. This whole thing with Clinton came to a head with the transiting Nodal axis in Virgo/Pisces. His Nodal axis is Sagittarius/Gemini. There's the square aspect. He certainly was looking at a crossroads, was he not? Kenneth Starr has a natal Mars/Venus conjunction in Virgo in his 8th house. This situation came to a head with the transiting North Node in Virgo, right there. Now is that 'coincidence' or something to do with synchronicity? You understand what I'm saying? (agreement) Why do the Nodes return to their natal position at age eighteen? If you study history, you will find that this was when, at least in Patriarchal societies, a man was meant to have his own kind of life direction. You see what I'm getting at? All these configurations I am talking about today are called evolutionary transitions, and they are very important events. The choices we make shape our life direction. They are the ones we really want to look at.

Of course all kinds of other astrological phenomena can also correlate with evolutionary transitions. A classic one is the Saturn cycle. Around seven years of age, transiting Saturn first squares its natal position. For most of us when we're seven or eight years old, we suddenly become aware of our mortality, Saturn: that we have a certain time frame or life span, Saturn, to live. This realization begins the emotional maturation process. It also sets in motion the primary conditioning of consciousness relative to the culture. This is when you start becoming aware that you're an American or a Tibetan or a Canadian. This is when the imprinting of culture begins shaping our sense of identity through the current cultural conditioning. Is this not a transitional state for all of us?

Saturn opposes itself at age fourteen. At the same time, we're having a Mars return at age twelve; we're having a Jupiter return at age twelve. Most of us remember those years between twelve and fourteen, don't we? Suddenly we have to oppose outside authority, whether it's high school, whether it's parents, whether it's society. There's a necessary rebellion. Why? The Soul is trying to discover its own authority. It's an acceleration of the emotional maturing process. Is this not a transitional moment? How many of you have children? (Many hands are raised) You've probably all heard the phrase 'the terrible twos'? This connects to the first Mars return. Mars has a two year cycle. What's the baby trying to do? Assert its own individuality. Because of this need to assert, the baby is not taking kindly to the limits that the parents want to impose. That's why we call it 'the terrible twos'. But this is a necessary transition for the baby. If you just watch babies in this way, they have these two year cycles. And when you're a parent, you're always trying to catch up with where the baby's going. You get used to where they are and then . . . oops, they've moved on. It's really interesting. Since I've raised nine kids, this has been a fascinating thing for me.

Let's illustrate with Clinton a little bit. He's got his natal South Node in Sagittarius, and a Mars/Neptune conjunction in Libra. When this whole thing came apart, the transiting Nodes were in Virgo/Pisces, as we've seen. Let's bring in this distinction between the apparent issue and the actual issue. Right away, what did we see? We saw Judge Starr and the Republicans doing a lot of persecution of this man. Lots of criticism. So, with the transiting South Node in Clinton's 6th house, we would look for an apparent issue there. Can we not agree this was a 6th house phenomenon that Clinton was experiencing in his workplace?

Audience: Yes.

Jeffrey: Now, what planet rules that transiting Pisces South Node? Neptune! And so the actual underlying issue we can see here is that Mars/Neptune conjunction in the 1st house, a house whose natural ruler is Aries. What was the root issue, according to the critics? Was it not a sexual issue? What is the underlying issue for Clinton himself? What does this planetary configuration tell you if you see it in anybody's chart, not just Clinton's, in terms of where the individual might be coming from sexually? We're talking about a natal Mars/Neptune conjunction in Libra in the 1st house.

Audience: Intense sexual needs.

Jeffrey: Well, there is an intense sexual need that would also clearly be demonstrated by this man's Taurus Moon in the 8th squaring Pluto.

Audience: Confusion?

Jeffrey: What we may have here is a Soul who has given itself the personal right, over many lifetimes, to have the sexual experiences that it's wanted. Without any sense of limitation. We have Mars with Neptune in an Aries-associated house, the 1st. Aries wants no restrictions. It has desires and gives itself the right to fulfill those desires. Also, the whole sexual dimension for him has been linked to Neptune. Is this not a potential signature, in a man's case, for the attraction to 'pretty skirts'? Libra. What's that cliché, 'to be a fool for a pretty face'? Because of Neptune, he can have a lot of sexual fantasy here, in which the pretty skirt or the pretty face triggers the fantasy. But it's also going to be an attraction to people like Monica Lewinsky.

Look at the statement here with Mars. This is a Venus-ruled Mars, and she herself made the statement that even before she went to Washington, she wanted to go there, in her own words, "with Presidential kneepads". Yes or no?

Audience: Yes. (laughter)

Jeffrey: I think I'll leave now. (laughter)

I mean, she was, to use a little bit of vernacular here, a 'ballsy' woman. Mars, yes? He's going to have an attraction to that kind of woman, is he not? Not just the passive ones. And when you put this in the context of the Moon in the 8th house, when you have a sexuality conditioned by a lunar archetype, there's often a linkage to oral sex. And Pluto squares that Moon. For him, if you followed the story, it was 'safe' to be involved with a woman just for oral sex. The Moon squaring Pluto means there's some element of attraction to what's taboo, as well. So I hope you can see what my point is about the actual issue and the apparent issue. The whole morality play, remember? The whole trip around 'family values'. And yet at the same, all this other stuff coming to a head: the Pluto aspect.

The transiting North Node was in Virgo. So what does this symbolism suggest? It suggests to me that this man had to be used in his own way as a martyr: Remember that North Node was transiting through his 12th house. But what would be the intent of being used as a martyr? One intent could be to show the actual crisis, which is a crisis in the media, as if they're somehow disconnected from the rest of us, and are essentially trying to sell us: Sagittarius, what to believe. Remember, Mercury rules that transiting North Node: Mercury, the media. With Neptune and Uranus transiting through Aquarius, the majority of the population was rebelling against the media. Because the people in general understood the actual truth, Sagittarius, of what was actually happening here. The man had an affair. It was two consenting adults. Look what happened to the media. Has it not gone through its own Soul searching? They had to really look at themselves to figure out, Virgo, that they themselves were in a position of bias. What's been exposed is that the majority of the media were biased against Clinton. For example, there is a non-partisan organization in Washington DC that has been monitoring the evening news since the 1950s to determine how the Presidency is reported upon. Since that time, all the reports on whatever president have basically been fifty-fifty, until Clinton was President. When he became President, the ratio became seventy percent of all the evening news reports about him were negative, and thirty percent were positive. This fact, Virgo, is not reported by the US media at all. Why? Because that would mean exposure: Pluto.

Audience: Jeff, what were the issues though before he even did this?

Jeffrey: What were Clinton's own issues?

Audience: Yes.

Jeffrey: In my opinion it was emotional dishonesty. In this particular context, it had to do with his 8th house Moon squaring Pluto.

Audience: The whole thing was to be emotionally honest with himself before this event even occurred, then? About what was going on in his life?

Jeffrey: That's right, and to do that he had to attract the apparent issue of public humiliation, 6th house. In order to crack the fixity and intensity of his 8th house Moon squaring Pluto. So before we march along here, do you have questions about what has been presented up to this point?

Audience: Was it the square to Pluto that indicated emotional dishonesty to you?

Jeffrey: Yes. In this case, in this context we're examining today. Remember that astrology operates according to observed context, and that this case doesn't mean that everyone with the Moon in the 8th house squaring Pluto is emotionally dishonest. Look how this particular case reflects what we said in the beginning, about a potential cataclysm via stressful aspects to Pluto. That connects, in this context, to sexual issues and emotional dishonesty.

Audience: But if the square to Pluto wasn't there, then it wouldn't necessarily have that intention?

Jeffrey: That's right. What's phenomenal is that both Lewinsky and Starr also have Taurus Moons, conjuncting Clinton's Moon in his 8th house. Starr's Mars and Venus in Virgo square Clinton's Nodal axis. And Starr's Mars and Venus in Virgo fall in Clinton's 12th house. You see how the synastry is starting to unfold here? When you deal with natural law, natural law shows up everywhere. As an example, let's go back to our last possible Presidential impeachment case, which was Richard Nixon. Nixon had a 10th house Pluto opposed to a 4th house Mars (see chart on next page).

His South Node was in Libra in the 1st house, and that South Node was ruled by Venus in Pisces in the Sixth. When Watergate came to a head, Pluto was transiting over his South Node in Libra in the 1st house, and that referred back to his South Node ruler, Venus in Pisces in the 6th. Did he not go through public humiliation? And how does this connect with the transiting South Node in the 6th house for Clinton? See the correlations?

In Nixon's case, the whole thing was reflected in his 10th house Pluto. Remember his statement, "I am the President": meaning, 'my sense of personal identity is totally bound up with my social position'. His entire sense of unconscious security, Pluto, was defined by the need for 10th house social position. His evolutionary intent is reflected in the 4th house polarity point of that Pluto. What we have here is an individual who, in an evolutionary sense, needed to find a new sense of personal identity, independent of his social position. When he was informed about Watergate through his chief lieutenants: all of his 'yes men', who were like his alter egos reflected in his South Node in Libra: what was the choice he made? Pluto is choice making. What if he had made the choice to go forward, instead of trying to defend himself? That was a Pluto in the 10th house natural defensive response, like pioneers getting their wagon train in a circle. And because he wanted to circle up his wagons, so to speak, it caused his downfall. But what if he had made a different choice?

Do you see what I'm getting at? Nixon's impeachment crisis enforced a 4th house lesson, which is finding a sense of personal identity devoid of social position. When he went to rent an apartment after Watergate, the people in the apartment complex had the right to vote on who would live there. They would not let Nixon live there! That was more public humiliation. Do

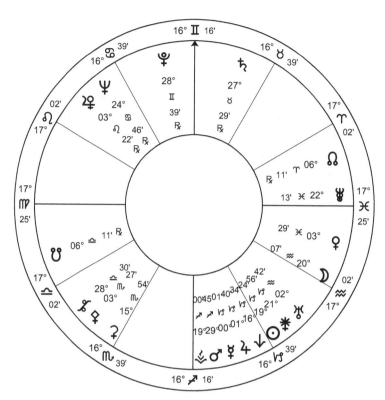

Richard Nixon 9 Jan 1913, 21:35 PST +8:00
Yorba Linda, California 33N53 117W48
Porphyry house system

you see how that could encourage someone to find a private and personal identity apart from his public position? Evolutionary necessity: relative to his 4th house polarity point of Pluto. What is the parallel to Clinton in terms of humiliation? Sometimes there has to be a severe event in these cases to unlock or change a rigid, fixed pattern, with the degree of the person's resistance determining the degree of severity of the event.

Audience: There's not necessarily going to be a cataclysmic event just because the South Node's in the 6th, but in this case, because Pluto was going to transit Clinton's natal South Node, it blew things way out of proportion because of his limelight in the media?

Jeffrey: In his particular case, it also created a cataclysmic event that might get him to change his ways.

Audience: On a personal level.

Jeffrey: On a personal level. He finally said the words, "I cannot": this is that 8th house Moon speaking. "I cannot defend the indefensible." Can not defend the indefensible. When he finally drew this psychological conclusion, he had changed. Yet it only came to pass through massive public exposure and humiliation. If you looked at his face through these events, did you not see a real change in it? A real change in his energy and where he was coming from? Didn't you see him suddenly age what seemed like ten years in three months? That's heavy duty change.

Here's something else you can see in the symbolism. Most of us have become aware of Clinton's mastery of the use of words: South Node in the 3rd and Uranus in Gemini. Not only is there mastery in and of itself, but he's so adept with the language that people think they're hearing one thing when he means something else. All of a sudden he's being evasive in terms of his language and his answers, diffuse and confusing. Here's what might be a useful exercise for all of us at the moment. The transiting South Node has just come out of Pisces. First, reflect on where you've been in the last eighteen months in the house or houses where Pisces falls in your chart. That was the apparent issue. More particularly, connect it to your natal Neptune in terms of the actual issue. Just take a moment to reflect on the last eighteen months of your life, with those two symbols in mind. See if you can make the connections to your own lives, (pause).

Is everybody making connections? Do you see it in your life experience? (agreement) Did that require any belief? Or was it simply a matter of validating actual experience? For those of you who are going to do astrological counseling, the transiting Nodes provide some of the deeper insights you can bring to a client, because most people get defined by the apparent issue and think that's the totality of the situation. If you can show your clients the actual issue, it's like turning on a light bulb for them. In terms of evolutionary transitions, there are lots of other symbols to consider. One of the more esoteric topics in astrology is the issue of all the planetary nodes. Not just the North and South Nodes of the Moon. All planets have their own nodes. Why should we limit ourselves to the Moon? If the Moon has its own past history, wouldn't it make sense that every other planet has its own archetypal correlations, and its own past? A past that brings you into each moment that you live, that leads you into your next step. My view is that we need to use all the planetary nodes. The planetary nodes also transit through the chart. Look how dramatic this can be. If you know the history of a person's Mars, or the history of their Venus, or their Mercury, etc., can you see what dimensions you could add to your understanding of that client? And if you know where the planetary nodes are transiting, can you see what the implications to the natal planets might be? You can bring in a dimension of interpretation that most astrologers simply do not employ.

The Greeks did a lot of astrology. They were also deeply into the symbolism of mathematics and numbers. The highest mathematical power they assigned to any astrological symbol was to the Nodes. They assigned them the number seven, which in their cosmology was the highest number of all.

Audience: Is that for all the planetary nodes or just the Moon's Nodes?

Jeffrey: The Moon's Nodes. But I think we should extend that to the planetary nodes as well. It relates to what I said last night. If I'm reading a book, to make sense of the current chapter, I probably should have read the chapters that preceded it. By understanding all the prior context, I will better understand the chapters to come. In a very similar way each planetary archetype has its own chapters in its own story, and those chapters are shown by the planetary nodes.

Audience: So you're saying you're supposed to look at the transits of the planetary nodes? To get more information about timing, is that right? In terms of what might be happening?

Jeffrey: To see the whole picture. Because, again, astrology operates relative to the person's actual context. Here's a simple example: during most of the 1920s, Uranus transited through Pisces In the context of this country (USA), it correlated to what we call the Roaring Twenties. In the context of Germany, it correlated to the most massive economic depression they've ever had. They needed huge amounts of money just to buy a loaf of bread. That's context! This is why one size does not fit all. We have to understand the pre-existing context. That is the essence of astrology: correlation and observation.

Audience: I have a specific question about the planetary nodes. I'm discovering the power of these things through Jeff. I never paid much attention to them until I began to work with him. I noticed that the planetary nodes are not always opposite each other, correct?

Jeffrey: Correct.

Audience: So you're using the true nodes?

Jeffrey: Right. I always use the true nodes.

Audience: With the Nodes of the Moon, I thought your practice was to use the mean Nodes, where they're precisely opposite. Do you use the true Nodes there as well? I know with the Moon it's generally just a tiny difference.

Jeffrey: Right. That's because, as you know, the motion of the other planets is not regular, the way it is with the Moon. As you know, the Node is when a planet is crossing north or south relative to the ecliptic. And therefore relative to planetary motion, which isn't regular, the planetary nodes are not always opposite one another. I do use the true Nodes for the Moon's Nodes, too. Check this out. We have just had the shift of the transiting South Node of the Moon into Aquarius and the transiting North Node into Leo. And we have a collective application of that transit, but we also have a personal application. Let's try to focus on one of the dimensions of Aquarius, which is the need for liberation from pre-existing conditions in order to grow. Let's work with just this one dimension of Aquarius, although it has many others, and let's think about where this transiting South Node is occurring in our own charts. What pre-existing conditions in your life are symbolized by the house that it's transiting? Are you trying to liberate yourself from them or rebel against them? Are you suddenly feeling psychologically detached from them? In order to take charge of your own destiny in some way, in order to create meaningful creative changes: North Node in Leo?

The transiting North Node in Leo demands that you take control of your life, sort of like when an artist first puts a paintbrush on the canvas.

Wherever the transiting North Node in Leo falls in your chart, that's where you need to begin to recreate your own picture, and liberate yourself from some pre-existing condition. Take a moment to reflect on where these transiting Nodes are in your chart at present. For those of you who feel brave, locate the planetary rulers of the transiting Nodes. Your natal Uranus is also connected to something in the past coming to a head, from which you're trying to liberate yourself. Think of your natal Sun, ruling that transiting North Node. What house is it in, and what sign? What aspects is it making? This will give you a core snapshot, a bottom line, to understand the emotional context of your life right now.

Audience: If you have the Sun conjunct Uranus, there's a connection where the past and the future are...

Jeffrey: They become the same thing. The real issue there is about choice. You make choices that reflect the past, or you make choices that reflect the future.

There are other dimensions to Aquarius. All of a sudden, insights come into your consciousness that connect to your past. But insights are also coming in, all of a sudden and out of nowhere, that reflect where you're trying to go. These will operate in a typically Uranian way: they simply appear in your brain. For the next eighteen months, all of us will be going through this process. All of us will begin to experience, because of the Moon's South Node transiting through Aquarius, a sense of increasing emotional and psychological detachment from the circumstances of our lives. In that sense, we will all begin to experience our lives somewhat like a movie. You have a sense of distance between what's happening on the screen and where you're sitting in the audience. What might be the evolutionary intent of our experiencing our lives in this detached sort of way for the next eighteen months?

Audience: It gives you perspective, doesn't it?

Jeffrey: Yes. Perspective comes from objectification, Aquarius. And we can only arrive at objectification through detachment. That is the intent, exactly. If we understand this process it's easier to deal with it, because feeling detached can be very confusing for some people. "I was totally engaged in my life, but, suddenly I'm feeling really detached from it all. Why?" Confused people may start drawing conclusions or taking actions that don't reflect the intent of this transit.

If you're a counseling astrologer and you know these underlying transiting Nodal archetypes, when clients come to you with these feelings, you can help them. You can give them a clear perspective on why this particular transit is happening. As we all become more objective about our lives, because of the detachment that's stimulated by the transit of the Moon's South Node through Aquarius, we'll be able to survey our circumstances with a better and clearer perspective. That clearer perspective will help us understand what we need to change in order to take charge of ourselves, in order to grow, in order to create the life that we need. Do you see what I'm getting at? That's not necessarily a pleasant process for anyone, because the transiting lunar Nodes mean that we're dealing with the nature of the Moon, i.e. what has meant security for us. How many of us really want to embrace insecurity? When we're dealing with the nature of the Moon, we're dealing with our own self-image, and how to integrate it into our lives on a daily basis. We're dealing with our emotional reality. And all of these things are now coming under the influence of the Aquarian archetype via the Moon's South Node transiting through that sign. How many of you like feeling totally detached from your lives? (laughter)

Audience: I've been feeling like this and wondering if I was losing my mind, recently. But it's just the detachment.

Jeffrey: Yes! If you just understand the intent behind the transit, then you can sustain that perspective, and you won't overreact.

Audience: It's like a light bulb went on. It makes sense.

Jeffrey: There you are. It becomes particularly problematic now that Pluto's in Sagittarius, because one of the dimensions of Sagittarius, Jupiter, and the 9th house is how we interpret and understand life. And most people understand life in the context of their existing beliefs, which of course are rooted in the past.

Here's an example. Keep in mind that Sagittarius primarily has a correlation to the right brain, the non-linear, intuitive brain. The left brain is the linear brain and is connected to short term memory. Since Pluto went into Sagittarius, more and more people have become, in quotes, 'absent-minded'. Let's say you're on the phone and you have trouble remembering what you said three sentences back. That's because the center of gravity in our collective consciousness is shifting to the right brain, to the non-linear. This is particularly interesting because, given our culture's fear of Alzheimer's disease, many people start jumping to conclusions: "I must be getting Alzheimer's". But all that this apparent absent-mindedness reflects is our progressive evolutionary need to shift our center of consciousness from our left brain to our right brain. Aquarius and Uranus connect to the entire brain and the dendrites. When we make new dendrites, the brain is evolving. Every time we have an 'ah ha' experience, this is a new dendrite being made. Shifting the gravity of collective consciousness to the right brain, the non-linear brain, reflects our need to accelerate the evolution of our brains.

Audience: Relative to the transiting Nodes in Aquarius/Leo, you said that through the transiting Aquarian South Node, you detach and gain perspective. Is the transiting Leo North Node the principle of new creative actualization in the house where the Leo North Node falls?

Jeffrey: Yes. Remember my illustration of my own case, where I made decisions on an airplane about a radical shift in the orientation and direction of my own work? There's the North Node connection.

We still have some other evolutionary transition symbols to consider. When you put your natal planetary nodes in your birth chart, you will find dimensions that you did not see before. Then when you start looking at the transits of the planetary nodes they will bring in still more dimensions that you would not otherwise see. For example, what happens if the transiting nodal axis of Mars is beginning to square the natal Mars? Most astrologers wouldn't look at this sort of symbol. But you can look at it, and you can understand what that symbolism might mean.

Audience: With the nodal axis of Mars squaring natal Mars, are you concentrating on the South Node, the North Node, or either one? Since the transiting Nodes aren't opposite, which one is more critical?

Jeffrey: To me it would always be the South Node. Because most of us are always being defined by our past.

Audience: I don't understand why you say they're not opposite. Aren't they opposite?

Jeffrey: No, not the true nodes.

Audience: The true nodes are not opposite each other?

Jeffrey: No, because the motions of the planets are not regular.

Audience: But it's on an axis. So shouldn't you have one hundred and eighty degrees?

Jeffrey: The axis is determined by when the planet actually crosses north or south of the ecliptic, not by the plane of the planet's orbit. That's why we have to take the planetary motion into account. Planetary motion is not regular the way the Moon's motion is regular, so we get planetary nodes that are far from being opposite one another. Still looking at evolutionary transitions, now we can get into some much more basic astrology. We have the classic Saturn cycle, which is dramatic. This is where we live. Saturn connects to our life experience on Earth. We have our feet literally grounded on the surface of this planet. Saturn has everything to do with how your natural consciousness becomes conditioned, conditioned initially by the nature of your early parental environment. Capricorn, which is ruled by Saturn, is in opposition to Cancer, and your original imprinting or conditioning comes through your parents.

It also comes through the nature of your unconscious memories, via your prior lifetimes. As we start to get older, i.e. at the first Saturn square to its natal placement at around age seven, that conditioning process is accelerated by our awareness of culture and mortality. All of you in this room can say, "I am an American". What does that imply? It's very different than saying, "I'm an Aborigine", or "I'm a Navajo" or "I'm a Tibetan". These are Saturn statements, and they condition your sense of reality: Saturn. Do you think the 'reality', in quotes, of a typical American is the same reality as that of a typical Tibetan? It's simply in the nature of this sort of conditioning that it defines, Saturn, our sense of personal and social reality. That sense of reality then goes through its own evolutionary transitions via Saturn's transits, especially Saturn's squares to its natal position, its opposition to its natal position, and its return to its natal position. These transiting aspects occur at approximately ages seven, fourteen, twenty-one, twenty-eight: you have to check them out specifically for each person's actual timing. These transiting aspects represent archetypal transitional events or moments in the development of human consciousness, independent of the particular conditioning of that consciousness: in other words, independent of whether that person is American or Tibetan. This is how natural consciousness works.

So we have the Saturn cycle. For roughly their first twenty-one to twenty-eight years of age, most people will more or less define their lives not only in relation to their current social and parental conditioning, but also in relation to their unconscious memories from other lifetimes. Therefore, most people have not truly prepared for the purposes of their current lives. This is why the first Saturn return is truly difficult for so many people, because they've already made life choices that have created a certain kind of Saturnian reality that is in place around them. They have a sense of duty and obligation to that reality and those choices; they are defined by them. Then they have this first Saturn return, and if they haven't prepared for their current life's purpose, they feel stuck: Saturn. They might start getting into a cycle of depression and futility. Most people don't have the courage, at twenty-eight or twenty-nine years of age, to make a decision that reflects the real purpose of their lives. A little before the first Saturn return, the progressed Moon is returning to its natal position for the first time. So it can be tough on an emotional level too. Conversely, for those who have made preparations and are going in the direction they need to go, typically the first Saturn return brings into fruition or reality what they've prepared for, and it can be experienced in an incredibly positive way.

For an example, I'll use my own case again. I was informed I had to be an astrologer at age twenty-four, at my second Jupiter return. Believe me, it would not have been my conscious choice to be an astrologer in this lifetime! But I have a 12th house Jupiter, so when I was informed I said, "Fine", because my trip is around God. But I also said, "Lord, if you want me to be an astrologer, then you teach me astrology". Jupiter again. For the following six years, I had nothing but dreams in astrology. This is how I learned it. Wherever I was living in the world, I'd put up a sign saying 'Free Charts', and I would empirically validate what I was seeing in my dreams. I started this preparation at age twenty-four. And on the day of my first Saturn return, which happened on a Sunday in Seattle, where I'd just moved, I was walking down the street and there was this little tiny brand new astrology bookstore. They'd just started up. No one was supposed to be there, since it was Sunday. But I looked through the window and there was the owner of the store. She waved me in, and there you have it. I got my first gig as a professional astrologer on that day. The very day of my first Saturn return! That's an example of what can happen if somebody makes preparations.

We have a Jupiter cycle to deal with, too, a natural twelve year cycle. We are starting to see cycles within cycles, yes? Again, these are natural laws that operate independent of any social conditioning. Let's try to remove one of the illusions of Jupiter, by the way, because most of you who have been dependent on books have learned that Jupiter connects to pure opportunity, and that some magical growth thing is going to happen for you. But this is not the case. Jupiter really connects to the Vedantic god called Ganesh. Before you have an opportunity, Jupiter will typically tend to remove something from your life. And through its removal, you are given an opportunity to grow. Jupiter generally does connect to the idea of growth, and therefore we have the issue of evolution implied. But to grow, again, typically something has to be removed first. How many of you remember some Jupiter transits in which something had to be removed first, before you actually had an opportunity?

Another amazing evolutionary cycle that people really underestimate in Western astrology is the Mars cycle. Remember that Mars is a lower octave of Pluto. All a 'lower octave' means is a denser vibration of something. Mars is linked, via Pluto, to Pluto's connection to your Soul and the entire intent of your life. Mars, then, is a like a denser vibration of the evolutionary impulse of the human Soul: a lower octave, subjective awareness of the Soul. Mars is in a continuous state of acting out, on a minute to minute, day to day, life to life basis, the desires manifesting from Pluto. Most of us are unconscious of our Souls. We're only really aware of them through the effects that they produce. Desires manifest in consciousness through your egocentric personality, through your Mars. These desires typically manifest as an instinct or an impulse to do something new.

This is why you read in the traditional books that Aries, the 1st house and Mars all require freedom, because Aries and Mars need freedom to act upon the desires manifesting from the Soul. A continuous process of becoming: that's your Mars experience. You become aware of your impulse to act: that's your Mars too. It has a two-year cycle. It begins, culminates two years later and then starts all over again. The Mars cycle should be seen in the context of the Jupiter cycle, the Saturn cycle, and all the other planetary cycles. A lot of our clients really want to know the future. "Tell me about my future." Are you beginning to see that if you really embrace that dimension of cycles in astrology, then the ways you have to look at 'the future' are infinitely more complex than what you've read in books? You can't just focus on 'transiting Saturn is in your 6th house'. That's like looking at the tip of the proverbial iceberg.

Audience: Going back to the Mars cycle, I'm going through a Mars return at the moment, among several others. Are you saying that because Mars is this impulse to act, that every two years you have this new impulse to act? But it's always coming back to the same sign. I don't understand how it works.

Jeffrey: Because there's evolution within the symbol. It's not a static symbol. Nothing's static. You have an original impulse wherever your natal Mars is. That's a life impulse, and it refers to the natal Pluto. That's a life statement. But you also have a whole potential in that symbol, Mars, or in any other symbol. The development of that entire potential occurs over time. The Mars cycle gradually unlocks the deeper dimensions of the whole potential of your natal Mars. Every two years we're given this opportunity to develop it further.

Audience: Would you repeat that, please? I'm sorry; I'm not quite getting it.

Jeffrey: Imagine I have a whole book in front of me. There's a whole story in this book. That's your natal Mars. Now imagine the first Mars return at age two. I've just read a few pages in that book. Throughout our lives, every two years we uncover a few more pages until we get through the whole book. Do you get that now? You do? Good.

   OK, before we wrap it up, are there any questions or comments on the first part?

Audience: You mentioned that Mars is the desires of the Soul. Could you contrast that with what Venus is?

Jeffrey: Mars acts out or acts upon the desires of the Soul. Venus correlates with the essential needs within the person's life that facilitate that Soul's evolutionary intent. How many of you have learned, for example, that Venus connects to your inner relationship with yourself? Most of you have learned in traditional books that Venus is your external relationships. But it also connects to your inner relationship to yourself. From an evolutionary point of view, why would we have Venus in this sign, and not that sign? For example, say you come into this life with Venus in Virgo, which would define your inner relationship to yourself. From an evolutionary point of view, why would you have this kind of inner relationship to yourself in this life? How does it link to your overall evolutionary intent? That's how we want to approach these things. And if we approach them from an evolutionary point of view, we suspend judgments that are linked with our own belief systems. Because now we just see things for what they are. Wouldn't you rather see a counselor who's approaching you in this way, just seeing you for who you are, validating what you are, versus somebody projecting his or her own belief system onto you?

I'll give you kind of a dramatic example. Some of you have heard this example before. It involves a client of mine who was going through, if I remember right, Mars transiting in opposition to her Pluto. She happened to have a Mars/Pluto opposition natally, therefore she was also having a Mars return. The astrologer she saw told her, "You need to stay in your house for the next six months. If you leave your house, you'll be raped". Imagine you'd been told something like that! Try to see how the astrological energies in a chart fit into that client's evolutionary intent, versus projecting your own belief system about Mars/Pluto or whatever onto that client.

The Venus function connects, ultimately, to why we have this sort of inner relationship to ourselves in this lifetime, and to how that inner relationship is changing in response to the transits. That's the evolutionary intent. Any other questions or comments?

Audience: It seems as if the Sun will be really important for the next eighteen months because it rules Leo, the sign that the North Node will be passing through. Can you talk about that a little bit? The Sun being the

integration of the chart, right? And how with this Nodal transit through Leo, we're all going to have a lot of emphasis on our Suns?
Jeffrey: And on our natal Uranus, through the South Node rulership.
Audience: Right.

Jeffrey: Again, to understand why something is emphasized is to understand its context: meaning, in this case about the Sun, we've really got to begin with the transiting lunar South Node in Aquarius. This goes back to our need to stand back a bit from our existing life circumstances in order to become more objective about them. Through this process of objectification, we can then see what we need to change in order to grow. Once we have that knowledge, we access the Sun. Now we have to take charge of those insights and actually apply them in order to integrate the change: those are Sun actions. That'll be all of our jobs for the next eighteen months.

Audience: When you have clients coming in, that's going to be the big piece.

Jeffrey: Yes. Look at exactly where these signatures occur in your clients' charts. Understand the general archetype, then make it specific to each person.

Audience: Where can we look up the nodes of the other planets?

Jeffrey: There are only a couple of sources. One is the Solar Fire astrology program that lists the planetary geocentric nodes. I hear that Alphee Lavoie's going to put them in his AIR Software programs. I want to say something more about the Mars transit. I said earlier that most people really underestimate the function and effect of Mars in their lives. If you observe its transits, you will see just how dramatic they are, because in many ways Mars connects to our experience of the continuous state of becoming. In effect, transiting Mars is the leading edge of your evolutionary change in each moment, both as it refers to the natal Mars, and as the natal Mars itself refers to the natal Pluto.

The Mars transit always refers back to natal Mars, to the actual house and sign it was in at birth, and how they reflect the evolutionary desires of the Soul as symbolized even more clearly in the natal Pluto. Here again I'll use my own life as an illustration. One day, transiting Mars was in direct opposition to my natal Pluto. And my natal Pluto is in the 9th house and Mars was transiting the 3rd. I lived in Maui for two years. If you've lived in Hawaii, you know you can't drive in that place. You just get island-bound. Right after we moved to Boulder, I had to do a lecture down in Phoenix, and being a Sagittarian man I said, "Yeah! I finally get to drive someplace!" So I got in my Bronco and drove to Phoenix. On the way back, at the minute of the exact opposition of transiting Mars to my natal Pluto, this woman tried to pass me on the shoulder of the road at seventy miles an hour. Think of transiting Mars in Aquarius in the 3rd, opposing my 9th house Pluto! She hit the right rear quarter panel of the Bronco, and they're like tanks, those Broncos. My Bronco went spinning; it rolled five times across the Interstate. They thought my neck was broken. They pumped me full of some sort of drug, and I was airlifted out of there in a helicopter. Imagine what that was like for me, because I had been in Vietnam and Vietnam was full of helicopters, and I'd also been captured there. They pumped this drug into me and I flashed out on being back in Vietnam. I wasn't in a helicopter in 1996 or whenever the car crash happened. And because of being flashed out on Vietnam, I was going crazy. Because when they think your neck's broken, you're all contained and strapped in. Look at this kind of intense, cataclysmic type of evolutionary event being triggered by a Mars transit! So don't underestimate them. Try to observe them in your own life.

Any other questions or comments? Have you found something you could use, take out and apply with your own clients?

Good!

Thank you.

8

Medical Astrology: Anatomy, Physiology, and the Chakra System

(Please note: none of the material in this chapter is intended to be used in the diagnosis or treatment of any medical, physical or emotional condition. Jeffrey Wolf Green will assume no responsibility or liability for any reactions to any use of any part of this chapter's material. For your health care concerns, please see the qualified health care providers of your choice.)

Jeffrey: Good morning. This morning's talk is on medical astrology. This will not be a totally comprehensive presentation, because we don't have enough time for that. But it will serve to get your feet wet, so to speak. We're going to look at two different systems. One will be the traditional Western system and, of course, astrological correlations to basic anatomy and physiology. Then we'll go into the Eastern system, that we can call the chakra system, and show you how we could also do a health analysis from a chakra point of view. You will see that when you combine the two systems, because they should be combined, you have a total system that, once you are proficient, allows for a very accurate diagnosis of what's going on in any particular physical body.

What we'll do first is go through the Western system of anatomy and physiology. This first part is basically for those who are interested and are going to write down a lot of astrological correlations to various physiological and anatomical functions. When we get into the chakra system, it will be a bit more lively. In fact, what I'd like to do, for those of you who are interested, is teach you a form of yoga which is not practiced much here in the West. It will allow you to actually hear the natural sounds that emanate from each chakra. In the East it's called laya yoga, which means 'body union'. Each chakra correlates with what in the East are called 'lokas', which in English means 'sphere', so one of the neat things in this yoga is that each loka basically correlates to a universe.

Relative to each chakra is a teaching unique to that chakra. A goal of laya yoga is to be able to tune in and hear these natural sounds. The ultimate goal is to create the situation of the 'non-listener', meaning that the ego's no longer involved. When this happens, the soul becomes the recipient of the teachings that are intrinsic and unique to each of the chakras. So that's the function of laya yoga, but a byproduct of it is that when you get proficient, it becomes a form of self-healing, because what you can learn to do is to direct your consciousness to the interior of your body, and at that point you're drawing cosmic healing energy through your medulla. The medulla in the old days was called 'the mouth of God'. It's sort of like putting on a coal miner's hat with a flashlight on it, and bringing the flashlight of your consciousness to your interior. By directing this cosmic healing energy consciously, with your own will, you can send it to an affected part of your body.

In 1982 when AIDS first began to appear widely, I had a client who had a severe case of it, and they didn't have the technology then that they do today. He was desperate and I taught him this yoga, because he had a very active and totally sincere desire to know God, which is the key. He began practicing this stuff and within, I think it was three weeks, the virus was gone. And he took himself to a University of Washington hospital, and they indeed documented that it was gone. But they would not accept how he had done it! That should tell us something right there. In any case, how many of you would like to learn this yoga? Lots of hands are up!

Great. As I said, we'll start with our Western anatomy and physiology correlations. The first and most important one involves the genetic structure, the RNA and DNA themselves, and the chromosomes. The genetic structure is specifically correlated to Pluto. Think of this concept from the point of view of evolution. Why is it that one soul goes into this body type, and another soul goes into that body type? The soul chooses, as it chooses everything, the entire set of conditions for its life, including its body type. In essence, the soul determines the genetics which produce the body type that expresses the soul's evolutionary necessities.

You will find that when Pluto is heavily emphasized, or when Scorpio is, or when there's a dominant 8th house theme, that you're looking at the possibility of a genetic problem in that Soul. Anything linked with genetic damage is a Plutonian issue. When Pluto moved through Scorpio, we had a tremendous amount of genetic alteration, and there was a lot of research into unlocking the mystery of the genetic codes in many forms of life, including human beings. Pluto, then, has a direct connection to your genetic structure, RNA and DNA. It's also specifically connected to enzymes. All enzymes are Pluto. Pluto also has a direct correlation with the pancreas. The pancreas's job is to regulate the levels of digestive enzymes, and of course the levels of insulin. With the Moon, Pluto has co-rulership of the stomach and duodenum, and co-rulership with Jupiter of the liver. Pluto directly correlates to your intestine, your colon and their health. An unhealthy colon can produce another Plutonian phenomenon called polyps. Pluto has a specific connection with abscesses and tumors. It can have a direct link to cancer and the mutation of cells. It has a specific correlation to the appendix, which long ago was part of the original immune system. It has a direct association with conditions like colitis. In its most severe form, this can correlate with rectal bleeding, as Pluto produces alteration in the lining of the colon and the intestine. The actual peristaltic action of the colon, the intestine, is specific to Mercury and/or Virgo. Pluto also has a direct connection to the gonads. With Jupiter, it co-rules the prostate gland. In combination with Mars, it correlates with the sphincter muscles. Pluto has a co-rulership with Mars of the testes and the penis in the man. It has a direct link with the quality of the sperm. And in the woman, Pluto in relationship to the Moon is associated with the nature of the sexual fluids that the woman emits, and the quality of the eggs that her ovaries produce. Pluto also correlates to the spine and, combined with Saturn, to the spinal discs.

All toxins correlate to Pluto. The phenomenon of conception is also Pluto. Mars in relation to Pluto has a direct correlation with muscles, tendons, ligaments and connective tissue. This is an interesting correlation, because we live in a country which is a pretty lazy kind of nation from the point of view of the Third World, where your life can be full of physical labor. We're pretty much a 'sit down' culture, aren't we? So what begins to happen to our muscle tone, tendons, ligaments and connective tissue? Why are so many men in this culture having prostate problems? In Ecuador in the jungle they aren't having prostate problems. One reason is our sit down culture, so men are sitting on their prostate and therefore decreasing their circulation patterns, which can generate inflammation. Another reason is that the prostate needs a mineral called zinc. We're in a culture which is pretty much deficient in zinc, because zinc is primarily in vegetables and fruits, and here it's mostly processed out of them. In the Middle East, many men carry a little bag of pumpkin seeds as a snack. Pumpkin seeds are full of zinc. Lo and behold, there are fewer prostate problems in the Middle East.

Mars directly correlates with anything acidic. With Venus, Mars co-rules the adrenal glands. The adrenals regulate the levels of adrenaline and cortisone. Adrenaline is specifically Mars; cortisone is Venus. These glands in the female regulate the levels of progesterone, which is Mars, and estrogen, which is Venus. These two critical hormones in women are secondarily related to the ovaries. The ovaries themselves are connected to Venus and Pluto. Why are so many women in our culture having hormonal problems? So many women have out of balance progesterone and estrogen levels. It's a really interesting question, because of the direct link to the adrenal glands, adrenaline and cortisone. I have a long logical thread to follow for this question, so stay with me. The adrenals are regulated through the parasympathetic and sympathetic nervous systems, and they are on either side of the spine. When you have any stress in your life, whatever the reason, then you're automatically affecting them. The parasympathetic and sympathetic nervous systems are directly linked to the hypothalamus, which is ruled by Uranus. Uranus also rules the parasympathetic and sympathetic nervous systems themselves. The hypothalamus emits chemical messages, specifically to the primary brain. The primary brain is correlated to Mars, the Moon and Pluto, and it regulates the entire instinctual function of your body: breathing, defecation, sexual impulses, etc.

Consciousness actually manifests from your primary brain. This is why when you get a broken neck, you're dead. But the primary brain itself is unconditioned. It operates instinctually, not conceptually. As a result, it's directly linked with everything we call 'natural law'. But we also have a cerebral cortex that is the recipient of conditioning patterns from the external environment. What happens when external conditioning represses or suppresses the biological impulses and instincts that are connected with the primary brain and with natural law? A condition of psychological and emotional stress is created. This stress will trickle down to the parasympathetic and sympathetic nervous systems. When they become affected, they begin to affect the energy available to the adrenal glands. When stressful conditions occur, what also happens via the mechanism of the hypothalamus and the primary brain, which have an interpretive function, is that the primary brain instinctually causes the secretion of lactic acids, Mars, into the bloodstream. When the lactic acid builds up, it creates muscular inflammation, Mars, in the lower back which then clamps down on the adrenals. When the adrenals are clamped down upon, it disrupts the balance of not only progesterone, estrogen, adrenaline and cortisone in women, but also the balance of the sexual hormone, testosterone, in men. This is why so many men in our culture have very unpredictable sexual rhythms. One day they have all this energy, and the next day it seems to evaporate. Unpredictability is Uranian.

Why are so many people having these problems? The ultimate answer is this issue of the primary brain's functioning via natural law, and the stress that occurs when natural impulses and instincts get repressed by current social conditioning.

Audience: OK, you're saying that the primary brain is working over here, and when it gets out of balance with natural law, because that gets repressed, then the hypothalamus, which is Uranus, kicks in?

Jeffrey: It's a simultaneous action. Mars is also directly linked with your red blood cells. Venus is your white blood cells. Again, Venus is cortisone and Mars is adrenaline. Venus has a specific connection to your white blood cells, arteries, capillaries and veins. In the female, it co-rules the ovaries, with Pluto. The Moon is specific to the uterus or the womb. The Moon in a woman is the vagina. The Moon also has a direct connection to the body's water and fluid levels. Most of you know that about seventy percent of your body is water. Water is ruled by the Moon. When the Moon is full, high tides are higher, right?

Which is exactly why when we have a full Moon, we have an emotional high tide, so to speak, and the Moon also affects the fluid in the body. The Moon has a direct connection to the left eye in the man. The Sun in the man is the right eye. In the female, the Sun is the left eye and the Moon is the right eye. The optic nerve is co-ruled by the Moon and Mercury. The Moon has a specific correlation to your sinuses, and a direct connection to a key substance in the body called mucus. Mucus is one of the body's natural ways of isolating and eliminating some toxins. It's a line of defense. Yet our culture is making all these addictive nasal sprays, and they interfere with this elimination process. So the Moon has a very critical function. In combination with Neptune, for example, it has co-rulership of the tonsils. How many of you are aware that the tonsils are actually part of your immune system? They're the last line of defense. They're a vehicle, again, by which the body eliminates toxins. This is why you get sore throats. But what happened in the 1950s in this country? Snip, snip: a lot of them got removed. The tonsils and the adenoids, which are also Moon/Neptune.

Audience: Mine grew back.

Jeffrey: I'm not surprised. I think that in about twenty percent of the folks who had these things removed, they grew back, Moon/Neptune. Meaning the body wants these things; it doesn't want to have them removed.

So the tonsils are actually part of the immune system. In combination with Pluto and the Moon, the correlation is to your lymphatic system, and in combination with Neptune and Pluto to the endocrine system. These are very critical systems for keeping the body clean or free of toxins. Neptune connects to what is called the etheric body or the astral body. These are just levels of energy. If any of you can actually see auras, then you know that the energy bands within the etheric body are forever changing. They're directly connected with your chakra system. There's a Western term for chakra: spinal plexus. Spinal plexus or chakras have nerves that affect various areas of the body; we'll get into all that in a moment. They're connected with your etheric or astral body. You can learn a tremendous amount about someone on a physiological, anatomical basis if you have this kind of perceptive ability. Neptune is directly linked to your entire immune system, including a specific correlation to the thymus gland. This concept is very, very critical, because the thymus gland is analogous to the conductor in an orchestra. It issues directions that we could call coding. What is being coded; where are the directions going? To the B and T cells which emanate from your bone marrow. B and T cells in astrology are connected to Saturn, just as the skeletal system and the bone marrow are. The B and T cells emanate from the bone marrow, and the thymus then gives them coding or direction. This process is connected to the immune system.

When people have an autoimmune disorder, it's linked with a loss of integrity in the quality and structure of the B and T cells. One of the best ways to work with autoimmune problems is to re-establish the integrity of the B and T cells and the quality of the bone marrow. This can be done in non-extreme cases with cell salt supplements. One is calc-phos and the other is mag-phos. When they are ingested, it immediately affects your B and T cells, the integrity of the bone marrow and, in a larger sense, the overall health of your skeletal system. Arthritis is typically caused by dehydration or lack of synovial fluid. In mild cases, you will find that by supplementing with calc-phos and mag-phos at a high dosage taken faithfully over time, you can decrease, not always eliminate but decrease, the severity of the symptoms. The B and T cells, then, are directly connected to Saturn. Another critical component of bone marrow correlates to the receptor cells. They receive, Venus, growth hormone. Growth hormone emanates from the thyroid and pituitary. The thyroid and the pituitary are both co-ruled by Saturn and Jupiter. Let me give you a quick snapshot into recent history, and then you'll see the dramatic evidence of these rulerships. Let's consider the phenomenon of time perception. How we perceive time is a function of our metabolic rate. Most of us have probably had a summer day when too many flies got into the house, right? When you try to swat a fly, all too often it escapes, doesn't it? From a fly's metabolic rate and perception of time, it sees your arm moving about like this. (Jeffrey pantomimes holding a fly swatter and swinging it very, very slowly. Laughter).

So the fly has plenty of time to dodge! The perception of time is related to metabolism. Metabolism is a function of the thyroid, so the perception of time is dependent on a key substance called iodine. Let's take another look at modern history. All of us survived the transits of Neptune and Uranus through Capricorn, right? (laughter) I lecture everywhere so I can take kind of an informal world survey, and we've all had the same experience. During the seven or eight years when Uranus was in Capricorn, didn't most of us have a real sense of time speeding up?

Audience: (many responses) Yeah! You bet!

Jeffrey: But there were still twenty-four hours in a day, so it was a perceptual issue. Time didn't actually speed up. Do you understand my point?

Now consider that Uranus also correlates to the atmosphere, and Capricorn correlates to iodine which affects our metabolism. The phenomenon of time and space as a concept or an abstraction is also Capricorn. One of the physiological actions of Uranus is dehydration, and one of its psychological actions is acceleration. We went through a collective moment, an eight year time period, in which Uranus transited through Capricorn. During that period we had a collective dehydration of iodine relative to our thyroid, affecting our collective perception of time. The thyroid also connects to growth hormones, what are called T-4 hormones, and to the pituitary, which most people know is the master gland in the entire body. The two halves of the pituitary correlate with our life experience. In the first half of life, basically from birth to, nowadays, around age forty-six, we're in a Jupiter mode. Everything continues to be an adventure, something new to do, a process of discovery. We're going somewhere.

Suddenly we hit the late forties, and then we have another perception of life, one that points toward its closure. This is a perceptual shift from Jupiter to Saturn, so to speak. The pituitary generates an enzyme which is connected to the natural ageing of the system. The point is that the physical death of the body is genetically programmed. There are all sorts of reasons for this from the point of view of consciousness, psychology, and emotional reality.

Remember that one of the meanings of Neptune is timelessness or immortality. What happened with Neptune moving through Capricorn and Pluto through Scorpio? A bunch of doctors went on a delusional quest, Neptune, seeking medical vehicles of immortality, as if they were playing God. How many of you would like to find yourself in the same body for two thousand years? Wake up every morning and see the same face for two thousand years? (laughter)

Concrete or asphalt was developed when Neptune was transiting Capricorn in the 1820s. When Neptune went through Capricorn, people were exploring cryogenic suspension. It was in ice, not concrete, but they were freezing themselves forever, thinking they were going to wake up one day.

Neptune also correlates to the pineal gland and, in combination with Pluto, to a key hormone called melatonin. A derivative of this is melanin which correlates to the pigmentation or the color of the skin. The spine itself is Pluto. The vertebrae and the spinal discs are Saturn. The left brain, the left hemisphere, is Mercury. The right hemisphere is Jupiter. There's also a component of the brain called the limbic system. Although shamans have known this forever, science is now saying that the limbic system contains the entire structure of what they're calling 'genetic memory'. We can translate that as the area of the brain that contains all the memories of what the soul's journey has been prior to the current life. All of you have heard about near-death experiences, where someone seems to go down a tunnel and see a light. In brain research, they've actually found the point in the brain that, when stimulated, will produce the experience of the tunnel. That means it's actually intrinsic to the structure of the human organism. They can reproduce the tunnel, but they can't reproduce the light! That means the light only happens when you actually physically die. Think of this the next time you run into a skeptic about reincarnation.

That area of the brain is right next to the limbic system. The dendrites in the brain which correlate to its evolution are ruled by Uranus. The brain as a phenomenon, as an operating whole, is Uranus. The structure of the brain is Saturn. The lungs are Uranian. With Neptune and Uranus coming into Aquarius, we now have a collective link to the lungs. As we speak, about twenty to thirty percent of the Earth's population has tuberculosis latent in the lungs. Also, we now have a connection between Neptune and the immune system, and between Uranus and the lungs and the atmosphere. Can you see what I'm getting at here? What is the possibility of all this latent tuberculosis becoming activated? Especially given the fact that most forms of it have mutated again, Pluto, to the point where they cannot be controlled with allopathic drugs. One of the phenomena connected with Aquarius, Uranus and the 11th house is contagion. You can have contagion at any level: social contagion, by which I mean a rebellion or a reaction, and contagious disease.

In Europe in 1348, during the Black Plague epidemic, Neptune was transiting from the first to the second decant of Aquarius. Today we have the AIDS epidemic. Right now about forty percent of the people in India are contaminated with AIDS. In a country like Uganda, it's about sixty percent.

We already have a plague underway, and there could be more. It connects to this phenomenon called contagion, and it goes back to what we were talking about last night, Pluto in Sagittarius, and the tremendous violation of natural laws and natural principles. Gaia, the Earth, is reacting to the human organism in order to cull it out, in order for the totality of the Earth's system to survive.

Audience: Is Pluto in Sagittarius igniting it too, instead of just Uranus in Aquarius?

Jeffrey: The ignition point is Pluto/Sagittarius, the forces of nature as they begin to react to any system that threatens nature's existence. Remember Sagittarius's natural inconjunct to Taurus? That's the whole survival instinct. You can see the implied crisis, especially since Sagittarius also inconjuncts Cancer. Uranus, then, directly connects to the lungs. As a result, in combination with the Moon, it connects to a lung disease called pleurisy.

What have we left out? The larynx, your voice box, is Mercury. The anatomy of your ears is Mercury. The psychology of hearing, by the way, is Venus. Mercury is its anatomy, but the actual psychology of hearing is Venus. Here's a simple example. How many of you, in your intimate relationships, have always felt that you've been heard by your partner in exactly the way that you meant something? (laughter) Why does that happen? It's one of the worst forms of externalized Venus, conditional love. "I will love you if, and I mean if, you meet my needs." When our needs are not being met, or when we're feeling threatened by our partner's voice because our partner is ignoring our needs, we tend to hear differently, subjectively. So Venus is the psychology of hearing, whereas Mercury is the anatomy of the ears. Uranus also has a direct correlation to what are called 'free radicals'. We all take in free radicals through the atmosphere. One of the actions of these free radicals is to bombard the membranes of the various cellular structures within the body in such a way as to degrade their viability. In turn, this can cause an acceleration of the ageing process, or disease. One of the best ways to remove these free radicals from your system is through ingesting a compound called lipoic acid. If there are systems I've forgotten to mention, please ask me about them.

Audience: The heart?

Jeffrey: The heart is the Sun. Your overall constitutional strength is the Sun. By the way, a good cell salt that deals with constitutional vitality is called silicia. It has a dramatic effect on constitutional strengthening. The Sun also correlates to the heart as an organ, to blood pressure, to the heart rate, and to the overall integrity of the various components of the heart. The feet are Neptune. The sciatic nerve, a very important nerve, is Jupiter. Many people in cultures like ours have problems with sciatica. This nerve emanates from your lower back, comes down your buttocks and through your legs to your feet.

The skin is Saturn. The skin is an organ. And for those who are having toxicity problems, that's why you're having skin problems. The skin is one of the organs that eliminates toxins. Saturn also correlates to some key minerals in the body such as calcium, phosphorus, magnesium and iron.

Audience: Let me go back to the sciatic nerve for a minute. If it's ruled by Jupiter and Jupiter likes motion, is it because we're such a sit down society that people are having trouble with their sciatic nerves?

Jeffrey: That, and the accumulation of stress. Beyond the fact that we're a sit down culture, we're in a highly stressful culture.

Audience: So how would that relate to a problem with Jupiter?

Jeffrey: Because this stress generates muscular inflammation in the lower back, and that clamps down on the sciatic nerve.
     Anything that you call toxins or poisons in the body are Pluto. Again, all things linked with cancer are Pluto. Any abnormalities such as cysts, tumors or boils are Pluto.

Audience: What about mold?

Jeffrey: Mold is also Pluto, in combination with the Moon.
     The phenomenon of parasites is Pluto. Bacteria and viruses are Pluto. The very first form of life on this planet was bacteria, and it will probably be the last one here, too. This is the life-form that mutates the fastest and can adapt to any condition. There's a form of bacteria that can live in the middle of a nuclear reactor.

Audience: Allergies?

Jeffrey: Allergies are an immune system reaction to the environment. But the causative factors in all allergies are emotional issues, so to treat an allergy is to treat an emotional issue. Any other questions?

Audience: How about insanity?

Jeffrey: Overall, that's Neptune. Manic depression is Saturn. Psychosis itself is Neptune. Schizophrenia, neurosis, hysteria, displaced hysteria and personality disorder are Neptune. They're all related to an imbalance in melatonin and saratonin within the brain. This is why you hear therapeutic circles talk about "chemical imbalances in the brain".

Audience: Migraine headaches?

Jeffrey: They're caused by a Saturnian psychological condition that creates restriction of the circulatory patterns in the body. One of the byproducts of restricting the circulatory system are migraines.

Audience: I'm fascinated by the lack of physical movement in our culture. Can you link that with a planetary ruler?

Jeffrey: We're in a Cancer country. We sit down. Same as in Canada, also in Holland; Holland's a Cancer country too.

Audience: Hepatitis?

Jeffrey: That's Pluto in combination with Jupiter: the liver.

Audience: Because of toxins, right?

Jeffrey: That's a byproduct of hepatitis. So we're back to Pluto, aren't we?

Let's get into the chakra system. Imagine you have a client reporting massive stomach and/or digestive problems. If we were limited to just the Western system, for a stomach issue most astrologers would look at Cancer, the 4th house or the Moon. Maybe the client is also complaining of ulcers. Ulcers are Pluto. Yet the Moon seems fine, and what's happening in the 4th house seems fine, and the planetary ruler of the 4th seems fine. You can't locate the problem. But now let's also employ the chakra system. The navel chakra and/or plexus, that which correlates with that region of the body, is connected to the stomach. We look at the birth chart and we find Mars and Pluto in opposition. They rule the navel chakra, and Pluto rules ulcers. This is why we want to combine the Western system and the chakra system. The relevant planetary correlations with each chakra can tell you something right away.

The root chakra and the nerves that emanate from it correlate with everything underneath that chakra: the legs, the feet, etc. It also correlates in the man with the penis and testes, and with the gall bladder – the gall bladder is ruled by the Moon – the perineum, the sphincter muscles and the anal opening. In the second or sacral chakra. look at the interesting connections to Jupiter and Neptune. This chakra correlates with the sexual functioning of the body. It's the chakra from which the nerves emanate that affect these areas: the penis, the testes, the anal canal, and in the woman the yoni and uterus and clitoris. We're obviously in a cultural era when sexuality has been subjected to Neptune and Jupiter type of glamorization. It's so extreme that for many people, sexuality and its imagery is somehow the ultimate meaning, Neptune, of their lives. Their whole lives revolve around their sexual impulse. When you have collective consciousness glamorizing sexual imagery, making sex somehow the ultimate meaning that we seek, then we have a situation where decisions about the sexual union between two people are not being made with any kind of psychological or emotional discrimination. People are simply tending to follow their glamorized impulses without taking anything else into account. This tendency is overriding natural law, in this case, it's overriding the natural and instinctual selection of a partner.

Most of us in this room today have probably had more than one lover, right? How many of you have had the feeling with person X, after you've made love and you're holding each other, that you just can't get close enough, as if you want to climb right into the middle of this person and stay there? It isn't a sexual feeling any more, because you've just made love. But then when you sleep with person Y, as soon as you come together, you have an instinctive reaction of repulsion. You have this instinct to get away. But you have sex with person Y anyway, going against natural law and natural selection. There would of course be psychological reasons why you did that, but the point is the same: you're still going against natural law and natural selection. For a long time now, about eight thousand years, natural selection has been progressively violated. We haven't been exercising our soul-level, psychological and emotional discrimination. That's one cause of sexual disease, which is a reaction to ignoring the natural laws of partner selection. At one time there was no AIDS or syphilis or herpes. By the way, for the information of the women here today, there is a new form of cancer. It's manifesting through a fungus that latches onto the cervix. It was just discovered within maybe the last thirteen or fourteen months, and it's another reaction to this overriding of natural law.

For all of you, here's what I'm getting at about the necessity of exercising discrimination in your sexual choices: if you're contemplating being with someone, but you have an instinct beyond your psychology or your emotional needs, and that body instinct is telling you, "Wait a minute", then honor that instinct. Think twice about that person. With this chakra, we can see the connection to the immune system, Neptune, and to Jupiter belief systems. Do you see how we can take in a belief system about sexuality? Is that a belief system in harmony with Jupiter, with natural law, or in violation of it? Again, if it's in violation, that belief system could create problems in this area of the body. In order to have a healthy psychology in general, and also a naturally operating and self-regulating sexual function, we need to be aligned with natural law relative to this chakra.

The sound that emanates from your sacral chakra, which in the East is called Krishna's chakra, is like a flute. It's the most beautiful thing you will ever hear. The root chakra's sound is like a bumble bee. Sometimes when it first opens and you first begin to hear it, it will sound like a cricket. Now we move up to the navel. The obvious rulers here are Mars and Pluto.

Psychologically speaking, this chakra correlates to the person's will, and how it interacts with the wills of others. It also relates to the soul's need, in the end, to harmonize its personal will with the will of God. All of that is happening in this one particular chakra; that's why the Chinese call it *chi*. You can probably see its links to various areas of the body. We have the stomach, duodenum, liver, pancreas, spleen and kidneys all in this region. The sound that comes from this chakra is like a really beautiful harp.

The heart chakra is specific to Venus and everything connected to the emotional body. Believe it or not, the liberation point for all souls in time/space realities like ours is specific to the emotional body. This chakra regulates, when you access it through laya yoga, the teaching of the truths that are unique and specific to the entire realm of emotion. Consider the psychology of what we like and dislike. That's an emotional response, which then creates a thought about that emotion. The whole issue of love, both conditional and unconditional, is located here in the heart chakra. The issue of psychological needs is located here too, along with the whole dynamic of being able to give and receive. From a systems point of view, we're looking at the lungs, the lining of the lungs, the heart as an organ, all the arteries connecting to the heart, and that area of the human back. How many of you have ever had a masseuse try to open up this area? What have you felt when she does that, and why? Frozen emotions, as in emotional wounds, get stored there. This region connects with the heart chakra. You can really improve a person's constitutional vitality by bodywork in that area, because it's connected to the heart. It's a releasing thing. It's like popping bubbles, but it's not champagne! (laughter) There's no Lawrence Welk hanging out there.

Audience: Lawrence is Saturn. (laughter)

Jeffrey: Many times over! That's why he needed the bubbly. The sound that comes out of this place is like a gong or a giant church bell. It's really fascinating.

Then we get up to the throat chakra, which of course will be Mercury. It correlates to all the areas in that region of the body, and particularly to the tonality of your voice. There are no two people on earth who have exactly the same voice quality, just as there are no two people with the same fingerprints. What does this mean in terms of evolution? Why have this type or that type of voice? Because every human being responds to vibrations, whether we like or dislike a particular vibration, and speech is vibration. The sound that comes from here is like a conch shell. All these chakras have specific color correlations that can be seen in the auric body. The color that is natural to the throat is yellow. That which emanates from the heart is green. That which emanates from the navel chakra is red, purple or black. For those of you who are doing healing work, let's say that your client is being too affected by the will of those around him or her. Two of the gemstones you could work with for this navel chakra issue would be obsidian or black onyx. They would help thwart or block the intake of external will. They can also help align someone's will with the higher will. The colors that come out of your sacral chakra are various shades of purple, blue and green. That which emanates from the root chakra, depending on the person, could be black, yellow, green or red. Sometimes it's reported as electric blue.

Let's go to the medulla. It's directly correlated to the Moon, and this is in fact the seat of consciousness of the human ego. How many of you have seen the third eye? Even though you see it here (Jeffrey points to his forehead), it's actually projected from the medulla, like a movie projector. In East Indian iconography, when they put the Moon on the image's forehead, it means that the ego is liberated, that the ego has identified with God and not itself. This chakra, which is called ajna, is the Sun. In Eastern systems there are no planets beyond Saturn, so the association here is to the Sun, not Neptune. So when you see the Moon here in an Indian image, it means that the ego has been burned up, so to speak, and no longer identifies only with itself.

Audience: Is it a full Moon or a crescent Moon?

Jeffrey: The iconography always uses a crescent Moon.

The medulla is where we take in the energy from the universal Source or from God. After conception, the very first cells that are formed are the medulla. It's the area that actually determines, in relationship to the crown chakra, when a baby will be born. The baby emanates a hormone that triggers the womb to go into labor, and it comes from the crown and the medulla simultaneously. So in the old days, this was called the mouth of God. It correlates to all these areas of the body, including the hypothalamus and the primary brain. If you've ever tried Eastern spiritual life, one of the first things you read is that your job is to get rid of your ego. I've said this before: that's impossible. One of the functions of the ego is to generate a self-image. If you didn't have an ego, you couldn't even say your name. Even from a medical point of view, this is one of the very few areas of the body that can't be operated on because of the nexus of nerves there, and that alone should tell us something. The issue isn't the ego itself: the issue is that with which the ego is identified.

Is it identified only with itself, as most people are? Or is it identified with the source of the ego, called the soul, which can be identified with its own source, called God? When that's the case, that's when Indian imagery shows a Moon on the forehead. That's the function of the medulla. It directly correlates with the Moon. In combination with the ajna, the Sun, it's like seeing two sides of the same coin. By the way, the sound of the ajna-medulla, when they're united, is in fact the original sound of Creation, which is what most people call 'Om'. When you actually hear 'Om' within, you'll find that you cannot reproduce the actual sound out loud. There is no other sound that will ever come close. It's the ultimate, original sound of Creation. The crown chakra is related to leaving the body, either by dying or in an out-of-body experience. People who are very ill can have out-of-body experiences. You can see the symbolism of Neptune linked with illness here. Have any of you ever had an out of body experience? (Some audience members raise their hands). Some of you. Then you know that the whole system goes into what appears to be rigor mortis. While fully conscious, you can no longer control the muscular or nervous systems. On a cellular level, when the body gets critically ill, the soul can be freed of that pain or illness by leaving the body. But in order to leave it, the molecular density of the body has to shift, so it can look like rigor mortis. Because so many folks are so identified with their egos, when they begin to have this experience of lifting out of the body and realize they can't control anything, they will often panic. Even if they try to scream, the body's not engaged, so they can't. Why is there a fear reaction? Very probably because the consciousness isn't totally linked with that which created it, because if it were, the soul wouldn't want to come back. It would just say, "Yeah! Let's go for it!"

The crown chakra is that which correlates to these key systems in the brain that we were discussing: the pineal gland, the limbic system, and so on. The color that comes out of the crown chakra is the purest of blues that you will ever see. This connection with blue is fascinating, because when they developed pictures taken inside the body, the pineal gland was blue. When they split the atom, the color that came from it was the same blue. In the East, there are said to be two lines on the spine. One is called ida and one is called pingala. In Western terminology they would correspond to your parasympathetic and sympathetic nervous systems. And the energy, the circulation, of these two systems is determined by your inhalation and exhalation. You can see that flow of energy linked with the nodal axis: south and north Nodes, past and future. When we are breathing out: the past. When we are breathing in: the future. It's that simple, along with the interaction at all times between the past and the future that describes our present moment. Any questions on the chakra system?

Audience: What's the sound connected to the crown chakra?

Jeffrey: By the time you move out to the crown chakra, you're not concerned with sound anymore. All you hear is a rushing sound as you exit the system. It's like a gigantic wind.

Audience: The color of the ajna medulla?

Jeffrey: Yellow or gold. When it's evolved there are three colors: yellow, white and blue.

Audience: What is the ajna connected to?

Jeffrey: The Sun.

Audience: What planet is connected to the throat chakra?

Jeffrey: Mercury.
    For those of you who will hear a sound through the laya yoga technique I'm about to teach you, roughly seventy percent of you will initially hear the Mercury chakra. That's because of our current conditioning which is oriented to the left brain. We have thirty minutes left. That's good, because it will allow you to go deeper. For those who want to try it, go ahead and practice and don't worry about the time limit. When the time is up, I'll clap my hands, and that will mean it's time for you to open your eyes.

[Editor's note: during the laya yoga exercise, the workshop was not taped. Jeffrey provides readers with the gist of the exercise below:

1. Sit as upright as you can. Keep the spine straight.

2. Press the thumbs against the cartilage on the ear that can be pressed in over the ear canal, to 'stop up' the ears.

3. Place the little fingers over the outer top of the eyelids, pressing very gently.

4. Let the remainder of the hands and fingers lie upon the forehead.

5. Breathe normally, while focusing the attention on the sensation of air entering and exiting the top of the nose. In time and with practice, you'll begin to hear the natural sounds of the chakras. First you'll hear the sound of the nervous system, like a giant transmission line. Then you'll hear the sound of the blood system pumping. Then, underneath this blood system sound, the sounds from the chakras can be heard. The goal is to unite your consciousness with whatever chakra sound you hear, with the additional

goal of uniting so completely that there is no more 'listener', and it's as if you become one with the sound.

The natural sounds that emanate from the chakras are:

1. the root chakra correlates to the sound of bumble bees, and is sometimes first heard as the sound of crickets;

2. the sacral chakra correlates to the sound of a flute;

3. the navel chakra correlates to the sound of a harp;

4. the heart chakra correlates to the sound of a giant church bell;

5. the throat chakra correlates to a sound like a conch shell;

6. the medulla/ajna correlates to the sound of 'om'.]

Jeffrey: Those of you who heard the sounds now know that they really exist. If you truly practice, the goal here is, in essence, full absorption with that chakra or loka. The ego's not listening, yet you are the recipient of the full teaching unique to that chakra. It's really dramatic. Again, the byproduct is a self-healing yoga. Any questions on the laya yoga exercise, or anything else we've done this morning?

Audience: Why was I getting two sounds at once in both ears?

Jeffrey: It means you have hemispheric switching.

Audience: I missed part of your talk about the perception of time speeding up. I got that Capricorn corresponds to iodine and also to time and space. Then I missed the part where you were saying that Uranus corresponds to what in relation to them?

Jeffrey: On a physiological level, it can correlate to a dehydrating action. On a psychological level, to a sense of acceleration, like going from thirty to sixty meters in an instant. Any other questions? Did you find some meaning for yourself with this material today, and maybe some use for it?

Well, great!

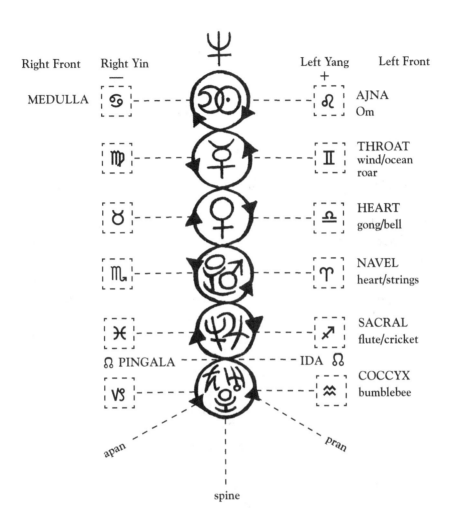

Right Front Right Yin   Left Yang Left Front
                    —   +

MEDULLA   ♋   ♌   AJNA
                                Om

           ♍   ♊   THROAT
                                wind/ocean
                                roar

           ♉   ♎   HEART
                                gong/bell

           ♏   ♈   NAVEL
                                heart/strings

           ♓   ♐   SACRAL
                                flute/cricket

♌ PINGALA   IDA ♌   COCCYX
           ♑   ♒   bumblebee

      apan   pran

           spine

The Chakra System

9

The 6th House and Issues in Self - Improvement that allow the Soul to Grow

Jeffrey: Good morning. You all awake and ready? Yes? This morning's talk is on the 6th house and the theme is issues in self-improvement. The first thing to know about the 6th house and/or Virgo is that it is a transitional archetype, a transitional archetype between houses and/or signs of houses one through five, and then seven through twelve. And as in all my lectures, if you have questions, go ahead and ask them at the point you have the question.

The 12th house, which is the natural polarity to the 6th house, is itself a transitional archetype. So then we can ask the logical question, what's that about? What's the transition about? The point here is that from the 1st house and/or Aries to the 5th house (Leo) the whole focus is on subjective development. In other words, the 1st house correlates to the instinct in all folks to initiate experiences through which they begin to arrive at their own essential individuality. That journey continues right on through the 5th house in which that individuality is now known and creatively actualized in a strictly egocentric subjective way. The 5th house, as an example, can be correlated to what is called delusions of grandeur or the peacock syndrome. And thankfully we have a 6th house and/or Virgo.

From the 6th house and/or Virgo point of view there's a great Taoist saying that applies here called "the axe falls on the tallest tree". The axe falls on the tallest tree, meaning if you're projecting yourself via delusions of grandeur and/or in a Leonian way, expecting all things to revolve around you or acting like you are the center of the universe, then the axe will fall on the tallest tree. How does that happen?

Keep in mind that the 6th house in and of itself is a naturally Yin house, a feminine house. Virgo is naturally mutable, naturally earth orientated. This correlates to inner self-analysis. Through that self-analysis you're mentally aware of that which you need to improve, perfect and/or adjust and/or eliminate in order for the journey of perfection to occur. What is being analyzed is the ego, the self-image. And then the effort is made to perfect it. This then creates an inner criticism – An inner criticism. I mean all of us are aware of our junk right? So, of course, this is also projected, meaning in a typically yin-like way we can receive criticism.

So in respect to the axe falling on the tallest tree, needing to go through ego blows at some point in our life, we simply create situations through which we attract the appropriate circumstances to receive the appropriate messages, keeping in mind that Virgo is naturally ruled by Mercury. So we get the appropriate messages at the appropriate time. But since you have a naturally introspective archetype this then means that most of us are already aware of what we need to fix and where our deficiencies are. So the point here, since we are already aware of these things, is that we will naturally have a critical and/or defensive response with respect to received criticism. We don't need to hear it, we think.

So what then happens if we drop into too much of a negative spiral with the thing? Via the 12th house polarity we can begin to feel victimized or persecuted or conspired against, somehow thinking that things are happening to us in an unjust way, and we don't receive the message. We now use this as a typically 6th house excuse to justify what we're maintaining.

So the archetypes of the 6th house are yin, earth, mutable. So on the one level you've got the mutable archetype, i.e. the need to grow the ever shifting spiral, and yet earth in and of itself wants to give definition and structure to reality and, therefore, security. And you have a naturally yin archetype which means energy returning to the center, i.e. your core. So where does the growth then occur? Can't you see the basic symbolism here where the growth occurs through self-introspection and by adjusting ourselves in this self-analysis, and trying to become inwardly aware of that which not only needs to be adjusted but also becoming aware of the specific strategies, 6th house – strategies – Mercury ruled, that we must actualize in our life to affect ongoing self-improvement?

So the key becomes this: You have this natural mutable yin conflict taking place on earth, and one of the inherent traps because of this archetype is to induce procrastination and/or laziness. Creating mental reasons, rationales/ excuses of why you're not going to do the thing that you know you should do when you should do it. You have this natural 12th house polarity creating that sense of self-undermining. So then we can ask this question, why? Why does this happen?

One of the basic issues in Virgo and the 6th house that most of us don't realize is that Virgo/6th house correlates to a sense of guilt that cannot be intellectualized, cannot be rationalized. You can't put your conscious finger on the thing and say that's why. And because of this inherent guilt – keeping in mind that one of the archetypes of the 6th is purification – when any time you set up the need to purify, it implies something else, doesn't it? Impurity, which itself can be connected to this sense of guilt. So what happens is that the 6th house via the 12th house polarity creates the need to atone. One of the acts of atonement is not to do the thing for yourself you should do when you should do it. It's a subconscious voice that says I need this state of crisis, you see? I need this sense of pain. I need to have this sense that my life is not working quite right.

Audience: Is that then the motivator to make the change? That things get so heavy that you finally turn around and make the change?

Jeffrey: No, the key is to understand why it's happening. And the point here is that if we degenerate into a state of crisis, i.e. not doing the things we know we should do for ourselves when we should do them, and/or attracting circumstances in our life which make us feel like we're not working in all cylinders, feeling contained or inhibited or trapped by, this will always enforce a 6th house analysis. And it's through the analysis that one becomes aware of the dynamics generating the crisis in the first place. So crisis then serves – 6th house, serves – as a vehicle through which self-knowledge (Mercury ruled), takes place, because it puts the light of day, i.e. the crisis, upon the dynamics, through the analysis.

So, when you just break this down to basic astrology, whatever sign you have on your 6th house (inherent implication of negative, yin) implicates that the negative associations correlated with that sign are the very dynamics, and/or characteristics, and/or orientations, that have to be adjusted, improved. Because you have a natural polarity involved, the sign on your 12th house will represent the unconscious ideal to you, that which implies perfection. You see? And you always have this natural polarity back and forth.

So as an example, if we have Aries on the 6th house, what do you feel the inherent negatives would be that would have to be purified, adjusted, and improved? Don't you think it would be gross, egocentric displays? You see my point? Arian displays, the Me syndrome. And what's the idea implied on the Libra/12th house? Equality. Not who's superior, not who's inferior, not who's leading whom, not who's following, but equality: individual equality, and social equality. The ideal of giving rather than taking. The negative application of Aries is to take, isn't it? "Give to me!" Whereas the implied idea of Libra on the twelfth would be – let's give first, then we receive.

If you break it down to a basic 6th house issue of work and/or service, the negative Aries says what? With respect to employment and/or work issues, what do you think it would say? Look, Aries is the instinct in all people that makes you feel that you have something special to do that is unique to your own individuality. So if you link this to the 6th house, what is now instinctively related to that which is special? Can't you see the scene now? The negative Aries emerging in the work place. Here I am, you see! I am here! And of course, the projected criticism. Libra/12th house, all these other voices going, "Well, so what?"

The point is that Aries on the 6th is going to be learning how to work to cooperate in an equal way in the work space. Not wanting to dominate it, not wanting to be the superior. So the point here is that until such a realization is made via the 6th house Aries, that special work which is implied there will be denied. And it's that kind of crises, i.e. the denial, that enforces the analysis leading to the awareness of the dynamics, hopefully creating the reasons as to why, which then effects self-improvement and adjustment. Do you see what I'm getting at? Is it clear? I mean it's ten in the morning, is it clear? (Laughter) Where's my coffee?

You see, one of the problems that can be generated because of this self-analysis and this awareness of imperfection, and need to improve, is that it can also create the inner feelings of self-doubt. So when you start talking about work issues, if the individual excessively drops into these negative correlations, self-doubt or self-analysis, it can then lead to the feeling of, "I'm not ready", "I'm not prepared to do what my work capacity suggests". And through excuse making I only minimally develop the maximum of the potential. You see, you have a whole realm of potential there. But forever focusing on what I need to fix creates this self-doubt, which then creates the necessary excuses to justify the non-performance leading to minimal actualization of that which could be. Yet another crisis!

Audience: How do you move through that without getting totally bottled up?

Jeffrey: The key through the 6th house – keeping in mind you have this mutable, yin, earth archetype – one of the keys is to follow instinctual rhythm. In other words, the key to perfection lies through action, not sitting in one space analyzing it to tears. So what you have is that you have to be in conformity with the archetype. In other words, on a cyclic or rhythmic basis it will be appropriate to step back and to introspect, and then just as appropriate in the other rhythm to act and to follow those instincts. Too much of either equals being out of balance.

Audience: If there is a stellium in the 6th house and nothing in the 12 house to balance that, does that imply a different approach?

Jeffrey: No. It gives it a specific structure that is unique to that person. But here comes your answer from another point of view. The natural planetary ruler of the sign on your 6th house, where it's located by house and sign, the aspects to it, are the specific strategies that you must implement to effect on-going self-improvement that is continually developed through action. This is also true with respect to the planetary ruler on the 12th house. Because you're going to have the ideals implied on the sign on the 12th house which, through follow-through, are also linked to its planetary ruler through house and sign. So you have, on the one hand, the practical strategies of the 6th house to consistently actualize, act upon. And you have the planetary ruler of the 12th house having this total connection to the ideal. You see? So these themselves become areas of experience to act upon. And then you unite or synthesize the opposite. So as an example let's say we have Aries on the 6th house, and we put the planetary ruler Mars in Cancer, and we put that in the 9th house. Now what would you feel to be specific strategies – concrete, practical strategies – that the individual could actualize to affect its on-going self-improvement. What do you think?

Audience: Listening, studying.

Jeffrey: What would be listened to and what would be studied? Couldn't we just simply suggest to the person, no-matter what their evolutionary state was, to just simply invest themselves in reading literature of a higher-mind nature? In any given dynamic and/or structure, and/or form, it makes no difference. And by simply exposing the self to these higher mind ideas, what happens? You satisfy all the requirements. You have, of course, the requirement of humility (6th house). So what happens if I expose my ego to higher mind ideas? You see? Does this not begin to place some proper perspective on my sense of individuality in a metaphysical or religious context? You see?

I'm expanding my horizon, which through necessary cycles of reflection, i.e. self introspection, I also back off now and then and reflect on what is happening here, which itself creates adjustment of what is happening when I'm reading and/or going to school. And is this not going to have an impact on the emotional structure implicated in the security associated with the negative Aries ego? I mean just the basic strategy. Can't we also say that another practical thing to do in that kind of symbolism, because of the connection to the 9th house, Aries, action itself, when you feel like getting in the stupid car, Go! Don't make excuses for it. Meaning that, if you place yourself in physical motion – travel, 9th house – this will promote an inner processing that can only occur because of the physical motion, rather than sitting in the chair all the time and trying to analyze it to death, in which you just get lost in mental collapse.

Audience: You're saying action is the method because of Aries. Would it be a different method with another sign?

Jeffrey: No, we're giving you an archetype. By placing a sign there we're illustrating that archetype. As an example, take the same Aries and put Mars in Libra in the 11th house. You still have this archetype of Aries needing to be purified, but now what are the specific strategies? They change from the 9th/Cancer to the 11th/Libra. So, what are the strategies? Can't you see the classic case?

The individual instinctively (Aries) attracts to itself a diversity of people (Libra/11th house) who now all begin to have all these messages apparently (11th house) out of the blue, and yet here they come. What is the challenge? Are you going to tell the Aries/6th house, "Yes, these people are just conspiring to come down on your case?" Or are you going to say, "Objectively listen to the messages that you're receiving?" And maybe also suggest that the individual get involved with some sort of social cause and/or group of people who share a common purpose. And by creating this interaction effecting equality – Libra in the context of relationship to which individuality (Mars) – is adjusted. You see, basic things. Then you satisfy this Libra/12th house.

Now most of us have learned that when we say transitional archetype this means that transition is taking us into the 7th house and beyond. So what the transition amounts to is an adjustment from excessive ego-centric self identity, i.e. delusions of grandeur. We have to then experience the inherent lack and/or inferiority associated with the 6th house in order to re-enter the world, i.e. 7th house and beyond, hopefully as equals – not as inferiors, not as superiors, but as equals. From the 5th house point of view this correlates to what we call the pyramid archetype, in which the individual is sitting on top of their own pyramid expecting all things to revolve around it. Whereas the 6th house is what we call the inverted pyramid, in which all things are sitting on you, (laughs) and you're serving it. And this is why the 6th house correlates to the work issue.

Work obviously implies self-sacrifice. The 5th house wants to do its own trip; I'm on the stage of life. And yet the 6th house demands work and/or commitment and/or service to a larger whole, keeping in mind that the 6th is naturally linked to the 12th, society. In the 12th house commitment to a larger whole and the self-sacrifice of egocentric whims creates the necessary analysis, adjustments, humility, purification, and so on, and leads to the inverted pyramid. Now, obviously, in some societies the work assignment is fixed; i.e. in your more authoritarian regimes and/or in your caste systems, like in India, it's fixed, and you can see if it's fixed. But what if I feel I have the capacity to be some administrator at a government level and yet by coming into a fixed nation, fixed class, fixed caste, I'm required to be a welder? Or if I come into freer worlds in which I have the option of actualizing the work that is relevant to Me. Then what happens?

We have to submit ourselves to the Earth archetype – 2nd, 6th, and 10th – the customs, norms, taboos, laws, and regulations of the specific society that we're born into. In other words, if I want to be a psychologist, and I feel I have the inherent capacity to be a psychologist, if I am born into this country, this country says what? "Well far out, but you go to school for eight years, and you get your Ph.D!" Do you see my point now? The ego is submitted to a larger source or force of power that it cannot control, and it is the submission to that source that leads to the very same effects. And if I don't submit to it, I may still want to be a psychologist, but if I don't do what is required, what happens?

This issue in self-improvement is going on all the time. In other words, the planets that rule your 6th and 2nd houses are always transiting some place through your chart all the time. And this means all you have to do is locate the current transitory position of those two planets, and you will specifically find the issues, dynamics or experiences that are occurring that come under this theme of self-improvement and where the current strategies will lie to affect it, as well as where the current external criticism can occur – where the current inner criticism can be affected. Where the current sense of lack can be felt. Now just take a moment to ponder on your own charts right now. Locate the current transits to those points and see if you can identify this in your life.

Audience: In my case I have Cancer on the 6th house cusp, which is ruled by the Moon and the Moon moves around the chart at such a rapid rate.

Jeffrey: What does that suggest to you in terms of your own information? It suggests that you have a nature that is perpetually trying to catch up. And by always having the sense that you don't have enough time in your day and are always trying to catch up, how does this implicate and correlate to your sense of emotional security? Isn't the larger teaching: What is security in the first place? And the 12th house ideal becomes responsible for establishing your security, instead of trying to find your security linked with the work space, or trying to find your sense of personal authority projected only in what?

Now, of course, the 6th house itself can be transited; the natal ruler itself can be transited, and it can be progressed to, and it can progress. You're going to have a solar return 6th house and so on. In other words, if you look at it this way, you're going to have a tremendous volume of information to deal with at any moment in time. The point here, obviously, is that self-improvement correlates to the issue of growth, so that the journey of perfection can be realized.

To me, the 29 degree symbol is obviously a very potent symbol, just as zero and the one degree are; these come under the archetype of mutation. With respect to the 29 degree symbol, this correlates to culmination: an entire evolutionary cycle with respect to the sign on that 6th house at 29 degrees that's coming to culmination in this life. It implies whole evolutionary lifetimes before this that you've been dealing with it, and it's come into a point of culmination this time, and it's beginning to mutate. And because it's culminating, it means that whatever you haven't dealt with, all of that is re-experienced in this life.

We also must talk about this natural relationship i.e. mutable grand cross, between the 6th, 12th, 3rd, and 9th. The basic thrust of this archetype is for self-knowledge, self-expansion with respect to self-improvement. So, if you start with the 3rd house, the natural Gemini house, you have a situation which is also Mercury ruled, and this side of Mercury (in Gemini) sets us in motion to simply collect information about the nature of reality in general – the need to collect information, facts, and data. The need to give names to what we call phenomenal reality. In other words, from the point of view of the 9th house, this is phenomenal reality. This is not called a lectern in and of itself. The human mind projects a name upon it in order to connect it to another name, which is called a platform, in order to connect it to another name, which is called a floor, which is connected to the wall and so on. And we create intellectual structure: One fact leading to the next fact – logic – in order to feel secure. How many of us could live happily in a phenomenal universe, giving names to nothing, simply living in existential voids our whole life? Not many of us. So my point is that via the 3rd house, we do all this collection. We create our own unique intellectual structure, which creates the very basis of our opinions.

So via the 6th house, the Mercury function here, analyzes. It analyzes what it's taking in. One of the functions of the 6th house from another point of view is what is called discrimination: What facts am I going to take in, and what am I going to reject? And through classification and analysis, we put it together, making compartments, files and all this. This fact goes here, this fact goes here. And if that fact doesn't agree with my existing intellectual structure, I criticize it and reject it.

The point of view from the 6th house, the Mercury side, is that it correlates to the intrinsic capacity, through analysis, to pinpoint the weakest link in any intellectual argument, and by finding the weak link, tear the remaining argument down in order to justify its own existing point of view. And via the 9th house in its negative state, this now correlates to what we call the Billy Graham complex: the need to indoctrinate, convince or convert other people to your point of view in order to feel now intellectually and philosophically secure. Does this not now give rise to sectarian philosophies and religions that have ordered it in their own little ways? Now creating the

Mercury voice, "We're right, you're wrong"?

The point here is that the 9th house of itself correlates to the archetype of intuition, what others like to call the sixth sense. We're all linked to the universe, the galaxies and so on, and because of this very basic fact, most people at most times will (9th house) ponder or speculate or wonder what it all means. What does it all mean from a phenomenal point of view? And so with respect to our 3rd and 6th houses we create our convenient intellectual structures to put it together. Now check this thing out.

We all have intuition, so the point here is that which we call truth, i.e. 9th house, exists. We have a created universe so there must be some law, some truth to explain that which exists. In other words, truth can't be invented, it can only be realized. So whatever my specific intellectual orientation is, whatever my specific intellectual/emotional needs are, whatever kinds of questions are generated, my intuition is orientated to the universe in that way. In other words, if I think of religion from an agnostic point of view and that constitutes the basis of my intellect, then my intuition is tapped into the universe to intuit the structural truth of agnosticism. Do you see my point? And this is called picking up a portion of the truth.

Intuition is that part in all of us that simply knows what it knows without knowing how it knows it. It is the wisdom that is inherited from your own prior lives and bring in to this life. But then we ask the next question: Is what you know the whole truth or part of the truth? So this sets in motion – keeping in mind the 12th house polarity – the need to understand the whole truth, you see, not a portion. And you have this natural mutable grand cross so now what happens? We start to attract to ourselves intellectual and philosophical confrontations, arguments and disagreements. Now why is this happening? To make us aware of the limitations in our own intellectual orientation? And can this not create cyclic philosophical and intellectual crisis when my own points of view have now become criticized or attacked or exposed for their limitations? Does this not then enforce analysis? Does not the analysis now lead to the dynamics creating the situation? Can this now not be adjusted?

The problem from the point of view of the 6th house, in this culture, is that it correlates to what, philosophically speaking, is called deductive logic: trying to build the whole out of the parts. You know you read in your happy astrological calendars – can't see the forest for the trees. And the 12th house polarity: what is it trying to teach from a philosophical point of view? To learn how to transfer into inductive logic: Identifying the whole first – the whole – so that its specific parts are revealed in their natural order.

So what we're now talking about is the inherent conflict or discrepancy between opinion and truth. Approaching it from the 9th house point of view, if I'm teaching from the point of view of self-righteousness, i.e. "My point is right and yours isn't", is this really teaching or is it indoctrination? If I teach from a Socratic point of view, is this real teaching?

The problem when you were born into the Western world within the last 300 to 400 years is that the whole emphasis was on empiricism, you see, scientific fact, which promotes a linear intellect, a fact oriented intellect. It emphasized deductive logic. So from the point of view of the 6th house in this kind of world, the 12th house is perceived as irrational, contrasted with what is called rationalism or pragmatism or that which is practical. According to whom? That's my question! You're going to tell me what's practical? That's your form of practicality. You see what I'm getting at?

If you were born in the East, I mean even the language structure of the East is character, whole concepts – abstract principles are reflected – versus just a word, like in the West. And from the point of view of the East, that which is called rational in this culture is called irrational. Who's right? Who's wrong? You see? So all we're trying to suggest is that you all have a 3rd, 6th, 9th and 12th house. The signs that you have on this natural grand cross, their planetary rulers, and the aspects that they may be making, will show you specifically in your own case, how you experience this archetype and the inherent conflict within it. The ultimate challenge of any mutable archetype is to synthesize, so that this finally leads to a vision or the knowledge of the whole truth.

Now from a more individual point of view, this also means your own truth. The point here is that this natural mutable archetype (the grand cross implied) is trying to teach every single one of us to identify our own natural truth, our own natural law and to actualize it. Not to live somebody else's truth, but to identify your own. So the signs that you have on these points, the planets, show you the kinds of experiences that you inwardly orientate to and externally draw to enforce this realization. So when you try to illustrate these things, what if an individual had Capricorn on the 3rd house, Cancer on the 9th, Aries on the 6th and Libra on the 12th? What kinds of inner experiences/outer circumstances would the individual effect in order to arrive at his/her own natural truth? Let your intuition guide you now. Don't get hung up on 6th house analysis. (laughter)

Audience: The action to search.

Jeffrey: The action to search for what? This combination, in general, would tend to create the affect in which the individual would want to try and establish its own authority (Capricorn) its own voice (Aries) through which its self-image (Cancer) and security (Cancer/9th house) was realized, and via the Libra/12th house, how would this search for personal truth be projected on to the external environment?

Audience: So you're saying in an enlightened sense the individual would project his or her own natural truth from the point of view of relativity (12th house/Libra), "This is my version of the truth I'm just trying to share with you, and this is your version of the truth and we respect individuality". (Aries/6th house).

Jeffrey: And could we not also say with respect to Capricorn on the 3rd house, what the natural intellectual orientation of the individual would be with respect to collecting what kinds of information? What would be the natural draw here?

Audience: Business.

Jeffrey: That's a bit specific. Can't we just generally say – because we have to speak in generalities – couldn't we say, in general, that at least the individual would orientate to tradition, established authority. So then the question becomes, in a potential crisis, what authority and what tradition? And by aligning its own individuality with some existing tradition, this becomes the basis for its own authority because its connected to something other than just itself (Capricorn) through which its own individuality (Aries) is realized, which constitutes the element of inner security (Cancer/9th house), which constitutes the element of its beliefs, which is intellectually justified through the tradition itself.

Audience: I have exactly the opposite of that.

Jeffrey: What it that trying to suggest? Clearly with that combination you must learn to establish your own voice by breaking free from tradition and reformulating your sense of security in that individual discovery – learning how to honestly express to people (Libra on the sixth), at all times what is really on your mind.

Is this something you think you can apply in your own work now? I mean is it practical enough for you (6th house)? (laughter.)

So my basic point is very simple. Because you have this natural mutable archetype, you will have key cycles in your life in which you experience philosophical or intellectual crisis or for some spiritual crisis and for others religious crisis when the ideas that your orientated to become crystallized (Earth) no more productive – counter-productive, which then sets in motion this natural crisis, i.e. the search for new information (3rd house/9th house/12th house), which will add to your existing intellectual/philosophical foundation so that you can grow, with respect to the search for the whole truth. The point of view from the 12th house is to dissolve all intellectual and philosophical limitations which prevent knowledge of the whole truth. So we have these key cycles of crisis in which this happens. This can be measured through transits. It can be measured through progressions. It can be measured through solar returns. We all go through it.

So in terms of strategies of self improvement, just locate the ruler of your 6th house, locate the natural ruler of your 12th house, determine the aspects therein, focus upon the specific experience and activities that they suggest to be consistently acted upon, so that if this is done, it will minimize the intensity of any given crisis that you have to go through.

Audience: What if you have planets in the 6th house?

Jeffrey: Obviously, if you have planets in the 6th house every one of those psychological correlations or functions is being acted upon with respect to these archetypes throughout life. The signs that they naturally correlate to or rule, and their own house locality are, in effect, brought into this 6th house and acted upon throughout life. Throughout life. It's one of the life intentions.

Audience: So what would happen if you had the ruler of the 12th house in the 6th? I think it would help you by bringing it out because the 12th house is unconscious, so with the planet in the 6th wouldn't that externalize it?

Jeffrey: Yes, but you also have this problem: The 6th house is naturally inconjunct the ascendant and naturally opposed the 12th house, so with respect to the inconjunct, i.e. the Yod, the ideal implied in that 12th house planet being located in the 6th can seem so pure, so idealized that with respect to the individual self-analysis and the focusing on the lack, not feeling ready, do you see what I'm getting at? That it seems almost unattainable, and as a result generates the necessary excuses or reasons to not develop it. That is, in fact, the most common application. It is the rare individual who can consistently act, i.e. put one step in front of the other, to realize the full potential of that planet. As Brian was saying in his lecture, it becomes a projected phenomenon when you are trying to seek that sense of perfection in something else – It can be another person, it can be a family member, it can be a work structure – without developing it within. It's a very common problem.

But then you ask the question, "Why did that individual choose to be born with that kind of planetary placement, from an evolutionary point of view?" Nevertheless, that planet locality suggests the appropriate activities to initiate for what needs to be realized, and it just requires one step in front of the other. There's an old philosophy that came out of Taoism, China, one of the ways they would illustrate principles is through analogy or stories. So one of the stories they have that applies to the 6th house is the story of the centipede. Imagine now the centipede has a thousand legs and it's fine as long as it keeps walking, but as soon as it tries to figure out how leg forty-six works it becomes catatonic. So the little moral (9th house) is one step in front of the other. This is how perfection is realized. Not through excessive inaction, not through excessive analysis. Mutability requires action.

Any more questions?

OK, thank you for coming this morning!

10

The Planetary Method of Evolutionary Chart Analysis

Jeffrey: What I'd like to do is try to make this as experiential for you this morning as possible, and the way I would like to do that is for all of you to keep your own particular birth chart in your head now as we go through this specific method so you can apply it immediately to your own case.

This particular method is very sequential; it is very Virgo like, ABC in nature, leading to a very deductive and Virgo-like analysis. In total, you will then find that once you employ this particular methodology – ABC – this will lead to a Pisces kind of awareness, meaning inductive, wherein you can see the whole first and then immediately grasp all the parts. So it is like going from Virgo to Pisces. Now as we go through this system, when you have questions, please ask me when you have the question, because the intention is to keep this as clear as possible as we are moving through it.

So the very first way we want to start the system is, of course, with Pluto. This is number one on your list; meaning as we go through this it is going to be like an outline. So we want to start with Pluto. We can ask a Pluto question: Why? And what we have here from a Plutonian point of view, of course, is the direct connection to the Soul, the Soul itself. Now, of course, if we understand this, the Soul is going to create the overall personality structure in any given life that is uniquely orientated to phenomenal reality in such a way that that unique orientation experiences the phenomenal reality in a way that is consistent with the evolutionary intentions and karmic requirement that the Soul has in any given life.

So we want to locate the natal position of Pluto first by house and sign. What is this going to be demonstrating? We have to remember that the nature of the Soul linked with time and space reality is simultaneously linked with the principle that we call evolution. Evolution is a dynamic in time and space reality that is beyond debate. The simplest way to know evolution: Is it not true that everybody on this planet, everyone in this room, inwardly always has an inner feeling of being in a continuous state of becoming? Who does not have such a feeling? So you can see right away just through normal life experience that this is a principle, a truth if you will, that applies to all people everywhere as long as we are living in time-space reality.

Now, if we linked evolution to the principle of the Soul, we ask a logical question: What is, in fact, the inner mechanism or dynamic within the Soul that causes evolution? The answer is straightforward, simple, and basic as most natural truths are. The answer is, in fact, the very same answer that came out of the enlightenment of the famous Buddha under the famous Bodhi tree, when he pondered the nature of sorrow and pain, misery and the like. What was actually promoted in Buddhism terms as Nirvana was based on the awareness within him called desire.

In each Soul there are two competing and antithetical desires that create evolution. One desire is a separating desire, meaning to separate away from what we can call God. And these sorts of desires are many, myriad, manifesting in typical ways as the desire for the new lover, the new possession, the new career ambition, whatever. All Souls have these desires, and simultaneous with the desire and coequal to it is the desire to return to that which has created the Soul in the first place. So, in effect, the essence of the evolution of the Soul is simply based on the progressive elimination (Pluto) of all separating desires to the exclusion of only one desire which can remain, which is to unite with the source of the Soul itself.

This is a very simple natural truth that operates independent of what we call astrology and can be validated by every single one of us in this room. In fact, it can be validated by everybody on Earth. The simplest way to know it, again: Is not true that we can have whatever separating desire, oh we want this new thing over here, this, that or whatever, and we may have the ability to obtain that which we are desiring, and, of course, we have a momentary sense of satisfaction when we get it. But once we get it, what soon replaces the sense of satisfaction is, in effect, the sense of dissatisfaction, the sense of something more. It is exactly the sense of dissatisfaction that is mirroring and echoing this ultimate desire to return and to reunite with the source of all things. Who of you has not known this to be your own experience? You see, it is universal. So the evolution of the Soul is simply based on the progressive elimination of all separating desires. The duality of these antithetical desires is intrinsic within the Soul and is what the psychologists call the basis of free choice.

Now, when we look at the nature of the natal position of Pluto, we are looking at two simultaneous phenomena, which is why we are starting with this number A on our Virgo list. Number one, it will describe very succinctly the types of desires that the soul has had prior to the current life, relative to its evolutionary necessities, its evolutionary intentions. That does not mean, by the way, that that is going to correlate or reflect all the prior lives that the Soul has had. The point is that the Soul in any given life will only draw upon specific prior life times that have a direct connection to, or bearing on, the current life evolutionary intentions.

So, what the natal position of Pluto is demonstrating is the specific prior lifetimes and orientations that have direct bearing on the current lifetime. A simple example: What if we are dealing with a 9th house Pluto individual? We can make a very simple Piscean/ Virgo deduction that this would have been a Soul who, prior to the current life, one way or another, was desiring to understand its individual connection to the cosmological reality we call the universe, meaning natural desires to understand philosophy and cosmology and metaphysics, religion (even if that's atheism), anything that is a form of philosophy connected to the cosmos. Are we clear? Good.

And now what would that mean coming into the current life? And this is one of the secrets about Pluto that most people don't realize, i.e. when you read it in your happy books that it somehow connects to compulsion, obsession, defensiveness, resistance to change and all these things, and these things are accurate, but they never tell you why, and it is because at this point Pluto is going to correlate with the deepest sources of your unconscious sense of security. Keeping in mind that security is a function of self-consistency. Self-consistency is a function of the past, meaning what has come before. Again, how many of you would totally and wholly embrace the experience of absolute insecurity? No takers? Hmm? Ever wonder why we have compulsion, obsession? That's what psychologists call repetitive compulsion.

So by looking at the natal position of Pluto (house and sign), beyond the metaphysical point of view, you are describing in anybody's life the sources that correlate with the deepest sense of unconscious security in the person. And in coming into the current life, the person instinctually gravitates to those sources in order to maintain a sense of self-consistency equaling security. Now clearly, if the soul stayed right there, there would, in fact, be no evolution. So this becomes a first point to examine. The next point is to determine how it is that soul is going to grow or evolve in the current life. And the answer very happily is that the next step (evolution) is determined – because we have to remember that we are living in a universe, time/space, that of itself is defined by the law of polarity – by the opposite house and sign of the natal position of Pluto.

So, following our example of the 9th house, it is, of course, naturally in opposition to the 3rd house. Now, one of the natural problems in the 9th house/Sagittarius/Jupiter archetype is that it correlates, in essence, with the nature of phenomenal reality in total. And it is the 9th house in any chart – Jupiter/Sagittarius, archetypically natural law – that creates the awareness in the human organism, in each person, that we are in fact connected to something much larger than just the Earth itself. It creates the awareness that we are connected to a solar system, universes, and galaxies. And this sort of natural awareness gives rise to the philosophical questions that all human beings ask: What does it all mean? How are we connected to this thing?

One of the problems of the 9th house is that it will typically orientate to a portion of the overall truth, and then consider that particular portion to be the total truth, which is why we call it the Billy Graham Archetype, meaning the need to convince and convert other people to your particular point of view. Why? In order to feel secure. This is why in this case we are going to have a have a 3rd house polarity.

Most of us have already realized in our happy books that Gemini correlates with diversity, yes? Most of us realized – particularly for those that find yourself to be Gemini – that Gemini is a happy little sign because you put it in a bookstore, for example, and it is going to go around and do what? It is going to read two pages of this and one page of that, and maybe one right over here, but it is thinking that it is reading everything. And this means that it is trying to understand as much as possible relative to the whole phenomenon called creation. So when you have this polarity point to the 9th house Pluto, you can see the obvious evolutionary intention. The intention of the Soul is to evolve beyond the particular portion – part – of the truth that it has already realized. You understand the point?

So the Soul is like a computer, and it has its own program and in a typically Plutonian fashion, then, the Soul will actually literally program necessary philosophical confrontations (Pluto), meaning it will attract to itself other individuals that are more philosophically or cosmologically evolved than itself. These people will have the effect of penetrating (Pluto) to the weak link in this person's existing philosophical structure. And by identifying the weak link, well, guess what? That whole structure collapses. And this is induces the Gemini evolutionary intention. Understand the point? I mean we could go on and on, but we only have an hour and a half. So, on our Virgo list we start with Pluto, natal position, polarity point. Any questions on this aspect of it? So, we are clear on this particular point?

Next step – point B on your Virgo list. We want to, of course, examine the nature of the South Node of the Moon. Now, why do we want to examine this point? The reason is that the South Node of the Moon will specifically correlate to the types of egocentric structures that the soul has necessarily created in order to consciously actualize the evolutionary desires or intentions, which have, in fact, preceded the current life.

That is to say that the Moon, the South Node of the Moon specifically, correlates to what we call the ego. Now take this very seriously because, of course, I realize in astrology land that astrologers can assign the idea or the archetype of the ego to whatever planetary symbolism. Over the last 10-20 years it has been given to Saturn, Sun or whatever. But in reality in the astrology we do, the ego is specific to the Moon. The way you can prove this through natural law is very straightforward. As an example we can understand that the ego is that which correlates with what we can psychologically call a self-image.

Now, for example, if we make an ego connection to the Sun and we look into the nature of our solar system, of course, the Sun appears to be relatively fixed, does it not? Now, do you feel throughout your life that your own inner self-image has been fixed and constant? When we compare this to examining the Moon and its various phases, you can see the direct link to your own self-image and its evolution. Understand the point?

So, in effect, the Soul must create a necessary ego to create a self-image of the Soul itself. So the South Node is the conscious component that the soul generates or creates to actualize the desires that are intrinsic to the soul itself. As a simple example, let's still use our 9th house Pluto as our example, remembering that the 9th house Pluto is how I want to understand myself in the cosmos, etc. Now when we put the South Node in the 7th house, what are we looking at? We Are looking at a soul who prior to the current life, over a series of recent prior life times, has created egocentric structures that have been actualized through a 7th house archetype. What does it mean? It's going to mean that the soul has created a series of prior life egos that have been structured in such a way as to initiate a diversity of relationships, (7th house), who looked like what? 9th house teacher types. And by initiating this kind of relationships with teacher types, it has been collecting for itself, or attracting to itself, the kind of information that it has desired relative to the 9th house Pluto. You see the link?

Now, to show you why cookbook astrology is BS – I mean wrong – compare this to a 9th house Pluto, but put the South Node in the 1st house. You are going to still have the same complex of desires, but what types of personality structure, or egocentric structure has the Soul used that is very different from the 7th house? In the first case you have dependency on an external teacher, but when you put the South Node in the 1st house, in essence, what you now have is a soul who has the same desire structure, but now with this South Node in the 1st house you have an individual who has learned to ask and answer its own questions. You see why cookbook astrology is so wrong?

So in either case you still have a pre-existing orientation to reality. When that 9th house Pluto, South Node in the 7th person comes into life she/he will gravitate, as they have prior to the current life, in exactly that way. This is why there is going to be a thing called the North Node. You see the point? So in this 9th house Pluto/7th house South Node, we have a polarity point in the 3rd house, and we have a North Node in the 1st. So in essence, the North Node in this case, the conscious actualization, makes that 3rd house polarity occur, understand my point?

What that would actually mean in this life as the person begin to emotionally mature (Moon) in the current life, is that it progressively would begin to rebel against external teachers, their message and their voices. Because the intention (North Node/1st house) is that the person is meant to learn to ask and answer its own questions. This is going to create necessary intellectual, philosophical confrontation with external teacher types. You see?

In the second case, the person has been living in happy splendor, all within themselves in a form of narcissism (South Node/1st house). You see my point? So now why are we seeing the North Node in the 7th house? They must learn to open up and share themselves with other people and in so doing, in opening up to other people, they are going to attract (3rd house polarity), you see how it works. You apply this to all charts. You start just this way, A, B on your happy list. Questions? So we have got this down now?

The next step in our happy methodology is then to go to the Sun, by the house and sign of the Sun and the aspects it is making. Why? Because the Sun is going to correlate specifically to how we are integrating and giving purpose and meaning to our current life experience. So in essence we are describing an evolutionary transition in our A B list, an evolutionary transition from past to the current life. The Sun is now going to show you how that is integrated and given purpose and meaning in the context of the current life. How the Sun in Sagittarius integrates life experience, gives purpose and meaning, is going to be very different from how a Virgo Sun integrates life experience and gives purpose and meaning, you understand my point?

So once you get used to these methods you ultimately get to play the role of an evolutionary detective, why this Sun sign? You understand my point? So that is why our next step is to move right to the Sun. And again I want you to be able to apply this experientially to your own chart, so try to work with that as we move through it so you can see the reality of what we are talking about. So just take a moment right now and think about your own natal Pluto, polarity point, North and South Node and your Sun sign. Take a moment, don't ask a question, just take a moment!

Now, how many are completely stumped? Maybe in a moment it will become more clear for you.

Audience: How about if your Pluto is right on the cusp?

Jeffrey: On the cusp?

Audience: Yeah.

Jeffrey: What you have when Pluto is on the cusp is the archetype of initiation, but if you have it just before the cusp of moving into the next house, you have the archetype evolutionarily of culmination – an entire series of prior lives all culminating in the context of the current life.

Audience: But you would still interpret it in terms of the house that it is in?

Jeffrey: Yes. And see then what you have is as it progressively culminates – when Pluto is evolving into the next house – you still determine the polarity point, which allows for that evolutionary shift. This can by the way, psychologically create frustration, because the Soul already can feel where it is trying to go, but it also has to culminate, so it has this push-pull, yeah.

Audience: What if Pluto is conjunct the nodes – actually, let's take the North Node.

Jeffrey: That's a very unique evolutionary signature. When you find Pluto conjunct the North Node it means in all cases, that that soul has been working in that area of evolutionary development prior to the current life and is meant to completely focus on that area in the context of the current life. There is no polarity.

Audience: If Pluto and the North Node are in the same house but not conjunct, is that the same meaning or not?

Jeffrey: First, you want to determine if the Node is balsamic or new phase relative to Pluto, which creates its own archetypical meaning. And then there used to be an old phrase in astrology (I am going to date myself now) but it used to be called in mundo, meaning conjunct by sign. But unless you have technically an absolute conjunction, then you have a different kind of meaning depending on the phasal relationship between Pluto and the node itself.

The next step after understanding the integrative principle of the Sun and the purpose and meaning it is giving to life experience in general, our very next step is then to move to the Moon itself. Why? The current life Moon, the natal Moon, and the Nodes are going to reflect a spiritual law, the trinity, from the earth point of view the phenomenon of past, present, and future. We have the North and South Nodes of the Moon and what this is correlating to psychologically is a universal experience we call the dynamic tension that exist in all people between the past and the future, as experienced in each moment of our life. That's the natal Moon in relationship to its nodal axis. We have an evolving ego, i.e. from South Node to North Node. How that evolving ego is integrated on a consistent basis (Moon) is the natal Moon itself by house and sign.

Audience: Could you go over that again?

Jeffrey: We have a thing called the dynamic tension between the past and the future that we all experience, yes? That dynamic tension as experienced in each moment of our life is contained in your natal Moon. How we integrate the potential insecurity linked with our past and our future experienced in the moment is our natal Moon. It creates cohesion, self-consistency, understand? It's that place in you, the dynamic in you, that can say, "This is who I used to be, this is who I am trying to become". That voice is your natal Moon; do you understand my point?

Audience: Can you give an example of that?

Jeffrey: All of you in this room know as your life experience that you are in a dynamic state of becoming, yes? You know you have a past; you know you have a feeling to go into – toward – your future, which is the experience of the moment, yes? The experience of these two things in the moment is your Moon. How you experience that is your natal Moon by its own house and sign.

Audience: Let's say the Moon was conjunct one end or the other of the nodal path, for example, the North Node, would there be more orientation toward the future than the past and really more conflict about trying to integrate the South Node somehow with Pluto?

Jeffrey: Each case is unique and you have to always overlay this with karmic evolutionary requirements. The experience of it depends on the person, including the observed evolutionary state; one size does not fit all. If I had the Moon on the South Node and I am in consensus state, for example, how I am responding to that inwardly would be vastly different than if I had that Moon /South Node and I am in, say, an individuated state, or a spiritual state, you see. In all cases you are looking at the phenomenon of something being unresolved in a prior life, at an emotional level, that the person is bringing forward into the current life in order to re experience with the intention of resolving it.

If you have Moon square the Nodes, and really anytime you have a planet square the Nodes, including the Moon or Pluto, in evolutionary terms you have what are called skipped steps. And in the current context the person has been flip flopping back and forth, back and forth. And in evolutionary terms, karmic requirement, the person must recover those skipped steps in order to evolutionary proceed. Until that recovery is made they are blocked, you see my point now? Are we clear on the methodology as we are proceeding? That's my main intention at the moment, are we clear at the moment? Anybody still not clear? Good!

Now, another way of looking at this is why we are going to be using the Moon in this sequence. The Moon is how each of us lives with our self inwardly on a moment-to-moment basis. It is how we are giving personal form and definition to what we call our reality. It is way for us to make it personally secure. All human beings have a need to feel secure. Of course the issue is what constitutes security. But the phenomenon of feeling secure is a constant for all human beings. It is like the need to put an anchor in the sea instead of just letting the boat drift where it wants to go. That is your ego. That is your anchor in the sea. That is the anchor into your unconscious. That is the anchor into your soul. Do you understand my point?

That is the way for you to personally relate to what your evolutionary intentions are relative to the purpose that is described by the Sun. It is a way for you to live with it, to feel emotionally secure because of it. The house and sign of your Moon and the aspects it makes describe how that process is done. It is that simple. Yes?

Audience: I'm sorry, is that the security ...?

Jeffrey: Yes, this is why we have a triad among Cancer, Scorpio and Pisces. See this is the ultimate meaning when we have the Moon linked with Scorpio and Pisces. We have this natural triad, and very few astrologers will tell you that the ultimate secret of Cancer and the Moon is to realize that the Moon itself is the source of its own insecurity. This is why it is a Cardinal archetype, two steps forward and one step back. We want to initiate change and we freak out, and we want to recover our past, our existing reality in order to feel secure again.

But the ultimate teaching of the Moon is reflected in the dark side of the Moon, the side we never see. And the reason that the Moon creates its own insecurity is to ultimately realize (Pisces) security from within, linked with an inner reality that has nothing to do with the external environment. When you link this through Scorpio, this is why all of us at various points in our journey misapply our trust into people – in order to experience emotional betrayal, abandonment and loss to enforce inner security. This is why.

The next step in our Virgo sequence is Mercury. Why? Mercury is now going to provide the intellectual structure. Again, we are all living in a phenomenal reality, yes? We started with Pluto, the nodal axis of the Moon, Sun, and Moon. And now you can see if you look at this evolutionarily, you can see why the Soul (Pluto) was picking Mercury in whatever house, sign and aspect. That's the kind of intellectual structure, meaning how I am going to intellectually organize in rational ways. That is how I explain to myself what my life experience is about, which is ultimately reflecting its evolutionary intention. This is how I give the intellectual super structure to this process. So I create an intellectual structure that creates rational thinking within me that creates an explanation and justification, which I then communicate to other people. This is why you have your specific house and sign of any given Mercury. You understand the point?

You see, life is either random, or it is in fact some sort of inherent order, you see? And if we look at it this way, we are looking at life and astrology non-judgmentally. This eliminates all the 19th century crap – exaltations, falls – it is irrelevant. We replace all this terminology with two words: what is. This is why you can have your Mercury in whatever house or sign. It is the way that you need to put it together and understand it intellectually through your left brain. Mercury in astrology specifically relates to the left brain.

Audience: What if Mercury is like right on a house cusp?

Jeffrey: Again, if you always use your ultimate perspective to understand the chart and then use an evolutionary perspective – transitions between past, present, future – then you can answer your own question. Any planet on the cusp is going to correlate evolutionarily either to culmination, meaning the planet just before a given house, or if it is just within that house something has already culminated and a brand new cycle of evolutionary development is now proceeding. So if Mercury happens to be the operative symbol it is simple going to mean a soul who is deciding to think, in this life, in altogether radically different ways than it has ever thought before.

OK, next step in our Virgo sequence. Venus, of course, is going to correlate specifically to the nature of the value associations that you make for yourself. Values equal a sense of meaning that you are giving to your life. How many people on earth do you think can live without a sense of meaning? The sense of meaning in life, archetypally through astrology, is specific to Venus. Meaning is specific to that which you value. That which you value is in its own way conditioning or contributing to what you decide to believe. Understand my point?

So the Soul in any given life must orientate to a specific type of value associations that provide a specific sense of meaning. That now is specifically linked with the evolutionary intentions for the life itself. So here we determine and can see from the point of view of Soul/Pluto why Venus is in this house, and in this sign, making those aspects. Understand now?

The next step in our happy Virgo sequence is Mars. Some of you have learned in your happy books that Mars is a lower octave of Pluto. And if you have heard this, ask yourself the following question: What is a lower octave of something? See, here is a happy example of cultures like this where we can understand words, but we don't really know what they mean. A lower octave is simply a denser vibration of something. So why then is Mars a lower octave? The answer is straightforward; again the essence of the Soul's evolution is based on desire. Mars in our subjective consciousness simply instinctually reflects and acts out desires emanating from the Soul itself. This is why you read in the happy books about Aries and Mars and the necessity of freedom. The Soul must have the necessary element, or level, of freedom in this life to initiate experiences that the Soul deems necessary relative to its evolutionary requirements and intentions, understand?

How that is done is specific to the house and sign and aspects that Mars is making. Got it? And this is why the necessity of freedom. That is also going to be correlating, by the way, to the necessary kind of sexual experiences. Sexual experiences are like any other experience of life in which the Soul learns about itself. Remember that sexual desires emanate specifically from the point of view of the primary brain. The primary brain in astrology correlates with Pluto, Mars and Moon. We have to understand that the primary brain in and of itself is unconditioned. It is specific to that which is called natural law. This sets in motion its own potential conflicts and collisions of what we call Will (Mars/Pluto). Meaning, the will of a normal society that is telling you what is right and wrong. What if the kind of sexual desires you have do not conform to your morality telling you this is right and that is wrong? Do you understand what potential conflicts are happening?

From a Patriarchal point of view, linked with the primary brain, this is going to have the archetype that Thomas Moore called Dark Eros. The dark can only be linked, or applied, from the point of view of Patriarchal judgment, understand my point? The only time any sexual desire is wrong is when it is linked with an intent to consciously hurt someone, anything other than what is normal and natural.

Most of you are familiar – most of you are old enough to remember – a series of books written, I think, in the late seventies or early eighties by a woman named Nancy Friday – *Women's Sexual Fantasies, Men's Sexual Fantasies*. So often you would hear in those books: Well I can have this in my fantasy, but I would never act it out. Now you understand this issue, don't you?

So Mars is simply the conscious component that instinctually registers the desires emanating from the unconscious life, Soul. Desires that are specific to the evolutionary needs and requirements of the Soul itself. It requires the necessary freedom in order to act out.

So we are still clear on the sequence? You are still trying to apply this to your chart? How many are starting to see your chart in a new way? Good. My point is that if you get used to doing it for yourself, well, guess what? You can do for your clients. Maybe you are beginning to see what this is finally going to lead to, the Piscean leap, called inductive logic, when you see it all at once. I mean you will get to the point where you don't have to spend three hours studying the chart before the client comes, and then you can do it instantly. So, any questions before we move on? Clear enough? Good.

Next step Jupiter. Following the sequence you can now logically see through your Virgo logic how Jupiter specifically is going to correlate with the types of belief structures that you need to draw upon in order to rationally explain, through your belief structure, the entire process we have described so far. Keeping in mind the nature of belief systems determines how you are interpreting the nature of phenomenal reality. How you are interpreting this reality comes right back to Mercury, how you are communicating it. From the point of view of brain, of consciousness, Jupiter specifically correlates to your right brain, the intuitive, the non-linear, the image based. There is that exact place in your consciousness that makes you aware, again, that we are connected to something much larger than just the earth.

So in effect, from an evolutionary point of view, why are we going to have Jupiter in this house, this sign, and making these aspects? It is the type of belief structure the Soul requires, without judgment, in order to facilitate the entire process of its evolutionary journey and intentions we are describing to this point. Got it?

As an example, do you think that a Soul that decided to have Jupiter in Aries is going to happily conform to a Capricorn version of reality? Why not? What is the evolutionary intent of having Jupiter in Aries? You see my point now? I mean they are trying to strike out on their own to think and understand and conceive for themselves. The phenomenon of conception, abstraction, to make abstract, is a Jupiter process.

It is one of the wonderful things about the great Yogananda. This man happened to have Jupiter in Aries and despite Vedantic tradition, which is essentially Patriarchal, the essence of his teachings was all defined around the Divine Mother, not the Divine Father.

So, the next step in our happy Virgo sequence is Saturn. Here I am going to share a secret with you about Saturn that you are not going to read in any of your happy books. Saturn is the very structural nature of consciousness in general. One of the essential functions of Saturn is to provide a conditioning function. So for example, what if an individual happens to have Saturn in Leo? That means the entire structural definition of that consciousness is defined around the Leo archetype. And that then means that every other astrological function, Venus, Mercury, Mars, Pluto, etc. is defined and conditioned by, in this case, by the Leo archetype – meaning the principle, the self-creative principle, the inner given right for creative self-actualization.

Understand this issue? For example, what do you typically read in your happy cookbook when Saturn is squaring Venus? Let's put Saturn in Leo and Venus in Scorpio. The typical cookbook interpretation will tell you what? That this individual will attempt to dominate and control and limit (Scorpio) the creative development of its partner relative to existing inner insecurity. This is wrong. The structural consciousness is defined by

Saturn in Leo, so this then means (and to show you the opposite) that this individual is giving itself the right to creatively actualize itself in any way it deems necessary and will necessary have conflict with (Venus in Scorpio) partners who are so insecure that they are trying to undermine its creative self development. The Saturn in Leo defining the structural nature of that consciousness will then mean what? A desire to have partners that were doing the same thing.

So you can see the weakness in these stupid cookbooks, because it never made the leap that Saturn is the defining principle in the structural nature of consciousness itself, which is conditioning every other function in that consciousness. Do you see my point now? So, from a point of view of evolution, the happy sequence we have developed we now understand the structural nature of the consciousness that the Soul is creating to facilitate its evolutionary lessons, requirements and intentions. Yes?

Audience: You are saying that Saturn is the overall structure given to things, the Sun then is more like how we sense things because I was looking at the Sun...

Jeffrey: Sensing is a Venus principle.

Audience: Well, you are saying it correlates to how we integrate our current life experiences. Is integrating, which you are associating with the Sun, different from structuring, which you are associating with Saturn?

Jeffrey: Yes.

Audience: Can you explain that?

Jeffrey: This is a structure (Saturn). How we give purpose and meaning to the structure is the Sun.

Audience: OK.

Jeffrey: Yes?
Audience: (Looking at a chart) Why do we have Mercury or Venus before we do, for instance, Saturn or Jupiter?

Jeffrey: I just explained that. That's why I am trying to go through this sequence very slowly. And it is a very deliberate sequence, one thing leading to the next thing. This is intentional to create cohesion, deductive analysis, not jumping around.

Jeffrey: Another Question? Yes?

Audience: With Saturn retrograde it is always desiring to redefine itself?

Jeffrey: Completely. Saturn retrograde has a very simple meaning: it is a structure of consciousness that is forever redefining and restructuring itself.

The problem with Saturn as an archetype intrinsically – this is what you read in the happy books – is the potentiality of crystallization. You have to remember everything is operating through polarity. What is the polarity of Capricorn, i.e. Saturn? It is the Moon and Cancer; it comes right back to security issues. Particularly as we emotionally mature and get older most people start to want to not grow anymore. They want to have their Winnebago and their patio tools, "Oh, I am comfortable now I am not growing anymore". There is a typical example of crystallization linked with security.

If you happen to have Saturn retrograde, you have a structural nature of consciousness that is always restless and will never reach a point in time that says, "Aha! That's it". It wants to forever redefine itself relative to the evolutionary impulse to evolve and to grow.

Audience: How does that relate to all the other planets?

Jeffrey: Then it will have an oblique retrograde function to all the other planetary functions, not direct, oblique. Understand? Direct is like this, oblique is like this. So if I had Saturn retrograde it is having an oblique function to every other planetary function. It doesn't even have to be necessary in a direct aspect. We are talking about the structural nature of consciousness that is defining every other function. This is not something you read in some book, but it turns out to be actual reality. The essence of astrology is observation and correlation, and I am sharing with you the results of correlation and observation of over 15,000 clients all over the planet, not just America. Yes ma'm?

Audience: So actually having a retrograde planet might not be a negative thing at all?

Jeffrey: It is not negative or positive. It simply is what it is. A retrograde archetype accelerates growth relative to the Jungian idea of individuation. Think about the symbol (Rx) to rebel, understand my point? To rebel against what? The status quo expectation of how the function defined by retrograde is meant to operate. And by having a rebellion function we have an individuation function, which is accelerating the growth of individuation or evolution through the function that is retrograde.

Karmically and evolutionary we also have retrogrades: the need to repeat, or relive something from prior lives that was (retrograde) not resolved. This can create its own kind of frustration. What if I have Venus retrograde in Scorpio linked with my relationship formation? And I have this need to repeat and relive x amount of intimate liaisons – karmically and evolutionary dictated – and I am now in a fixed pattern of Scorpio. Meaning all my relationship dynamics, despite my intellectual intention to change it, are fated to be repeated. Is this not going to create some potential frustration with our partner? Meaning the psychology of no matter what I do, I keep re-attracting the same thing. You see my point? These are things you don't read in the happy books.

Audience: So how do you bring that to an end? How do you stop?

Jeffrey: It is stopped once it is completed. It is completed when you finally see the retrograde symbol going to direct through progression, and not until.

Audience: What about when by progression a planet goes retrograde?

Jeffrey: Then you have entered a timeframe where you are repeating something from the past and/or redefining your overall reality in general, through individuation.

OK, so now we move into ever understandable Uranus. From the point of view of Saturn, Saturn is going to describe – for most people – the interfacing between what we are consciously aware of, meaning our subjective consciousness or what we call personality, and the unconscious. It is that natural boundary, or barrier, or threshold. And for most people this is necessary because it goes right back to the idea of the Moon, the anchor in the sea, which creates stability. This is also why, by the way, that most people do not have spontaneous natural access to their prior life memories. The point is that if most people had access to their prior life memories, those prior life memories, which are contained by Uranus, would overwhelm the current sense of reality (Saturn) in such a way it would become so consumed (Pluto) with what happened or didn't happen, what went right, what went wrong, we would not get on with the business of this life. That's why there is a necessary boundary (Saturn) that prevents this awareness. It can only really truly open to the Soul who begins it natural process of evolution back to the Source itself in an active conscious way. Understand my point?

So, Uranus correlates in Jungian terminology to what is called the individuated unconscious, or in Freudian terminology to the subconscious. In either case, I don't care about your the terminology, the Uranian element of your consciousness contains three components. You have learned, as an example, that it is a higher octave of Mercury. Mercury correlates with short-term memory. Uranus correlates with long-term memory. This also includes the long-term memories of other lifetimes. Just look at it logically. How many of you can remember in total detail what you did three days ago? Where did those memories go? Now we are looking at Uranus. So one dimension of Uranus correlates with where all the prior life memories that you have that are contributing to the current life are stored.

It also correlates to the component of our unconscious, dynamics that Saturn represses: dynamics in ourselves that we are having a problem accepting and, therefore, suppressing. This can also include the nature of trauma that is not resolved and is stuck into the subconscious. And Uranus also correlates to – connects to – what we can call the larger blueprint for the Soul's evolutionary future. This is why we have the principal of liberation. To liberate from what? Saturn, the existing conditions of our life that can equal what we can euphemistically call our own personal status quo. That equals our own sense of security (Moon) equaling the anchor in the sea that has been crystallized. So in effect, Uranus is always knocking on Saturn's door. When you go through an act of a Uranian transit, through linkage, the symbolism is very basic. That's what we call the hand grenade in a steel box. The steel box is your Saturn; the hand grenade is your Uranus. In the last analysis the hand grenade will prevail.

As an example, if I make a bomb go off right here, obviously everything is flying about, goes up into the air, fractured. Through the natural laws of returning (gravity), it is meant to come back to the earth, but it comes back in a new way. And that is really the function of Uranus. To remove whatever binding forces in our reality that are preventing necessary evolutionary growth. So whatever house and sign your Uranus is in and the aspects it is making, this is showing you how your own personal liberation in your own Saturnian conditions of your life is necessarily and naturally meant to occur.

It will also tell you, graphically, what kind of subconscious or unconscious memories the individual has, linked with their own prior life times, which is subconsciously conditioning their approach to their current life. This is where you can play astrological detective yet again. It can also show you the potential of unresolved karma as occurred and still may be operating subconsciously in such a way as to influence the behavior of the current life.

Now we come to the end of our Virgo sequence, and you can see now we come almost back to Pluto, meaning Neptune. And, of course, Neptune from a Patriarchal point of view is called the archetype of transcendence. From the point of view of natural law, it is called the archetype of unity. The Patriarchy teaches you that there is something to transcend, which itself is roughly the same as the delusive Patriarchal idea that there is a natural conflict between spirit and flesh. That is why you have the word transcendence. This is utter BS. An obsolete opinion invented by men to subjugate women. Through natural law the correct word of Neptune is union: to unite with the totality of creation, not to transcend it. And it is through absolute union that a natural expansion of consciousness occurs. There is nothing to transcend. And there is nothing to redeem. Despite what you've read in the happy books. That is reinforcing the Patriarchy.

The issue here is that Neptune specifically correlates to the phenomenon of consciousness, in total, in every one. Consciousness is very analogous to water. Water in and of itself has no form. Consciousness permeates and is the essence of creation. If I put water into this cup, then the consciousness in that water assumes the shape, form and function of the cup. If I put water /consciousness in human form, it is assuming the function and form of this body. If I put it in this plant, this animal etc., etc. Form and function is inherently limited – inherently limited – which is why you have read in your astrology books the need to go beyond the perception and experience of limitation. This is the inner action between Pisces and Scorpio.

Now, to make it very graphic to you, you all have consciousness, and it is all right now in a human body. And I will show you right away the limitation of consciousness in human form. Ready? What created God? You have just reached your limit, which exactly gives rise ultimately to the desire in all Souls to reunite with the source of all things, meaning to dissolve (Neptune) the apparent extinction of the separating form and to realize through union how the appearance of all manifested form is rooted in the original creation point. For you to do this naturally – for you to do this naturally – determine the house and sign of your Neptune and the aspects it is making. This is your own natural way, not according to any book or any teacher, understand the point? So has this now made a little bit of sense to you this morning?

Any last questions?

God Bless you and thank you for coming.

11

Trauma and the Outer Planets

The subject of trauma is a subject rarely dealt with by astrologers, yet it is a dynamic and experience that *many* people have. Accordingly, we as astrologers would do well to understand the nature of trauma in general, and specifically to be able to help our clients who are experiencing the effects of trauma. In this spirit the following is presented.

We will be examining in this section just exactly what is trauma: consider possible causes of it, and examine the effects that it produces. Specifically, we will examine trauma from the point of view of types of trauma. These types will be (I) mental, (2) emotional, (3) spiritual, (4) physical, and (5) collective trauma. Within these considerations we will examine the astrological correlations (planets, signs, houses) to these types of trauma, and specific case histories in order to uncover possible astrological signatures in birth charts that reflect higher probability rates for trauma.

Also, in this section, we will include Saturn even though it is not considered to be an outer planet. The reason we will do this is that Saturn correlates to the outer threshold of our conscious awareness, the boundary defining the interface between conscious awareness and the unconscious. Because Saturn correlates to the psychological function of repression or suppression which is based on the act of denial of some dynamic or experience, its linkage as a causal factor in certain types of trauma is implicated. Saturn will also be included because of its correlation to the inner and outer structure of the physical body, thus it has a linkage to physical trauma of the body.

So, what is trauma? A succinct definition will suffice. Trauma is an intense mental, emotional, physical or spiritual/psychic disturbance resulting from stress or shock that can have a lasting psychic or psychological effect. *An intense disturbance caused by shock or stress that can have a lasting effect.* Yes, this statement can probably describe the state of affairs for the entire planet right now because of what psychologists have termed the Delayed Stress Syndrome. Astrologically, this is a function of Saturn, Capricorn, or the

10th house. Delayed stress infers some dynamic or event that has been suppressed, repressed, or ignored.

All that one has to do, in this country for example, is to tune into one of the talk shows to witness yet another person, or set of people, talking about some horrible event: rape, sexual or psychological abuse etc., to understand the effects of delayed stress caused by trauma. Or the Vietnam Veteran's problems, or the collective (Neptune) search for the inner, wounded child. The wounded child syndrome infers 'origin issues' and how these issues define one's sense of identity. When Saturn, Uranus, and Neptune began their transits through Capricorn, the delayed stress of childhood surfaced into the collective consciousness of many within the Western World. Because Capricorn is a Cardinal Archetype there has been and is a need to go backwards, in the sense of recovering the inner child, by bringing to light the nature of the psychological and emotional imprinting that occurred in childhood. This must occur in order to go forwards through becoming free or liberated (Uranus) from these early conditioning (Saturn) patterns.

On a larger level, there is a collective need all over the planet to politically, economically, and philosophically restructure (Uranus transiting Capricorn) the internal nature of each society/country in order to be free (Uranus) from outmoded or crystallized political, economical, and philosophical structures that are impeding the evolutionary growth (Pluto) and needs of the planet, and each nation on the planet. The revolutions within Eastern Europe, the Soviet Union, the restructuring of the Middle East, the 'new world order', the progressive enforcement powers extended to the United Nations, the rebellion within the Canadian Provinces, the replacement of dictators within South America with freely elected officials, all attest to an individual and collective stress and trauma that will have lasting effects.

Delayed stress is implied in all of this because we are living in very transitional times in which everything has to change. The old ways of doing things do not work any more, yet to confront new and unknown ways of doing thing is to create a fear of the unknown. Fear of the unknown creates an individual and collective insecurity. The essence of feeling secure lies in the need for self or collective consistency. So the tension or stress between the old and the new, the transition therein, leads to the delayed stress syndrome because the resistance (Pluto) to necessary change generates a suppression or ignoring of the 'signs' that change is necessary. When evolutionary needs are ignored or suppressed then the need to change, now suppressed or ignored, increasingly compresses and intensifies, like the increasing friction in a fault line, until change can no longer be avoided. This resistance can lead to cataclysmic change, which produces intense forms of individual or collective trauma.

The Gaia of the Earth as a biosphere has been generating many such signs for many years now. The breakdown in the ozone layer, the greenhouse effect, the contamination of the water, the contamination of the food chain, the alteration of weather patterns all attest to a trauma within Nature that will have lasting effects. The signs have been and are many and yet the necessary changes to adjust to the scientific and empirical facts have been and are too slow. The delayed stress in the Gaia of our planet will mushroom into possible cataclysmic events that will have long range consequences leading to irrevocable change.

This may occur in many ways including the accelerated (Uranus) mutation (Pluto) within the genetic structure and coding with many forms of life within Nature, as all forms of life seek to adapt and adjust to the increasing trauma within the biosphere of Earth. This includes the forms of life called viruses and bacteria's as they attempt to sustain their own lives through accelerated mutation within their own genetic structures. Uncontrolled disease is the result, the AIDS virus being but the first manifestation of the planetary trauma.

This is interesting to consider from the point of view of the Gaia. Astrologically, Neptune correlates to the overall functioning of the immune system, and specifically to the pineal and thymus glands. Saturn or Capricorn correlates to the overall structural integrity of the human body. Uranus correlates to the overall atmosphere of the planet, and, among other anatomical and physiological correlations, to the respiratory system of the human body: specifically, the lining of the lungs. Pluto, again, correlates to the phenomena of evolution, metamorphosis, mutation, and the genetic coding in all forms of life.

So what do we have here? The delayed stress within the Gaia of the biosphere is now manifesting as an acceleration within the breakdown of the atmosphere; Uranus transiting Capricorn. This breakdown is fundamentally and radically altering the nature and quality of 'light' within the atmosphere of Earth. The functioning of the pineal gland within the brain is determined by the quality and nature of light entering the retina of the eyes within all living organisms. By altering the quality of light entering the biosphere the simultaneous altering of the pineal gland and immune system occurs within all living organisms. In effect, this alteration will initially weaken or depress (Capricorn) the immune system as it seeks to adjust to these new conditions (Uranus in Capricorn).

In conjunction with this are mutations of the various forms of viruses and bacteria as they seek to adjust to these new conditions as well (Pluto in Scorpio). Thus, we have the AIDS virus which is known as a retrograde virus, a function of delayed stress, which has the capacity to merge (Scorpio) itself within the RNA/DNA genetic structure and coding in such a way as to turn the immune system in upon itself (lupus in the worst form) to the point of killing the organism (the human body) that it has invaded. This condition is but the first warning to mankind that the Gaia is out of balance due to the activities of humankind. With Neptune leading Uranus (as of this writing) through Capricorn, the immune system is that which suffers first from the effect of delayed stress within the Gaia. As Uranus catches up with Neptune the next major disease that will likely occur will be specific to the respiratory system. By way of viruses that have mutated through evolutionary necessities this will manifest as multi-drug resistant forms of viruses and bacteria's that will spread through the casual contact with other people; by simply sharing the same air or atmosphere with other human beings, in conjunction with immune systems that are being altered or weakened, the impact of such disease has incredible implications for the planet. And, from the point of view of the Gaia, this just may be a way that Nature adapts to the out of balance state that it is in. Maybe this is Nature's way of culling organisms in to order rebalance itself into a state of structural integrity once again.

On a collective psychological/emotional level, the breakdown (Uranus) and dissolution (Neptune) within consensus societal beliefs and values (Saturn, Capricorn) i.e. the American Dream, has been and will continue to generate an increasing collective futility, depression, anxiety, angst, and hopelessness that has potentially far reaching sociopolitical /economic implications that will radically (Uranus) alter 'the system' as currently structured. This kind of collective trauma is necessary because it forces the collective and individual consciousness to invert (Saturn/Capricorn), to withdraw from the individual and collective 'system' so that new ideas, realizations, and directions can be realized that reflect and symbolize the new and necessary way. A quick glimpse in into modern history when Uranus and Neptune were transiting through Capricorn the last time they were together, the 1820s, reveals this dynamic relative to the Industrial Revolution of that time. The Industrial Revolution totally altered and restructured western societies whose imprint we still live with today. And it is this imprint or structure that is once again demanding radical change.

The point of citing delayed stress as an example of trauma is that it is one of the most common forms of trauma that generates a collective or individual reality that is defined (Saturn /Capricorn) by the effects of the trauma itself. Yet, the behavioral effects that are generated are not recognized as caused by the trauma itself. It is not recognized because of the suppression or repression within the collective and/or within the individual. And, of course, the reasons of the suppression or repression are that the nature of the specific trauma is so severe that the individual or collective can not accept that the trauma has or is occurring in the first place. Yet, the suppressed trauma continues to dictate behavior, the dictation of the behavior operating at a subconscious level (Uranus). Operating in this way, the effects of the trauma produces many 'signs' within the behavioral patterns at any level of reality, i.e. breakdown in the ozone layer, irrational rage in an individuals behavioral patterns, economic structures that produce increasing homelessness, bankruptcy, mergers of corporations, insane budget deficits etc, that tell us something is amiss. As of this writing, one out of ten Americans is currently on Food Stamps. One out of ten!

If we focus on the individual, such signs can be classified as (1) personality disorders of various types such as agoraphobia, pathological lying, extreme forms of masochistic or sadistic behavior, intense or irrational rage that permeates an individual's behavior, and all forms of pathological or repetitive compulsive behavior, (2) sociopathic behavior, (3) multi or split personalities, and (4) neurosis or psychosis. And even though these 'signs' of behavioral disorder define the nature of one's identity, the individual typically does not recognize or 'own' the behavior until the nature of the specific trauma is unlocked. Once unlocked within the individual it becomes imperative that treatment or therapy is entered into so that a reintegration of the personality can occur. This does not necessarily mean that the effects of the trauma can be permanently erased as if the trauma never happened, but it can mean that the effect of the trauma is changed because it has been brought up from the unconscious into the full light of consciousness.

In this way a perpetual awareness of the effects relative to the affect can be sustained in such a way that the individual over time can consciously change his or her behavior, the repetitive compulsion syndrome linked with traumatic behavior fundamentally altered.

The delayed stress syndrome caused by specific trauma is but one type of reaction to trauma even though the most common and pervading. Behavioral reactions to it are not dependent on suppression of a specific trauma. This means an individual can experience trauma and not suppress it, and yet the effects of that trauma will alter the individual's behavior anyway, this alteration can continue on into a potentially indefinite amount of time until the effect of the trauma is worked out in some way. The behavioral alteration is a function of the stress associated with the trauma even though the trauma is not suppressed.

Trauma occurs, again, to the mental, emotional, physical, and spiritual or psychic bodies. And, as will be seen, these bodies, when trauma occurs, can interact in a chain reaction like way, i.e. severe physical trauma causing a trauma to the mental, emotional, or spiritual bodies. Let us examine in detail, through case studies, the types of trauma associated with these different bodies and provide the appropriate astrological associations for them.

The Mental Body: astrologically this will correlate with Uranus as primary significator, and its lower octave Mercury as secondary significator. The types of trauma associated with the mental body are stroke, various types of psychological or psychiatric disorders, epilepsy, various diseases of the brain, sudden, unexpected changes that alter the psychological reality of the individual, and the external structures of his or her reality that have defined their sense of identity up until the unexpected changes begin to occur.

The Emotional Body: astrologically this will correlate with Pluto as primary ruler, and the Moon and Neptune as secondary rulers. The types of trauma associated with betrayal, abandonment and gross misuse through misapplied trust, psychological and sexual abuse, sudden loss, experiencing cataclysmic events of an individual or collective nature, anticipation of events that appear to be fated or beyond the control of the individual, etc.

The Physical Body: astrologically this will correlate with Saturn. The types of trauma associated with the physical body are various physical traumas such as severe injuries of various types, rape, torture, intense physical illness, degeneration of the body through various causes such as disease, birth disorders such as cerebral palsy, spinal bifida, etc.

The Spiritual Body: astrologically this will correlate with Neptune. The types of trauma associated with the spiritual body are loss of faith, loss of beliefs, loss of values, massive disillusionment, and in rare cases being possessed by an unwanted spirit.

Again, a key point to remember is that even though trauma can occur in one of the specific bodies, i.e. physical, there is almost always a chain reaction effect that impacts the entire organism, the other bodies, in a variety of ways.

At this point I would like to example Saturn, Uranus, Neptune and Pluto through the houses in order to illustrate where and how the various traumas can manifest when they do. As in all astrological work an entire horoscope must be evaluated to determine the exact application to any given individual. The following statements and descriptions are only relative to one factor: a planet in a house. These statements are not presented as if they are fated. They are only suggestive of what kind of traumas can exist.

Physical Trauma and Saturn

Saturn in the 1st house or Aries: physical trauma that can occur include severe injuries to the head, stunted growth of the skeletal system, imbalance within the white and red blood cells that can cause various problems, malformed genitals, various forms of arthritis due to dehydration of the synovial fluids, osteoporosis in females after menopause, severe anemia, and prostrate problems in men.

Saturn in the 2nd house or Taurus: physical trauma that can occur include severe injury to the lower back, blockage of the ducts within the kidneys, kidney disease, build up of deposits within the veins or arteries leading to a variety of problems such as phlebitis, imbalance in the white and red blood cells that could lead to leukemia, ovarian cysts or cancer, tipped wombs in females impacting on ability to conceive, disease linked to the cervix, womb or vagina, problems within the inner ear that can cause vertigo and unexplained dizziness.

Saturn in the 3rd house or Gemini: physical trauma that can occur include severe accidents to the hands or arms, nerve damage impacting on motor skills, problems impacting on the autonomous nervous system, various degrees of hearing loss associated with the nerves being diseased or dying within the ear, disease with the larynx, tumors on the left side of the brain, synapse dysfunction on the left side of the brain.

Saturn in the 4th house or Cancer: physical trauma that can occur include disease of the lymphatic system, ulcerations within the stomach or duodenum, cancer of the stomach or intestinal tract, gall stones, chronic constipation leading to progressive infusion of toxins throughout the system, glaucoma, cataracts, and disease associated with the eyes, prolapsed wombs, and chronic fatigue syndrome generated through yeast infections.

Saturn in the 5th house or Leo: physical trauma that can occur include malformed hearts, disease of the heart, heart murmurs, high or low blood pressure, circulatory problems, retinal detachment, progressive degeneration of the nerves within the eyes, night blindness, stroke, heart attacks, angina, anemia and general constitutional weakness of the life force available to the entire system.

Saturn in the 6th house or Virgo: physical trauma that can occur include breakdown in various magnitudes within the immune system leading to uncontrolled infections of all kinds, various forms of arthritis, motor skill dysfunction, dysfunction of disease with the throat or larynx, skeletal diseases and breakdowns within the bone marrow's ability to produce healthy, functional B and T cells.

Saturn in the 7th house or Libra: same as the 2nd house.

Saturn in the 8th house or Scorpio: physical trauma that can occur include disease of dysfunction of the pancreas, colon, intestine, stomach, liver, duodenum, various cancers, prostritus, cervical, uterine or ovarian growths, cysts, or cancer, genetic birth defects, disease or dysfunction of the endocrine or lymphatic systems, candida or yeast infections, improper levels of enzymes regulated through the pancreas and liver, problems associated with the spinal column such as curvature of the spine, disintegrating spinal discs, fusion of the vertebra, etc.

Saturn in the 9th house or Sagittarius: physical trauma that can occur include dysfunction or disease of the thyroid and pituitary glands, insufficient constitutional strength through a lack of zinc and/or silica, naturally accident prone because of a general absentmindedness which can lead to physical injuries of various magnitudes, restrictions within the sciatic nerves that produces improper circulation within the legs and a state of chronic muscular tension in the less and feet, liver dysfunction generating toxic conditions throughout the system, and digestive problems associated with enzyme levels controlled by the liver.

Saturn in the 10th house or Capricorn: physical trauma that can occur include various forms of arthritis, osteoporosis, breakdowns within the B and T cells emanating from the bone marrow that implicates the integrity of the immune system, disease or dysfunction of the pituitary or thyroid glands, severe problems with the skin, cancer or dysfunction within the digestive tract, growth disorders, skeletal disorders.

Saturn in the 11th house or Aquarius: physical trauma that can occur include stroke, all manner of dysfunction or disease of the brain, damage to the brain leading to various conditions such as cerebral palsy, respiratory disease or dysfunction, inherent or genetic weakness in the lining of the lungs, dysfunction or disease of the hypothalamus and thalamus glands, dysfunction or disease within the overall nervous system.

Saturn in the 12th house or Pisces: physical trauma that can occur include auto-immune syndrome, any manner of disease or dysfunction of the immune system, endocrine and lymphatic systems disease or dysfunction, abnormalities linked with the feet, severe water retention, and apparently unresolved or wrongly diagnosed chronic systemic issues that create the effect of never being really well, or truly healthy.

Mental Trauma and Uranus

Uranus in the 1st house or Aries: mental trauma can occur to these individuals because of an inability to accept physically, psychologically or karmically prescribed limitations that create the effect of blocking them from achieving their inner sense of special destiny, of not being able to do anything or everything that they feel they could do. Typically, these individuals have a 'superhuman' complex that requires circumstantial restraint in order to realign the ego into a state of balance or equality with other individuals. The natural power of leadership and breaking new ground exists within these people, yet they must learn how to integrate this capacity within the 'system' as currently defined so that these intrinsic abilities can be actualized. Subconsciously many of these individuals will have memories of premature or early life endings from other lives. This can create irrational fears of loosing control, or of going too far from their immediate environment in which they feel safe. Uranus in transit through the 1st house, forming a stressful aspect through transit to the planetary ruler of the 1st house, Mars, or to natal planets in the 1st house can generate this type of trauma.

Uranus in the 2nd house or Taurus: mental trauma can occur when these individuals are forced to change the nature of their value systems, values that have defined their identity and overall reality for a long time. Everything that has been held dear and cherished becomes lost: this can include material loss as well. Because of this trauma these individuals must realign themselves with a new set of values, or at least adjust or modify the existing ones, which will allow them to relate to themselves and others in a totally different way. Subconsciously many of these individuals will have vague memories of physical or emotional destitution which can create the effect of desperately hanging on to what they have, as well as a fixity of values that have defined their sense of meaning in life. The transit of Uranus in the 2nd house, or the transit forming a stressful aspect to the planetary ruler of the 2nd house, or to Venus, or to planets within the 2nd house can generate this type of trauma.

Uranus in the 3rd house or Gemini: mental trauma can occur when these people experience life situations that directly confront the way in which they understand life via their ideas, opinions and mental constructions.

The intensity of the confrontations or experiences forces them to question and restructure their mental constructions so that a new ideational system occurs. The transition between the new and the old systems is the period of greatest trauma and psychological instability. Subconsciously, many of these individuals can have memories of a knowledge based on understandings that are not present, or part of, the current life reality as reflected in other people or society in general. The frustration of trying to communicate or relate such knowledge creates a state of psychological confinement because of the sense of being 'different', or wide gap, that they experience within themselves in contrast to those around them. This frustration can generate its own mental trauma that is defined by a state of alienation from others and society. When Uranus transits the 3rd house, forms a stressful aspect by transit to the planetary ruler of the 3rd house, or Mercury, or to natal planets in the 3rd house it can generate this type of trauma.

Uranus in the 4th house or Cancer: mental trauma can occur when these individuals experience an intense lack of emotional understanding, and a lack of nurturing, related to their biological parents. Through extension, this same lack is experienced as adults because of the displaced emotions of childhood. This creates a core insecurity, and an unresolved inner child, that can project emotional demands onto others in an effort to recover or experience the emotional nurturing that they desire. This can generate quite erratic and unpredictable emotional states and moods that affect themselves and others in adverse ways. These individuals will continue to generate environmental or circumstantial experiences that have the effect of throwing them back in upon themselves until they understand that the nurturing and security that they are seeking is wholly within themselves. This will occur because Uranus here will cyclically remove or radically change their life forced to learn this lesson. This can clearly generate psychological trauma. Subconsciously, many of these individuals have memories of many other lifetimes in which this same dynamic has been operative. This only adds to and intensifies the projected emotional demands and needs which in turn only intensifies the effect of not having these needs met at the most crucial of times. When Uranus transits the 4th house, forms stressful aspects by transit to the planetary ruler of the 4th house, or the Moon, or to planets in the natal 4th house it can generate this type of trauma.

Uranus in the 5th house or Leo: mental trauma can occur when these individuals experience an indifference or non-acknowledgement from society or others. This is so because these people have a need to be acknowledged as special, to be acclaimed and validated as a Zarathustra or superhuman as measured against other people. This experience of indifference or non-acknowledgement can occur throughout life, or it can occur cyclically as these individuals may achieve relatively great heights or achievement for a time only to experience a fall from grace. Thus, periods of time of no acclaim or achievement. This effect can also occur when Uranus transits the Sun in any chart or begins a transit of the 5th house, or forms a stressful aspect via transits to the planetary ruler of the 5th house. Typically this generates the evolutionary need to almost totally change, restructure or redefine how an individual's sense of purpose in life has been actualized, and how the individual has understood the very meaning of his or her life in relation to that purpose. This period of disassociation, and the consequent need to re-associate one's sense of purpose and meaning in new ways, can he truly psychologically traumatic. This is because the very core of the individuals' being seems to have so radically changed. The period of disassociation can fracture the ego or personality in potentially horrendous ways. A bomb has gone off, and the pieces that are falling back to earth in a new way. Being responsive to this necessary change, versus trying to maintain what was, is the key leading to psychological stability and reintegration. Many of these individuals will have subconscious memories of achieving great fame, acclaim or heights from other lifetimes, some having memories of being part of some royal family. This can only fuel the frustration of not being acknowledged as special in this life.

Uranus in the 6th house or Virgo: Mental trauma can occur when these individuals focus upon and experience a sense of psychological separation, of isolation, from their immediate environment. And within this isolation or separation they can interpret their overall environment in general, and others specifically, as being unduly critical or persecutory towards them. Other people seem to be conspiring against them in one way or another. In addition these people can experience trauma with respect to the type of work that they find themselves in because they typically feel that they have a very different approach to work in general, and a very different ability or capacity that remains un-actualized specifically. The underlying subconscious memories that these individuals have suggest that they are not good enough or ready to actualize their sense of larger capacity. This creates its own trauma because of the implied crisis of not actualizing what the individual senses to be possible. This sense of inner and outer containment creates a dynamic of rebellion in which these people can create one crisis condition after another. Each crisis, large and small, creates the effect of being in an almost perpetual state of trauma in one way or another. Many of these individuals will have subconscious memories from other lifetimes of intense, irrational persecution and ridicule. This creates the effect of not only feeling victimized, but also one of trying to appear normal in their lives, even though they do not feel normal. This form of compensation creates the sense of frustration and isolation. When Uranus transits the 6th house, when through transit it forms a stressful aspect to the planetary ruler of the 6th house, or Mercury, or to planets in the 6th house it can generate these types of trauma.

Uranus in the 7th house or Libra: mental trauma can occur to these individuals when they experience sudden, unexpected disruptions, fracturing, or outright termination within their relationships, intimate and otherwise. This can occur by another, or others, projecting their own subconscious realities or dynamics upon these individuals, or because of these individuals projecting their own stuff upon other people. In both scenarios this type of projection creates a high degree of irrationality into the composite effect of the relationship that can lead to psychological instability or trauma. In addition, these individuals have an intrinsic sense of fair play, of justice, and of equality. When these intrinsic principles are consistently violated in relationship the cumulative stress can induce a psychologically traumatic state. When this occurs these individuals must reevaluate themselves in terms of their expectations about reality in general, and relationship dynamics specifically. And because these individuals will rebel against the feeling of being overly confined, or enmeshed, in a relationship they can create trauma for themselves and their partners when they begin to look for the exit sign. Many of these individuals will have subconscious memories of sudden loss within relationships that intensifies a core detachment from people in general, and those that they are intimate with specifically. This inner, subconscious vibration can thus attract others who seem to be just as detached at a core level as they are. This can create trauma for both because neither will have the feeling of being totally connected to each other. When Uranus transits the 7th house, or forms stressful aspects through transits to Venus, planets within the natal 7th house, or to the planetary ruler of the 7th house these types of trauma can occur.

Uranus in the 8th house or Scorpio: mental trauma can occur to these individuals when absolute betrayals of trust occur. This can occur when an individual that they have extended trust to ends up totally violating this trust to the extent of becoming a totally different person relative to how they had seemed or appeared to the individual when the trust was initially extended. This violation of trust thus generates the experience of abandonment and intense loss that can lead to psychologically cataclysmic states. By experiencing others 'turning upon' them they can experience quite intense states of psychological abuse that can border on sadistic abuse. The abuse dynamic linked with violations of trust can also include sexual abuse in a variety of ways. The sudden loss linked with partnerships wherein a merging of resources and realities has occurred is that which can create fundamentally psychological trauma that impacts on these people's ability to trust ever again. In many ways Uranus in the 8th house is an intensification of Uranus in the 7th house. This is so because these people can project psychological intentions, motives, or agendas onto others, and have others project the same upon them. This is problematic in that these individuals have very keen and accurate perception into how others are motivated and psychologically structured on the one hand, and on the other hand they can mix-up and project their own subconscious dynamics onto others. This produces intense psychological confrontations and tests of will between these people and others that can generate its own set of traumatic conditions. In addition, many of these people will have subconscious memories concerning these dynamics which can only intensify these problems in life. Also, these individuals commonly have had, and have, desires to experience and know the different uses and forms of sexual energy that go beyond normal pro-creational or conventional expressions. The potential for misuse of sexual desire and experience can create karmic conditions wherein others can misuse or abuse these individuals sexually as a result. Conversely, some of these individuals, through evolutionary development, may have known, or come to know, the highest form and right use of sexual energy that is possible. When Uranus transits the 8th house, or forms stressful aspects through transits to Pluto, natal planets in the 8th house, or to the planetary ruler of the 8th house these types of trauma can occur.

Uranus in the 9th house or Sagittarius: mental trauma can occur to these individuals by the very nature of their beliefs because those beliefs are typically at odds with consensus held beliefs. The trauma occurs through others who isolate these people because of their beliefs, this isolation occurring, through ridicule, persecution or outright attack. In turn, these individuals can create traumatic effects for others as they challenge and rebel against the belief structures of anyone who is not in sympathy with, or supportive of, their own beliefs. Trauma can also occur for these individuals when traumatic experiences occur at such a level as to make them question the nature of what they believe in. This type of trauma or traumas have occurred in the first place because their existing beliefs can not account for or explain why the trauma could occur. An example of this could be an individual who fervently believed in a Christian God who, while in Vietnam, experienced his friend being blown to bits while reading the Bible in his bunker during a rocket attack. The shards of a blood-stained Bible being all that remained, the bloodied pulp of his friend staining the sand. This person could then find himself in a theological /existential void of despair which will alter his beliefs forever. When Uranus transits the 9th house, forms a stressful aspect through a transit to the planetary ruler of the 9th house, or Jupiter, or to planets in the 9th house it can generate these types of trauma.

Uranus in the 10th house or Capricorn: mental trauma can occur to these people by way of their family or origin wherein one or both parents are dysfunctional in some way, absent, emotionally unavailable, or through sudden loss of a partner. Trauma can also occur through not being validated or acknowledged for who they are by the parents. As adults, these same dynamics can occur through non-acceptance by mainstream people or society, of being severely misjudged by those in their career field of choice, by sudden loss of social position or career, and through feeling psychologically misplaced in their overall environment. In addition, these individuals can suffer from severe forms of depression and psychologically self-defeating attitudes towards life in general. These states are created because of the experience of feeling blocked or thwarted by the environment. This can generate a feeling that it is pointless to work towards any goal or objective because it does not mean anything, anyway. These attitudes reflect subconscious memories that reflect other lifetimes of being 'defeated' by forces that they can not control, of memories that reflect lifetimes in which the promised rewards linked with goals that were so hardly worked towards, never materialized. A permeating sarcasm and pessimism underlies these individuals very way of being, this type of psychology but the effect of these types of trauma. When Uranus transits the 10th house, forms stressful aspects to the planetary ruler of the 10th house through transit, or to Saturn, or planets in the natal 10th house it can generate these types of trauma.

Uranus in the 11th house or Aquarius: mental trauma can occur when these individuals realize that they have been living a lie. This lie is one wherein they have not actualized a life or lifestyle that is reflective of their inner self. This inner self is one wherein the individual feels fundamentally different than the consensus reality that constitutes the environment in which these individuals find themselves. And yet, because of this fundamentally different inner self, these individuals will compensate by adopting the external appearance of normalcy. The act of compensation is that which generates the lie. Psychological trauma occurs relative to this realization and the need to radically alter their life. There is a need to rebel against the normal, consensus life. Yet there is also a fear in doing just that. This fear can implode on these individuals in such a way as to not act towards change, this implosion being similar to the famous Dutch Boy putting his fingers in the leaking dike. This creates its own state of instability. To fully act upon the impulse to caste off the consensus life also creates a period of instability that may be undetectable to the observer until there is a sudden, unannounced rebellion; the husband or wife who simply did not come home one night. Trauma can also occur via a myriad of social connections and relationships that turn ugly, disruptive, or simply terminate almost overnight. Friendships go astray, unforeseen dynamics and issues suddenly and 'irrationally' appear. Many of these individuals will have subconscious memories that they have been persecuted or criticized for being different by others which can only fuel the psychology to compensate by adopting the appearance of normalcy. When Uranus transits the 11th house, through transits forms stressful aspects to the planetary ruler of the 11th house, forms aspects to itself, or when it forms stressful aspects through transit to planets in the natal 11th house it can generate this type of trauma.

Uranus in the 12th house or Pisces: mental trauma can occur to these individuals when their ego or personality begins to fracture, disintegrate, or dissolve due to stress externally experienced, or through an inner stress emanating from the unconscious. This inner stress is based on thoughts, or desire impulses to escape or run away from the mundane conditions that define their life. Anatomically and physiologically this impulse is rooted in the pineal gland within the brain. Uranus correlates to the electricity within the brain, thus a high degree of electrical impulse impacting on the pineal gland. This gland secrets a protein called melatonin which is responsible for what we call dreams, sleep, and the need for transcendence; to embrace a more holistic, inclusive, ultimate or spiritual reality. Failing to understand the right actualization of this impulse, i.e. to embrace spiritual realities, the individual becomes quite 'crazy' at a subconscious level which can manifest in any manner of psychosis, phobias, neurosis, personality disorders, split or multi-personalities, addictions and escapes of all kinds. Consider that Uranus was transiting Pisces for most of the 1920s and, in the US this decade became known as the Roaring 20s with respect to rampant alcoholism, drug use, the invention of credit spending, etc. Many of these individuals will have subconscious memories of being imprisoned or incarcerated against their wills, and of being severely persecuted by many people. This type of memory generates a fear that translates into 'hiding' from people. When Uranus transits the 12th house, forms stressful aspects through transit to the planetary ruler of the 12th house, or Neptune, or to natal planets in the 12th house through transit it can generate these types of trauma.

Neptune: Spiritual or Psychic Trauma

Neptune in the 1st house or Aries: idealistic expectations about self-potential that generates a sense of having something special to do. Yet the awareness and experience of self seems so small as unconsciously compared to the Universe, God, or the Other. This awareness makes it seem as though the idealistic expectations about self are impossible to achieve. A disillusionment within the self generates a disillusionment with the all, or Other: the Universal. The trauma is one of identity confusion, and how to actualize or make real that which is instinctively sensed as possible. When Neptune transits the Ascendant, forms stressful aspects through transit to the planetary ruler of the 1st house, or Mars, or to planets in the natal 1st house it can generate these issues and subsequent traumas.

Neptune in the 2nd house or Taurus: idealistic expectations about sharing, exchanging and giving that which constitutes the substance of life itself, a substance that allows for life to be sustained. This is the famous example of the individual who would give you the shirt off his or her own back. Thus, the individual by nature, owns nothing in the sense of egocentric identification with that which constitutes substance. Disillusionment through loss of natural values and beliefs occurs through, and because of, others who take advantage of the individual. This is done by taking away what is naturally shared and given freely without equally returning to the individual what constitutes their own substance of life; whatever it may be. Disillusioned the individual can unconsciously react by way of hoarding and taking because of a psychology that now feels that he or she is owed everything, by everyone. Irrational fear of destitution at all levels results from this. The psychic or spiritual trauma is one wherein God is not a giving, loving God, but an avenging, cruel God. It is evil. When Neptune transits the 2nd house, forms stressful aspects by transit to the planetary ruler of the 2nd house, or Venus, or to planets in the natal 2nd house it can generate these issues and subsequent traumas.

Neptune in the 3rd house or Gemini: an idealistic expectation linked with an inherent knowledge that there is a much larger reality than what is perceived or known by the logical, rational mind, and that others should understand and know this too. A frustration wherein their own inner expectation to be able to intellectualize, or put into logical mental sequence, that which is inwardly sensed can exist. The experience of a limited language as spoken by most of the people around them is that which frustrates their efforts to communicate that which is essentially incommunicable. It is as if these individuals are tuned into a radio station that no one else can hear. Disillusioned by their efforts to communicate in ways, and about things, that no one else seems to understand can generate a spiritual or psychic trauma wherein these people can simply give up all efforts at communicating, to inwardly withdraw to the point of total reclusion from the world. When Neptune transits the 3rd house, forms stressful aspects to the planetary ruler of the 3rd house through transit, or to Mercury, or to planets in the natal 3rd house it can generate these issues and subsequent traumas.

Neptune in the 4th house or Cancer: an idealistic expectation that the world, the universe, the origin of all things, the home, and the family is but a universal womb of purity, simplicity, of love, and of nurturing for and through all. This expectation produces a natural emotional empathy for all, a compassion linked to the common suffering of all. Disillusionment and spiritual trauma occurs to these people through the experience and perception of a natural innocence which exists within themselves, and others, becoming violated, abused, destroyed and contaminated. This experience is based on the ugly realization that impurity exists in others, that others can have malevolent intentions, that the world is no good, and that the soul can be corrupted. The natural child of innocence becomes lost, confused, and alienated within an impure world. An existential void of a godless world now haunts their souls. When Neptune transits the 4th house, forms stressful aspects through transit to the Moon, or the planetary ruler of the 4th house, or to planets in the natal 4th house these traumas can occur.

Neptune in the 5th house or Leo: an idealistic expectation that the Eternal spring and dynamic of Creativity is unlimited and unbound, that this principle and dynamic is at one's disposal, and that Creation should be perfect and beautiful. Disillusionment and psychic trauma occurs when one realizes that one is not God, that the ego can not create in and of itself. This realization occurs when the apparent well of Creativity runs dry, appears blocked, when these individuals are not acknowledged as special and godlike by others in the way that idealistically and unconsciously is expected. Trauma occurs when what is being created appears to be insignificant as compared to what is ultimately or idealistically sensed as possible, when what others achieve or create seems more spectacular and grand than what these individuals create for themselves, and when others are acknowledged or treated more special than they are. When Neptune transits the 5th house, forms stressful aspects by transit to the planetary ruler of the 5th house, or the Sun, or to planets in the natal 5th house it can generate these issues and subsequent traumas.

Neptune in the 6th house or Virgo: an idealistic expectation of collective and individual purity and perfection in all things, of right action. These expectations are judged against some ultimate standard of conduct. For these people purity and perfection is unconsciously linked to the desire to sacrifice oneself, the ego, to the principle of service to another, others, or the Whole. These people carry an unconscious yet pervading undefined guilt that needs to he atoned for. This leads to the creation of personal crisis and masochistic type behavior, a behavior defined by the unconscious that leads to personal crucifixion to that which is impure and unholy. Psychic or spiritual trauma occurs through creating a life of suffering in a variety of ways including physical illnesses which can not be explained, cured or properly diagnosed. Trauma occurs via an inability to understand why their suffering persists despite every effort to purify and atone for themselves through personal sacrifice. When Neptune transits the 6th house, forms stressful aspects through transits to natal Mercury, planets within the natal 6th house, or to the planetary ruler of the 6th house it can generate these issues and subsequent traumas.

Neptune in the 7th house or Libra: an idealistic expectation that all people are essentially pure and good in general, and those that they form intimate relationships with specifically. An unconscious desire to rescue or save people through masochistic self-sacrifice, a desire to heal the hurts of their intimate partners, and to have their own sufferings and hurts healed by others; and especially by their intimate partners. These individuals 'see' the potential and spirit in all people, their partners in particular, and expect that potential to be actualized. Through identifying with another's inner spirit these individuals can experience disillusionment and great pain when the other's actual reality prevails in ways that seem contradictory to what he or she wants to see or believe. Disillusionment and trauma can occur when these individuals realize that they have given themselves away to another, and that they have nothing to show for it but pain and needs that have gone unfulfilled. In addition, these individuals idealistically expect the dynamics of giving and receiving, of equality, of justice, and of fair play to prevail in all human interactions, and especially between themselves and their intimate other. When these expectations go unfulfilled, when life experience teaches them that these ideals rarely occur, tremendous disillusionment and trauma can occur. When Neptune transits the 7th house, forms stressful aspects through transit to Venus, natal planets in the 7th house, or to the planetary ruler of the 7th house it can generate these issues and subsequent traumas.

Neptune in the 8th house or Scorpio: this can be one of the most problematical positions for Neptune in that these people can unconsciously project a complex of fears, motives, or intentions onto people that creates the effect within themselves of being unable to open up to life in general, and others specifically, even though they desperately want to. There is an incredible level of intense suspicion that is projected onto people which is but a reflection of the impurity in themselves. This impurity reflects lifetimes of manipulating, using, and destroying others relative to their own purposes. When such behavior is pointed out these people create a stance of absolute denial. Through such inner denial they project that which they are onto others, the inner denial reflecting their own unconscious idealistic expectations of how they want to be, of how they want to see themselves. Psychic or spiritual trauma occurs when the holy mask that they create for themselves shatters into the nightmare of their actual reality, and when they realize that what they have projected onto others is but a reflection of themselves. The struggle between good and evil, masochistic and sadistic behavior is most emphasized when Neptune is in the 8th house or Scorpio. In addition, these individuals can have an unconscious fascination with 'taboo' forms of sexual expression, a need to be dominated or to dominate, a desire to dissolve the ego through consuming forms of sensation of a sexual nature, and at the same time deny all of this to themselves and others. Some, by way of denial, will even pretend that they have no sexual desire at all, or that sex is a function of evil. Others can develop a superstructure of fancy or groovy words reflecting high-minded intentions that only mask where they are actually coming from. A few will understand and experience the metamorphic and transcendent nature of sexual energy properly used. When Neptune transits the 8th house, forms stressful aspects through transit to Pluto or Mars, or the planetary ruler of the 8th house, or to natal planets in the 8th house it can generate these issues and subsequent traumas.

Neptune in the 9th house or Sagittarius: an idealistic expectation that the way in which these individuals view the world in general, and whatever specific views that they hold about the nature of some dynamic or experience that is occurring in their or another's life, is understood and shared by others. It is as if their 'truth' must be general truth for all. Disillusionment and trauma occur when they are forced to see that their truth or vision is but one against many other truths and visions. In addition, many of these individuals have a core feeling of inadequacy and impurity which can generate the need to compensate for this feeling. This compensation can take the form of becoming incredible liars, the basis of the lies to create an illusion that makes them appear holy, grand, sincere, and much 'larger' than they actually are within themselves. These lies can also be created to manoeuvre or manipulate others to do something that they want done for some devious and dishonest purpose. Disillusionment and trauma occurs when their lies are revealed, and when the actual reality of who they are becomes exposed and in their face. Some will have unconscious expectations that all people should be or are essentially honest. This is because this type of person is inwardly defined by this noble dynamic. Some are the very essence of unwavering honesty in all that they do, in the very nature of their being. Disillusionment and trauma occur when they experience the pain of dishonesty through others, when they become victimized by an unprincipled world. When Neptune transits the 9th house, forms stressful aspects through transit to Jupiter, planets within the natal 9th house, or to the planetary ruler of the 9th house it can generate these issues and subsequent trauma.

Neptune in the 10th house or Capricorn: idealistic expectations about the nature of family structures, societal structures, and the structure of the world itself. The essence of these expectations is based on the principle of sacrificing oneself, the ego, for a larger good; to others. The principle of sacrifice can have many forms, many applications. There is an unconscious expectation that purity and right action should define and prevail in any activity: large and small. These individuals are typically defined by an unconscious and uneasy feeling of guilt; that they have done something wrong, or that there is something wrong with them. Thus, there is a need to correct or atone for that guilt. As a result, this can generate life experiences in which their unconscious ideals of purity and right action, of egocentric self-sacrifice to the Other, are violated: the abusive father, the emotionally unavailable parent, the narcissistic husband or wife, the needy of this world who latch onto these people for dear life and abuse what is offered, the imperfect worlds that violates the expectation of purity and right action, etc. Over time these kinds of experiences can generate a horrible, depressive disillusionment and trauma that can create severe bouts of depression. This trauma can lead to a life in which these people struggle to throw off the undermining feelings of being continually defeated by life itself. In addition, disillusionment and trauma can occur through the experience that what is considered 'real' becomes 'unreal'. Nothing seems to be permanent, nothing seems to last, and that the very nature of 'reality' is but transitional images that come and go. And that what is 'real' is only real for the time that it actually exists. Accordingly, cycles of despair, of fighting off an inner feeling of being consumed by a dark, bottomless pit define the inner world of these individuals. As a result, these individuals create a fundamental fear of loosing control and, yet, longing to do so. Paradoxically, many of these people will seem like beacons of salvation light to others because of this inner world. This is because these people know their inner pain so well, that it serves to motivate them to heal the suffering of others. This symbol, Neptune in Capricorn, or the 10th house, is the ultimate symbol of the crucifixion of the ego. If you doubt this consider that Jesus was put on the Cross when Neptune transited Capricorn in his time. When Neptune transits the 10th house, forms stressful aspects through transits to Saturn, the planetary ruler of the 10th house, or to planets within the natal 10th house, it can generate these issues and subsequent traumas.

Neptune in the 11th house or Aquarius: idealistic expectations that all people everywhere should be treated equally and with justice. Expectations that all artificial barriers of caste, race, rich and poor should not exist, and that all social, economic, and political systems should be defined in ways that are equitable for all. These people have idealistic expectations, and a vision, that each member within a group has an important and equal function that contributes to the well being of the whole group. In addition, these individuals intrinsically expect that people should approach group activities with the spirit of how each person can add to the purposes of the group, versus what the group can do for the individual. Disillusionment and trauma occurs when all of these expectations are crushed by reality, when through experience these people realize that most people do not live or think in the ways that they do. Trauma and disillusionment occur when they experience one group dominating and taking advantage of another group, when they experience the horrible collective pain of people turning upon other people, when the awareness of so many people seems to be limited to the tip of their noses. This trauma can thus generate a total detachment from all external reality. This can create the effect of being extreme loners, removed from the fray that so many call life. Eccentric and iconoclastic, these people can experience a general uneasiness around other people, and others can also feel a vague uneasiness around them. They seem so 'different' to most people, and most people seem so different to them. This creates the 'Plexiglas' effect wherein these people can be seen but not touched. And, for these people, they can observe life but never really experience it. Somehow they are always on the outside looking in. When Neptune transits the 11th house, forms stressful aspects through transit to Uranus, the planetary ruler of the 11th house, or to planets within the natal 11th house these issues can be generated with the subsequent traumas.

Neptune in the 12th house or Pisces: this archetype symbolizes the sum total of all the astrological archetypes combined. Thus, issues concerning disillusionment and trauma as defined in this section on Neptune can occur in all the ways described for these individuals.

Pluto and Emotional Trauma

Pluto in the 1st house or Aries: emotional trauma can occur to these individuals for the following causes:

1. When the need to balance their desire for independence and relationships generates a reality of feeling trapped by the needs and demands of another in such a way as to block or restrain their desire to do whatever they need to do in order to become what they are becoming. Being forced to make choices regarding changing the conditions of the entrapment creates yet more trauma. That occurs because to consider termination of the relationship that he or she is feeling trapped within creates a feeling of emotional death. And to consider not making this choice which will allow for freedom of self-discovery also creates a feeling of death because it leads to sustaining the reality generating entrapment.

2. Emotional trauma can occur when these individuals create circumstances that enforce the awareness of egocentric limitations in order to counteract an underlying feeling of being 'superhuman'. In essence, the constraints that these people experience or create to reign in the ego leads to an emotional shock that generates a trauma of feeling limited at all levels of reality.

When Pluto transits the 1st house, forms stressful aspects through transit to Mars, the planetary ruler of the 1st house, or to planets in the natal 1st house it can generate these issues and subsequent traumas.

Pluto in the 2nd house or Taurus: emotional trauma can occur to these individuals for the following causes:

1. When life conditions are created that have the effect of forcing these individuals to evaluate their value system, and how these value systems define their sense of individual identity and meaning. Cyclically forced to reevaluate their meaning and values these people discover ever deeper levels of resources within themselves that creates new or refined values that allows them to relate differently to themselves and others. The will to survive is strong here and intense emotional trauma can occur when this will to survive and carry-on becomes weakened. Yet, the survival instinct is so strong in these folks that it does enforce the deepening of an inner awareness so that new values and ways of relating can emerge.

2. When their will to dominate another is met with equally or stronger wills that have the effect of generating intense confrontations that require the individual to grow beyond his or her existing reality, and ways of being. These confrontations call into play the nature of the individual's motives, intentions, and emotional agendas in such a way that the light of honesty creates harsh yet necessary realizations about the truth of their emotional reality and dynamics.

When Pluto transits the 2nd house, forms stressful aspects through transit to Venus, or to the planetary ruler of the 2nd house, or planets within the natal 2nd house these issues and subsequent traumas can occur.

Pluto in the 3rd house or Gemini: emotional trauma can occur for the following causes:

1. When the water tight intellectual constructions that define not only these individuals' sense of reality in general, but also the very core of their emotional security which is based on their intellectual constructions, becomes unraveled through intense, cataclysmic life experiences. The nature of these cataclysmic events forces them to change their way of thinking, of how they have understood the nature of things.

2. Emotional trauma can also occur when these people experience intense intellectual confrontations with others that poke holes in the water bags in such a way that they have no choice but to question their underlying assumptions about the nature of reality. Once the underlying assumptions

are questioned and changed, the rest of their complex intellectual network also falls and changes. The emotional trauma is defined by a core instability and insecurity because of the need to change the nature of their intellectual framework, and how they communicate their ideas and opinions. The period of insecurity or trauma is defined by the amount of time it takes for these individuals to evolve into new ways of understanding.

When Pluto transits the 3rd house, forms stressful aspects through transit to natal Mercury, or to the planetary ruler of the 3rd house, or to planets in the natal 3rd house these issues can be generated with the subsequent trauma.

Pluto in the 4th house or Cancer: emotional trauma can occur to these individuals for the following causes:

1. Intense emotional, psychological and/or sexual abuse with their family of origin. This can generate a deep, wounded child who has failed to learn how to internalize the mother and/or father in such a way that when they are not present the individual's sense of safety and security does not exist. This displaced emotional dynamic manifests in their adult lives in such a way as to recreate the early family dynamics in their adult relationships. This effectively creates a reality in which they project intense emotional demands upon their partners. Such partners will not be consistently available to them either. Emotional trauma can thus reoccur as the emotional demands and needs of the displaced inner child go cyclically unfulfilled.

2. When the very nature of their overall reality, how they have structured their lives, is threatened or destroyed: taken away against their wills. When this happens these individuals will experience a sense of emotional death, this experience being so total because the very essence of their emotional security, and sense of identity, is removed.

When Pluto transits the 4th house, forms stressful aspects through transit to the Moon, or to the planetary ruler of the 4th house, or to planets within the natal 4th house, it can generate these issues and subsequent traumas.

Pluto in the 5th house or Leo: emotional shocks or trauma can occur to these individuals for the following causes:

1. When life conditions occur to totally defeat egocentric delusions of grandeur. This deflation of the ego creates an inner sense of loss. This loss is

based in not being allowed to be at the center stage of life, of not being the self-appointed star of the play.

2. When life conditions occur in which these individuals feel an almost absolute powerlessness to change or alter how those life conditions are occurring. The awareness of 'forces larger than themselves' creates the sense of an ego death until these individuals incorporate and align their egos with those forces. When this occurs creative change begins in very positive ways. These changes can lead to very creative expansions of the overall life purpose.

When Pluto transits the 5th house, or forms stressful aspects through transit to the Sun, or the planetary ruler of the 5th house, or to planets within the natal 5th house these issues and subsequent traumas can occur.

Pluto in the 6th house or Virgo: emotional trauma can occur to these individuals for the following causes:

1. When life conditions occur in which the individual experiences an intense lack of meaning, or when their life conditions become meaningless. This sense of lack, of an existential void, generates a total state of crisis. This crisis is one of feeling totally displaced on an environmental basis, and a sense of acute inner aloneness in which they can feel victimized by the life conditions that they are experiencing.

2. When life conditions occur in which the individual feels intense persecution or criticism of an unjust nature. Not being able to understand why these conditions are contracted generates the trauma.

When Pluto transits the 6th house, forms stressful aspects to Mercury, or to the planetary ruler of the 6th house, or to planets in the natal 6th house these issues and subsequent traumas can occur.

Pluto in the 7th house or Libra: emotional trauma can occur to these individuals for the following causes:

1. When life conditions occur in which they are forced to realize that the sense of purpose and meaning that they are looking for is not embodied in another person, but is within themselves. These individuals' core sense of identity and security is bound up, linked with, the desire and need to be in intimate relationships. At key points in their lives these individuals

will experience fundamental breakdowns, confrontations, or cataclysmic loss within their existing relationship. This has the effect of forcing them in on themselves in order to learn to grow from within themselves, not through and because of another person. The compulsion of co-dependency is shattered.

When Pluto transits the 7th house, forms stressful aspects through transit to Venus, to the planetary ruler of the 7th house, or to planets within the natal 7th house it can generate such conditions within existing partnerships with the subsequent trauma.

Pluto in the 8th house or Scorpio: emotional trauma can occur to these individuals for the following causes:

1. When life conditions are created in which they experience severe and intense betrayal, and violations of trust.

2. When they experience being intensely used and manipulated by others.

3. When they experience intense sexual violations and misuse of such energy.

4. When they experience intense loss of those that are closest to them.

5. When life conditions are created in which they are forced to examine their own motives, intentions, and emotional agendas. This examination, at some point, will uncover the subtle and not so subtle ways in which they have manipulated others or situations in order to gain something that they need or want. The light of emotional honesty creates a cruel glare that exposes the inner lies that they create for themselves and others.

When Pluto transits the 8th house, forms stressful aspects to Mars and/or Pluto through transits, to the planetary ruler of the 8th house, or to planets within the natal 8th house it can generate these issues and subsequent traumas.

Pluto in the 9th house or Sagittarius: emotional trauma can occur to these individuals for the following causes:

1. By experiencing a core alienation relative to their country and culture and origin.

2. By experiencing intense belief system confrontations with others, or a society in which their beliefs are fundamentally at odds, or contradictory to the beliefs of most others.

3. When cataclysmic life events occur that forces them to examine the nature of their beliefs and underlying principles that generate those beliefs.

4. When they experience intense violations of truth, honesty, and the principle of justice relative to the truth of any given situation.

When Pluto transits the 9th house, forms stressful aspects through transit to Jupiter, the planetary ruler of the 9th house, or planets within the natal 9th house these issues and subsequent traumas can occur.

Pluto in the 10th house or Capricorn: emotional trauma can occur to these individuals for the following causes:

1. When they experience a total 'fall from grace', or from positions of power and/or social position. This can be extremely intense because these individuals are inwardly defined by their social position or role. The fall or loss of position requires an intense inner reformulation or metamorphosis of their sense of identity, an identity that is not defined by social power or position. Former President Nixon is an example of this dynamic.

2. When they are born into a family in which one or both parents are emotional dictators who expect the child to conform to their sense of reality. The child is thus not acknowledged for their own innate individuality. This type of trauma creates an adult who is emotionally closed and rigid because he or she has learned as a child to emotionally shut down in order not to be hurt. The delayed stress of childhood manifests as adults who try to control or shape the emotional lives of those that they interact with. This is done through confronting type judgments that they project onto others.

When Pluto transits the 10th house, forms stressful aspects through transit to Saturn, planets within the natal 10th house, or to the planetary ruler of the 10th house it can generate these issues and subsequent traumas.

Pluto in the 11th house or Aquarius: emotional trauma can occur for these individuals for the following causes:

1. When they realize that the lifestyle that they have been living is not

reflective of their actual nature, or when their lifestyle is radically altered through cataclysmic events which they seem powerless to alter.

2. When they experience being intensely used and manipulated by others who have been considered friends or lovers, or when their friends or lovers seem to turn against them for no apparent or legitimate reason.

3. When the overall culture treats these people as iconoclastic threats in such a way as to create a reality for them of always being on the outside looking in.

When Pluto transits the 11th house, forms stressful aspects through transit to Uranus, to planets within the natal 11th house, or to the planetary ruler of the 11th house these issues and subsequent traumas can occur.

Pluto in the 12th house or Pisces: emotional trauma can occur to these individuals for the following causes:

1. When their innate sense of ideals are so severely crushed through life conditions that they become lost souls; souls that become utterly aimless, ungrounded, and who simply wander the alleyways of life.

2. When these individuals create a reality that seems to be the embodiment of all that they have ever dreamed of only to have that reality destroyed. The degree of disillusionment can create a state of absolute emotional devastation in which the will to continue living can become weakened if not extinguished.

3. When their innate need to rescue, save or help those in need, or those who are unstable, weird, or fractured becomes over extended to the point of feeling all used up. The trauma is one of total emotional exhaustion wherein they begin to wall themselves off from life, to enclose themselves in order to create a protection from the emotional demands of those around them.

When Pluto transits the 12th house, forms stressful aspects through transit to Neptune, the planetary ruler of the 12th house, or to planets within the natal 12th house, these issues and subsequent traumas may occur.

Conclusion

I would like to mention that traumatic conditions are, of course, very difficult situations that can be very hard to deal with as they are occurring.

But, such conditions always have a way of resolving, and there is always some leap in our growth because of them. Once we understand the reasons or causes of the various types of traumas, the solutions and ways of resolving them can become apparent or known. The key is in the understanding, of the causes, of any given trauma. And then to resolve to take the positive actions necessary so that growth and change can take place.

12

The Evolutionary Meaning of
Retrograde Planets

Jeffrey: Today we will be talking about the nature of retrograde planets, and what they mean from the evolutionary point of view of the Soul. Please keep in mind that the phenomenon of a planet appearing retrograde is an apparent motion. That simply means their motion appears retrograde is relative to the Earth: it is not actually happening from the point of view of the Sun. So this is an apparent motion. Nonetheless, since it is applicable to the Earth, what we see from the surface of the Earth, there have been observed dynamics in human consciousness, and events on the Earth, that are specific to that apparent retrograde motion.

There are key archetypes that retrograde motion correlates to that are specific to retrograde archetypes. The first thing to understand is that the retrograde planet accelerates the evolutionary momentum of the Soul. The reason is that the retrograde is meant to retreat, reject or rebel against the status quo expectations of how that planet, its archetypal behavior, is expected to manifest and, thus, it accelerates the process of individuation. The retrograde function must, as an archetype, define for itself how that behavior, how that psychology, and how the circumstances which reflect that will be defined. In addition, the retrograde archetype is non-static: it rarely reaches a point in time where it goes, "Aha, that's it, no more". It emphasizes the need to continuously grow, and to continuously challenge existing limitations that promote the sense of stagnation, or non-growth. Thus, this creates a cyclic or perpetual need to redefine, retrograde, internal or external circumstances as necessary.

Again, it accelerates or emphasizes the individuation process. As a result, the function that is retrograde will place a premium on individuality, but, in so doing, it is also going to induce the sense of being different: different as measured against the status quo. For example, if we have Venus retrograde, this is going to demonstrate archetypally an individual who needs to uniquely define its own personal and social values which will then allow it to relate to itself, Venus, in a way that is reflective of its own individuality. As a result Venus retrograde will orient to relationships in such a way as to reject, rebel, retreat from the status quo expectation of how relationships, and how the roles within relationships, are meant to be played out from a societal, status quo, point of view. Thus, the person will feel different. If we apply this archetype to say a teenager in a middle class high school in Middle America who is growing up within a teenage peer group that has all kinds of social norms with equal expected ways to be in relationships and how the genders are meant to treat each other, how is this teenager going to be able to relate to his or her peer group? Is the retrograde Venus teenager going to feel different than this? As a result, is it possible that it is going to feel itself to be a social loner? Could this not set up all kinds of cruel accusations from its existing peer group? This is exactly where the issue of emotional, psychological compensation can exist. It is not uncommon for the retrograde archetype to compensate by giving the appearance of normalcy relative to whatever function is retrograde in order to feel socially, and thus individually, secure. Yet, in so doing, it is in violation of its own natural law: how the Soul is desiring to evolve.

There are such things as retrograde personality types. This is commonly linked to birth patterns in which you find four or more retrograde planets. Typically these people, unless they are psychologically compensating, are highly introverted: retrograde. They are extremely sensitive, shy, timid, and socially unsure. Now keep in mind this issue of compensation. Some can play a good game, and create the appearance which belies reality.

Audience: When does it become a game, and when does it become a balancing act? If we believe in the transmigration of Souls, there has been a certain point in the evolution when the planet has been direct and another time when the planet is going to be retrograde. Yet, one can go beyond that to a certain extent and balance the archetype which does have an inner and outer function.

Jeffrey: The balance that you are alluding to is for the Soul to create or design its circumstantial life to reflect its own inner essence: its intrinsic individuality. If that is done there can be a natural balance. If not, anything other than that is going to be an act of compensation in which balance can never be achieved. It is a very fine line.

Compensation is about protection. My point is that once the individual manifests the courage to define these archetypes which are retrograde to reflect its actual essence, that courage to do so will create an inner security that will withstand any sense of social insecurity that is based on not conforming to the status quo. The evolved retrograde attitude would be like the bumper sticker, 'Take it or leave it'.

Audience: What I think becomes important is that it is a highly individuating function, and if the function becomes paramount, and the person does this from an individual perspective rather than being forced into it collectively, then he or she can develop in a very unique way.

Jeffrey: Absolutely. And that is the key: to have it reflect their own individual law or nature. It does not mean forming group bonds with similarly alienated Souls, and adopting those alienated value systems. This is another possibility. But it would then become just another compensation relative to the consensus: the consensus now being a group of alienated people.

Audience: My son is 19 months old and has five planets retrograde including Pluto. I didn't understand the group thing.

Jeffrey: I said that some retrograde people opt for relationships with alienated Souls, Souls who are also feeling that they are not fitting into the status quo, and then adopt the consensus of the alienated peer group versus doing what retrograde demands which is to uniquely define whatever is retrograde to reflect the actual individuality or reality of the person themselves. The only way the group thing could work would be being within a group whose primary attitude is 'define yourself to reflect yourself'.

Audience: That's how I feel our whole family is.

Jeffrey: That is the whole point. Once the environment is created which reflects the individual, then the introversion doesn't exist because there is environmental permission to be who you are. The introversions of timidity and shyness are only in environments of a consensus in which the environmental message is not to be who you are. A parent who is able to give this permission to be who you are is clearly the combination that allows this safe to be opened.

Audience: When you speak of this individuating function, I find Saturn to be particularly important because that is, of course, the social collective and if the person can't overcome that, then the person can't individuate.

Jeffrey: Yes. That is difficult. Saturn retrograde is not an uncommon symbol: Venus is the rarest to be retrograde, every 542 days out of every cycle. That is a long time: it is almost a year and three quarters. The smallest number of people with a planet retrograde are Venus retrograde people. The most common is Pluto. It is retrograde half the year every year.

Audience: There are going to be cycles too like right now where the planets are bunched through Scorpio, Sagittarius and Capricorn where anyone born in opposition to that is going to have all of those retrograde.

Jeffrey: Yes. Going back to Saturn retrograde is going to be difficult but we always have to come back to this basic issue of evaluating the condition of the Soul. If we are observing a Soul which has already evolved to an individuated state, Saturn retrograde will not be problematic. That is only twenty percent of the population. Seventy percent of the Saturn retrogrades will be in the consensus state, and that is where the problems can exist. That is where these issues of compensation will be most observable. So this is a key point: observe the evolutionary state of the Soul. This cannot be overemphasized.

Audience: I have always felt (I have Venus retrograde) ostracized by the peer group, growing up and through the teen years and I never really felt like I was part of the classroom on the social scene. I always had to stand off most of the time. I could see what you would mean about a growth in the individuated: trying to find your own values. But with the retrograde it seems like it takes such a long time to find out what your values really are.

Jeffrey: Again, it is non-static. It is analogous to peeling the layers off an onion to arrive at the core: how quickly can that really be done? Especially when you have tears in the eyes, and you want to throw the onion away. But it again depends upon evolutionary station. I have Venus retrograde, and it is in Scorpio in the 1st house. I couldn't care less if I fit into whatever group, even astrology groups. I am a group of one, Aries, and I am quite happy.

Audience: What is an average number of planets retrograde? One or two? Is it rare for someone to have no retrogrades?

Jeffrey: No, it is not rare. Both of my children have no planets retrograde including the nodes.

Audience: I read in a book that three was normal.

Jeffrey: Based on my own experience through counseling I would say the average is two or three. Let's take a random sample in this room of how many of you have Venus retrograde given that it's the rarest of all retrogrades (the room that Jeffrey is in has about twenty five students). Four hands in the air. That's unusual, but not in a group like this, eh? And that's because groups like this, an astrology group, are *not part of the consensus in this society.*

Audience: What about Venus in Aquarius retrograde?

Jeffrey: I can only give you the archetype: the need to define your own unique values, individually, socially, to define uniquely how you need to be in a relationship, what you will and won't accept, what the partner should and shouldn't be. And then manifesting the courage to express that. If it doesn't look like anybody else's relationship with respect to the social milieu, so be it. There is simply a need to rebel, Aquarius, against the status quo expectations. From a karmic point of view, which is the next layer of retrograde, there can be some karmic implications with respect to many past lives in which you confused the issue of friendship and intimacy, and trying to turn a valued friend into an intimate other. This then created all kinds of problems in so doing. So then the retrograde means what?

The archetypal intent of the retrograde also applies to relearn, redo, repeat, and rethink. So, from an evolutionary and karmic point of view the retrograde can re-experience, relive dynamics, circumstances, people, events that are symbolic and reflective of other lifetimes because the lessons were not learned.

Audience: Do you think that would cause a person to have a lot of feelings or energies from past lives?

Jeffrey: Are you talking about images that occur into the consciousness?

Audience: Yes.

Jeffrey: Retrograde planets of themselves attempt to break down the barrier between conscious and unconscious and, specifically, the individuated unconscious. The retrograde archetype tries to actually access the Uranian archetype which is held in the individuated unconscious. So, of course such images can come forth as well as actually having the experience of reliving things from other times.

Audience: With Pluto retrograde you said that all intimate people that you have in your life, you have been with before.

Jeffrey: No. That is not in the Pluto book. I wrote it, I should know.

Audience: I thought you made that statement about the 8th house Pluto.

Jeffrey: Yes, that is about the 8th house Pluto, not Pluto retrograde in general.

Audience: How do those people come together?

Jeffrey: That choice, and that karmic requirement, if you look at it from this life's point of view, is established in other times. It comes under the category of fate or destiny. Generally, twenty percent any of our lives is fated, and eighty percent is free choice. When there is a karmic/evolutionary requirement to repeat or relive certain relationships with individuals in which something was not done right, finished, or completed, or even in certain cases where there is a condition of fruition, then those karmic and evolutionary requirements correlate to 'fate'. In this context fate then directs the show beyond the current personality. Circumstances have actually been created by the Soul, unbeknownst to the conscious personality, that lead people back together.

Audience: Can it be an archetype of something that needs to be repeated rather than something which is with an actual Soul that you have been with before?

Jeffrey: From an 8th house Pluto point of view? Yes, that 'something' can be inner dynamics that have created circumstances that need to be repeated. If that also turns out to be the need to repeat specific relationships with others then you want to look at Venus, and the ruler of the 8th house because that is essentially what is going on: what the dynamics have been. Look at the aspects that both are making in order to understand the total 'picture' of what has gone on and why. Within that to then understand what the resolutions are of these dynamics that are being repeated so that the Soul does not have to repeat them again.

Audience: This is true all during one's lifetime, and never stops? And does it continue into future lives?

Jeffrey: It totally depends on what choices are being made during this lifetime.

Classic example. A person we knew had a deep vision to be an alternative teacher. She had a natal 8th house retrograde Pluto, and a stacked 9th house. The vision that the person had was a wonderful vision, magnificent vision, which required her to have a teaching partner. She had done this before, in another lifetime, and had others that she had partnered with for this vision to become reality. And, yet, in that former life one of those partners, a business partner, 8th house Pluto retrograde, was utterly jealous of this person. She wanted to be this person herself. Thus, she was dishonest, and completely manipulative in terms of presenting her own motivations to this person: the reasons that she wanted to help her actualize this vision. Her inner motives in that life were to help this person actualize her vision, and then to sabotage her so that she could then take over the alternative school that this person had designed.

In that life when this began to occur the 8th house Pluto person refused to understand, grasp, and accept who that person really was, what their intentions and motives were. She just wanted to forgive that person, and made up all kids of excuses manifesting as reasons as to why that person did what they did. Thus, because of this, the 8th house Pluto retrograde person created karmic and evolutionary conditions in which they would have to repeat these dynamics again so as to relearn the truth of what actually happened, and why. This was necessary of course so that the 8th house Pluto person would not do this again, so they could then evolve. And, of course, it was necessary to experience this person in this life so that the 8th house Pluto retrograde person could finally call a spade a spade to this person's face.

So as she began to implement her vision she drew to herself a person who wanted to help her actualize this vision. Everyone else around her was telling her not to get involved with that person. And, of course, that person was that same person from the former life.

So even though everyone else around her was telling her not to get involved with this person she did so anyway: it was fated. So she went ahead a made the choice to go ahead with this person. Yet, because of that person not being honest, etc, events transpired that lead them to become arch enemies. This time she did not make excuses for her, and saw everything about her with crystal clarity. And that, indeed, was the resolution relative to the karmic and evolutionary need to repeat this relationship. The lesson for this 8th house Pluto retrograde person, relative to a stacked 9th house, was to trust her intuition, and to see this particular person clearly.

Audience: What would be different with a 2nd house Pluto retrograde, versus the 8th house Pluto retrograde?

Jeffrey: Because the issues and dynamics of the 8th house are diametrically different than the second: making choices equaling union, partnership, and marriage with another. Typically, the 8th house is involved with manipulation. And, typically, 8th house Pluto people deny rabidly that there is any manipulation taking place. The most common pattern with 8th house Pluto people is that they form relationships with people, or people form relationships with them, relative to need and once the need is satisfied there is no more use for the relationship. Thus, use and manipulation. So, unless is it openly stated in the beginning of the relationship that I will be here this amount of time, and when it is over I will be gone. That will then preclude any sort of karma at that level.

Audience: Would you say that there is more of a fated quality to retrogrades? The more retrogrades the more fated the life?

Jeffrey: Yes. That can be. Especially when the issue of relive and repeat is on the line. In my own case, I have a balsamic Mars/Venus: the culmination of a cycle relative to relationships: And my Venus, again, is retrograde in Scorpio in the 1st house, and square Pluto and Saturn which are also retrograde. It is also inconjunct Uranus in Gemini in the 8th house. So, how do you think I am culminating many relationships from many lifetimes? In the kind of work I am doing.

Audience: Through vicarious association?

Jeffrey: No. By doing it impersonally, so I don't have to get closely involved. The impersonal aspect of it is the Venus retrograde inconjuncting the Uranus retrograde in the 8th house Gemini. And this takes place in the contest of my work or career: the square from the Venus retrograde to Saturn retrograde. So it becomes like a revolving door, and becomes the quickest way to do it. And, sure, all the time there is that kind of recognition factor.

We must also understand that there is a collective issue with respect to retrogrades. If Mercury goes retrograde we all have to deal with the principles of redoing, redefining, and rethinking pertaining to Mercury. How many of you have experienced communications from people that you have known in this life that you have lost communication with for a period of time, and suddenly you have a re-communication? How many of you have experienced this when Mercury is retrograde? It is a common phenomenon. So what is being redone? What is being reestablished? What is the purpose?

It is a classic Mercury retrograde example that you have put together certain things in a Mercury kind of way, and strategies to accomplish them. What happens when Mercury goes retrograde is you have to rethink the whole thing. Suddenly, you are not quite so certain. What happens if you start making major decisions when Mercury is retrograde? Typically information win come to light after it goes direct that has bearing on the decision that was made when it was retrograde. So don't make major decisions when Mercury is retrograde. Always wait for it to go direct so as to become aware of that last vital piece of information to make a more logical decision. Mercury is retrograde about three weeks about three times a year.

Audience: Is it good to wait for it to get back to the degree where it went retrograde?

Jeffrey: Yes. That's a very good piece of advice.

Audience: People who have Mercury retrograde would naturally look at all angles because this for them is a deeper intensification of their mind.

Jeffrey: Actually, for people who have Mercury retrograde natally, it tends to promote a special clarity when it goes retrograde. So they get to sit back and get a great laugh while everyone else struggles, and sees what they go through throughout life!

Audience: Would that also be true for someone who has progressed Mercury retrograde?

Jeffrey: Yes. But not as strong as when it is a natal issue. But don't you see this Mercury retrograde issue right now with all these politicians questioning the nuclear arms treaty? Rethinking, redoing. Don't you see that certain of these politicians running for president are having to retract certain statements that they have made: for example Pat Robertson's ludicrous claim of missiles suddenly back in Cuba!

Audience: He has it on good authority!

Jeffrey: So, there are these collective implications.

Audience: What about stationary retrograde or direct?

Jeffrey: The stationary retrograde, or stationary direct, is a very interesting symbol because it right away is going to magnify itself: it concentrates. A student noticed that when Pluto would go retrograde, and then go stationary direct, major events would occur and yet at the point of the stationary direct it was not aspecting any other natal planets. His question was what does it mean. What it means, from Pluto's point of view, when it goes retrograde it sets in motion a gestational process, the gestation emanating from the Soul, in which the Soul is beginning to redefine certain aspects of its reality. So, by the time it goes stationary direct, it concentrates itself to induce inner or outer events which reflect what the gestation was all about. So, what the stationary does, then, is to bring into reality what the retrograde issue was trying to gestate: to rethink, redo, redefine, etc.

Audience: So, if you were born with a stationary direct, it would be an evolutionary thing, you have been in a retrograde before and are now moving direct.

Jeffrey: Yes. If you see it stationary, then this is the first life where that is taking place after that gestational process. This implies that there has been a series of prior lives in which it had been retrograde and relative to the natural evolutionary cycle, suddenly there is a life for the first time after a while in which it is now retrograde. It will move from birth through transits and progression and express itself, manifest itself, quite instinctually. Even though it will be instinctual the Soul will know how to do it, whatever it is.

Also, when you find planets that are retrograde which form aspects to planets that are not retrograde, this is called an 'oblique retrograde'. You can have an oblique retrograde Moon. If you have Uranus retrograde forming a square to the Moon, for example. You see? So, what would an oblique retrograde Moon actually mean?

Audience: Stabilizing and internalizing.

Jeffrey: Internalizing is the key in order to establish a state of inner emotional security. The whole intent of the retrograde is to introspect, and to internalize in order to individuate. So, relative to the Moon, the individual has decided to learn how to nurture itself, and to create a state of inner security. It infers that the person is learning to break free, to liberate, Uranus, from all external dependencies. It infers that there is a discrepancy between the parents' realities, and the child's realities. This is because the Moon is aspecting a retrograde planet.

A person could have a whole chart that is retrograde by aspect. The same applies to the Sun. If anyone has an oblique retrograde to the Sun, it means that the person cyclically or perpetually throughout life will redefine its whole sense of purpose, and how it creatively actualizes that purpose. And, within this, how it is interpreting and giving meaning to its experience relative to that.

For example, a person with a Sagittarius Sun. And let's say that person goes through some major traumatic event. The way that the person integrates itself and gives purpose to its life is uniquely Sagittarius. That is different than integrating oneself relative to Libra. If I go through a major hardship and I am integrating by way of a Sagittarius Sun, am I not going to tend to philosophize that trauma? I will be integrating it into my existing belief patterns, and using them as a basis of making a philosophical understanding of that trauma. Is that not going to be different from Sun in Taurus, or Libra or, Cancer?

Audience: What happens if a retrograde planet is aspecting another retrograde planet? Does that undo it or intensify it?

Jeffrey: It intensifies it.

Audience: With an oblique retrograde to the Moon, do you find that when the Moon moves slower, the speed of the Moon slowing down, that this relates to a retrograde function as opposed to a quick Moon?

Jeffrey: No. It does tend to make a person much more emotional than in the faster Moons. The average motion of the Moon is 12.5 degrees per day. It can move as quickly as fifteen degrees a day, or as slow as ten degrees in a day.

Audience: When a retrograde planet goes direct by progression, how would that affect it?

Jeffrey: That's a good question. It means that at that point in time, that which has been gestated, rethought, redone, redefined to reflect individuality tends to begin to stabilize. The person begins to put things together and tends to establish a foundation that reflects all that questioning that can be sustained for a great length of time. But, again, the natal impulse is always retrograde. It is always trying to refine, retrograde, that new structure. Just think of all those kinds of words that start with 're': relive, rebel, rethink, refine, redefine, etc.

Audience: Retread.

Jeffrey: If it is not retrograde at birth, and it goes retrograde by progression, then the retrograde archetype begins to operate. Now that directness is challenged, and that person begins to feel unstable relative to the function that is going retrograde.

Audience: How many days a year is Venus retrograde?

Jeffrey: It retrogrades every five hundred and forty two days, and stays retrograde two to three weeks. That is a large cycle of un-stabilization relative to relationships. That means that a bunch of people on the planet get to redo, rethink, reflect on their relationships which includes their own relationship to themself.

So let's go ahead and now talk about each planet when it is retrograde.

Mercury Retrograde
People who have Mercury retrograde are people who, evolutionarily over many lives, have, prior to Mercury going retrograde, indiscriminately collected information from a diversity of sources in the efforts to create logical structures which will allow them to intellectually explain the nature of their existence. Because the information has been indiscriminately collected their Souls have become a library of random information that has caused intellectual confusion because of all the different forms of information that has been collected conflicts within itself. Thus, the evolutionary intention of the Mercury retrograde is to rebel, reject, to throw out all unnecessary information. The intent within this is for the Soul to orient to information that is specific and particular to its own reason for being, and thus to intellectually simplify. It means to rebel or retreat from externally gained or accepted information systems. It means to internalize in such a way that the person can develop their own voice: to arrive at their own views relative to the nature of things. It means to personalize such information.

Audience: Personal truth as opposed to social truth?

Jeffrey: Yes. As a result we have a natural antithetical archetype.
That nature of Mercury is to externalize, yet the nature of retrograde is internalize. As a result, people with Mercury retrograde, when they are exposed to knowledge which does not reflect their personal purpose, information which is not needed, then there is an automatic stiff-arm, so to speak, in the Soul which does not allow them to take in unnecessary

information. This can create problems in cultures like this in which the premium, relative to educational models when we are children, is to memorize and parrot, not to conceptualize. This creates problems with the majority retrograde Mercury students. Some of these people are classically labeled slow learners. We have advocated for many years that there should be special schools taught by Mercury retrograde teachers to Mercury retrograde students. It would work: the Soul vibrations would be in harmony.

In addition, the Mercury retrograde is pointing from the left brain to the right brain. The left brain is linear, and the right brain is not. The left brain is fact-based. The right brain is intuitive. Mercury retrograde people, evolutionarily speaking, are beginning the process of relearning to rely upon and trusting their intuition as a source of information and knowledge that they are seeking. They may seek out external information sources but those sources of information would only be relative to the Mercury retrograde Souls own specific purposes and needs. When Mercury retrograde focuses on such information it can then have a photographic type memory in which that information is never forgotten. Mercury retrograde, when operating in harmony with its archetype, only speaks when there is a reason to speak. Mercury retrograde, when it is not in harmony with its archetype, gossips like crazy, and can talk non-stop. Going from one thing to the next thing, over an over.

Audience: I know this quite intimately relative to a plane ride I just took with respect to a fellow passenger.

Jeffrey: When Mercury goes retrograde collectively then, we all come under this impulse. When it goes retrograde through progression, this is what happens. Mercury retrograde points towards Jupiter.

Venus Retrograde
Venus is the rarest archetype to have retrograde motion and the need is to, archetypically, utterly and uniquely define one's values on a personal and social level which will then allow the person to harmoniously relate to itself. As a result of this the person can then relate to others from the point of view of being centered within itself. It places a premium on the lesson of Venus from a Taurus point of view called self-reliance. Retrograde Venus people, from a spiritual point of view, are learning that the ultimate relationship is with non human being. It is with the inner Godhead. Commonly, people

in monastic environments have Venus retrograde. Commonly, the artist has Venus retrograde. Commonly, the musician has Venus retrograde. The person forms a relationship with that which constitutes its work where that work is a reflection of the Soul's inner relationship to itself.

Retrograde Venus people commonly feel a high degree of social alienation through the un-relatedness, Venus, of the values systems that are shared, Venus, amongst the consensus relative to Soul's own unique and individual values. This conflict in values, of what is meaningful, of how we relate to others and why, creates a feeling of being very different with respect to the social milieu. The famous 'wallflower'.

Audience: I don't have retrograde planets, but I can really relate to that.

Jeffrey: If you have evolved beyond consensus state and you have planets in the social houses or the relationships houses, it can induce this effect. Anytime you have evolved out of the consensus, you are beginning to access the archetype of Uranus. Once you access the Uranus archetype consciously, that is the effect in general.

Commonly, retrograde Venus people, when they do participate in relationships, either draw individuals who are themselves rugged individualists, or they draw relationships in which they play the role of helper or counselor. The reason is that Venus correlates with the phenomena called magnetism. If you are around a person with Venus retrograde who has done the necessary inner work on themselves, then the nature of their magnetism is quite different than those who have not.

Audience: Sounds like a guru – to bring the divinity through a human being – one is able to see God through a human being – and therefore there is a relationship with a human being, not as themselves, but as bringing God through them.

Jeffrey: That can exist, but it is relative to the evolutionary state. The reason here is that people will commonly perceive in the Venus retrograde person that they truly have something to offer that is not consciously defined, and they are magnetically drawn to the person for counsel or advice. Typically happens.

The Venus retrograde principle points towards Uranus. Any retrograde archetype will point towards Uranus. It reflects the archetype of individuation, Uranus; of withdrawing from conditioning patterns outright. Venus retrograde also points to and emphasizes the Taurus side of Venus, not the Libra side. The Taurus side is all about one's inner relationship to oneself. It is also about the learning to be self reliant, and learning to identify one's own inner resources in order to sustain oneself. Within this the Taurus archetype is all about what constitutes meaning in one's life, and thus what one values. So with Venus retrograde these Souls are emphasizing this archetype within themselves.

Audience: So Aquarius in the 2nd house could have a similar effect to Venus retrograde?

Jeffrey: It depends on the condition of Uranus, and the evolutionary condition of the Soul. If it is strong in the chart, and the evolutionary condition of the Soul is individuated and beyond, then, yes, it can operate that way. Conversely, many within the Aquarian archetype simply bond with their peer group which is the majority outright.

From the Soul's point of view, Venus is mercifully retrograde the least of all. From a personal point of view, it can be an incredibly long winter. Even in the context of the best of relationships, such people still feel entirely alone. They may enjoy being alone yet the nature of human beings is that they are social animals. So this inner feeling of always being alone, even in the context of an intimate other, can be quite difficult at times to live with because of this feeling of inner isolation from everything.

But, it is also true that, by way of compensation, many Venus retrograde people go through a diversity of partners thinking that they can find someone who can relate to them. Rarely does a Venus retrograde person find the life partner in the first partner, because evolutionarily and karmically, there is also a need to repeat or relive relationships with Souls with which there have been these prior linkages in which something was not finished or resolved. Thus, the need to repeat or relive such relationships in order for a resolution, or completion, to occur. When Venus goes retrograde by transit this can correlate to a time in which any of us can attract to ourselves others whom we have known in the past that suddenly resurface into our lives for this reason.

When Venus goes retrograde through progression this can then correlate to a time, which can be the remainder of one's life in certain cases, in which the Soul progressively withdraws from the way it has been living its life. The Soul then goes deep within itself as it attempts, desires, to recreate to core sense of meaning for its life. In turn this creates a time in which the Soul will question the very meaning of life itself, and then to create a new sense of meaning for itself.

Thus, the very nature of what it values, its value systems, can change, and, as a result of how the Soul then relates to others, and how others relate to the Soul. The core intention of the Venus retrograde natally, through progression, or through transit is all about the Soul's inner relationship to itself, how it relates to itself, and that which constitutes to the very meaning of life in general, and, thus, what will constitute personal meaning for the Soul itself.

Mars Retrograde

The very nature of Mars is yang, the male principle, to project outwards. And here, again, we have a retrograde principle that wants to introvert, and to internalize. Mars, of itself, wants no limitations. It is an utterly instinctual process which reflects the actual desires emanating from the Soul. These desires, in themselves, reflect the evolutionary journey of the Soul and, thus, the instinctual need to assert or act upon any experience deemed necessary with a minimum of restriction in order to discover the reactions to the experience. It is the reactions to the initiated experience that produces knowledge. There is no forethought within Mars, of itself, no conscious intent. It is an utterly instinctual process that reflects the desires from the Soul.

The linkage of Mars and Pluto, by the way, is the archetype behind the Indian idea of maya: the illusion of separateness, the subjective ego of the Soul that is only identified with itself at a personality level, and thus the illusion of separateness. Mars also embodies the sexual instinct. So, if you turn this impulse retrograde, it can induce frustration because you certainly have a consciousness that is monitoring the nature of desires, and the intent behind any given action, or the desire behind any given experience. It is interrupting the natural instinctual flow. This can create problems.

Evolutionarily speaking, the intent is to only manifest experiences which are essential to the evolutionary purpose of the Soul, and thus not to waste time. Mars is analogous to the pinball machine: you pull the lever, the thing flies around, and it takes a while for the thing to find the final slot. Action-reaction. Action-reaction. Mars retrograde, however, only wants to initiate experiences that are essential. So, if you put such an archetype in a culture which is now putting a premium on freedom, and the person witnesses all around people who are operating antithetical to itself, what happens by way of comparison? What happens to the sexualized external instinct? What happens to sexual rhythm relative to this instinct? Is it constant, or does it fluctuate? What happens to the consciously acknowledged desire behind any given sexual attraction? It creates an automatic check or filter that allows for a conscious awareness of an archetype that is not normally conscious. That can be highly frustrating to the Mars.

Audience: Does it create sexual dysfunction or just reflection?

Jeffrey: In certain cases, it can lead into sexual dysfunction, in other cases, by way of compensation it can lead to the rabbit syndrome.

Audience: It sounds like these people have something on an instinctual level or process, and are working with it consciously which is implying responsibility in this case: a lot of responsibility. Would you say that Mars direct normally doesn't have that kind of responsibility?

Jeffrey: In and of itself, yes. Of course this can be conditioned by way of connections to other planets and/ or signs. For example Mars in aspect to Saturn can create that.

Audience: So, a more individual sense of right and wrong, rather than cultural, but the right and wrong of the Soul is the point.

Jeffrey: Right. That is the point. It is also obviously going to place a premium on the right to be an individual. It is going to place a premium on the need for freedom. From a spiritual point of view, it attempts to align the personal will at an egocentric level. Mars, with a higher will.

Audience: Even more so if it is in aspect to Pluto.

Jeffrey: Yes. It can lead to potential collisions, now emphasized, between its will and the will of other people that can make the person highly susceptible to the impact of other people's will. Mars rules the naval chakra with Pluto. This is where all of us take in the will, through the environment, of others.

So, with Mars retrograde, i.e. its natural action of Mars is to project outward, and therefore we have a natural repelling force that can thwart other people's wills. So when Mars is retrograde the person is now taking it right back into itself. This can perpetually or cyclically weaken the constitution. It can lead to digestion problems because of the linkage with the chakra that is now emanating the nerves leading to digestion: the stomach, pancreas, duodenum, liver, etc.

Audience: Would that be accentuated if the Mars is retrograde in the 1st or 6th house?

Jeffrey: That would be accentuated with Mars retrograde in the 4th or 8th houses, or in Scorpio or Cancer.

Audience: What if the Mars is in a mental sign in a mental house?

Jeffrey: There would be all kinds of verbal arguments relative to the collision of wills.

Audience: Like Mars in Gemini in the 7th house?

Jeffrey: Yes.

So the key in understanding Mars retrograde is that inverts the consciousness of the Soul so that it can determine the cause, the why, of any given desire that the Soul has. As a result, the Soul, when Mars is retrograde, is desiring to eliminate all unnecessary desires that have nothing to do with what the Soul needs by way of its ongoing evolutionary journey. And this includes inverting the natural sexual energy of the Soul: to determine the reason, or the why, of any given sexual desire that is perceived as a need. When Mars goes retrograde by way of a transit or progression this same need to determine these reasons, the why, of any given desire that has lead to the creation of its life to date, including sexual desires, occurs. As a result, the Soul will desire to eliminate or change anything in its life that no longer has anything to do with what the Soul actually needs to continue on its evolutionary journey. In the process of eliminating anything that has lead to the Soul's current state of reality the Soul will reflect on exactly what it does need, what it does desire, to move forwards on that journey. Thus, this can be a time of creating new and intensified desires to that end. And the Soul, via its will, Mars, will demand the freedom to so actualize those desires. In many, many ways when Mars goes retrograde through transit or progression it correlates to a time of Soul renewal because of this. When Mars is retrograde it points back to the Soul itself: Pluto.

Jupiter Retrograde

Jupiter is interesting to have retrograde. From an evolutionary point of view, the individual must eliminate all belief structures that it has accumulated over a period of many lifetimes in order to arrive at an individualized belief system, philosophical principals, abstracts, or cosmological views which are wholly arrived at, and defined, by itself.

This then places a premium on the intuitive development of the Souls nature. This is Jupiter retrograde. It creates a focus upon the right brain. As a result, these people's belief structures tend to be redefined or adjusted throughout their lives with respect to learning strategies, to which Jupiter correlates, which have to be highly tailored to reflect the individual reality of the Soul.

As in Mercury retrograde if this is not done, the person has a very hard time assimilating, accepting, or taking in new abstract principles. Sometimes, with Jupiter retrograde, depending on the evolutionary condition of the Soul, some individuals can find it extremely difficult to find linear words, logical sentence structure, to express what they are conceptualizing or intuiting. They can commonly have a psychology of inferiority relative to communication skills with respect to what they know.

Audience: It would be more prevalent in a left brain society such as ours.

Jeffrey: Exactly.

As a result, some of these people won't communicate even at times that they ought to communicate because of the imposed or learned inferiority. Linked with anatomy, some of these people have thyroid and pituitary issues. The thyroid is ruled by Jupiter, and the pituitary is co-ruled by Jupiter and Saturn. The pituitary is linked with the growth and decay of the entire organism: the master gland. The thyroid correlates to what you can assimilate on a nutritional level. It is not uncommon for these people to have an assimilation problem relative to the thyroid, and can have some degree of difficulty or disruption relative to the pituitary in terms of the ability to regulate the growth and decay of the organism. For example, commonly, people with Jupiter retrograde have a lack of iodine in their system which is critical to the thyroid and its ability to assimilate the nutrients that are put in the body. This can then lead to people who are very thin, and/or the opposite: very, very fat.

When Jupiter goes retrograde through transit, for all of us then all of these processes are afoot. For example, when Jupiter goes retrograde through transit in the natal chart that is an area where you can be taking a new look at: a new view. One of the correlative functions of Jupiter is to interpret phenomenal reality, and thus by way of interpretation, generate meaning. But the interpretation is based on the totality of your subjective reality which, itself, is a composite of exiting beliefs which then determines how you interpret phenomenal reality in general, and your own life, reality, specifically.

So let's say this occurs in your 6th house. This is the area that you will then be taking a new look at. And that can include your body, your physical health. This will then create a focus within your consciousness that creates an awareness of your body that leads to what needs to be adjusted in order to sustain physical well being. If the body is physically suffering in some way at that time it then leads to the awareness of what you need to change, of what to do, in order for it to be healthy again.

This transit will create an awareness within your consciousness of anything that needs to be adjusted, of that which leads to self improvement, relative to how you have been responding to the various elements in your overall reality including work, strategies of personal improvement which are based on the need to redefine, to interpret differently. It will make you look at the issues pertaining to the 6th house differently. And this will be true of the Jupiter retrograde transit in any house or sign that it is in. As a result, you have of expansion of your consciousness through redefinition.

Audience: Is the main difference between Jupiter retrograde, and Mercury retrograde the intuitive emphasis?

Jeffrey: Yes. Mercury is specific to how you logically order your reality in a very linear way: a, b, c, d. Jupiter is how you are putting together your reality abstractly, conceptually, based on principles which become the basis of the specific words that you use to describe your reality.

Audience: What is the difference in learning difficulty?

Jeffrey: Mercury is concerned with collecting information and logically connecting that information in order to build a whole out of it. That does not mean, of itself, understanding the meaning of it, the conceptual basis of it, the beliefs that have led to the logical ordering of the information itself. The information that Mercury is orienting to is specific to its personal needs which excludes any other level of information when it is retrograde. Jupiter retrograde desires to understand, needs to understand, the conceptual, abstract, basis of anything. It needs to understand the nature of beliefs themselves as beliefs lead to how phenomenal reality is then logically ordered because of the nature of whatever beliefs. If the Jupiter retrograde person can not understand, or accept, the abstract or conceptual basis of the information that it is subjected to then a disconnect happens in its right brain. And that disconnect then tunes out the information that is coming into it.

Audience: So, if you have both retrograde?

Jeffrey: You have both processes working. And from an evolutionary point of view it then becomes essential to understand why the Soul has those archetypes both retrograde. It becomes essential to understanding such a Soul so that any projections upon it in terms of how that Soul goes about learning what it needs to learn for its own evolutionary purposes. If the Soul is aligned with the information that it is taking in, and the conceptual basis for it, then such a Soul can be one of the best learners of all. They can take in vast amounts of information very rapidly, assimilate it, and continue to move on at rates that others simply can not do. There would be the very essence of a photographic memory then. All is remembered. Almost nothing is ever forgotten. Conversely, if the Soul is not aligned with the information that it is being subjected too, does not understand the conceptual basis for that information, then it can certainly create the appearance of learning almost nothing. Such a Soul will be tuned into itself, allowing for imagination, daydreams, random ponderings about whatever, simply staring into the sky, or the wave, or the Moon etc., to induce what it feels it needs to know.

Audience: I have Jupiter retrograde ruling Sagittarius rising. Does that accentuate the whole redefinition thing more?

Jeffrey: Yes. Because your planetary ruler is retrograde. So, that colors the entire chart, conditions the entire chart. Everything in the chart comes through the ascendant, so if the ruler of that ascendant is retrograde that is why throughout your life nothing will ever seem quite right, or completely right. There is a relationship between the 9th house and the 1st house in terms of how you are trying to understand your specific sense of identity, your individuality. It is going to have to have these cosmological wrappings which set in motion the existential search for truth which is perpetually being refined and/or redefined. Perpetually.

What happens with Jupiter retrograde at an oblique level like this, meaning because Jupiter retrograde is the ruler of your ascendant it is making your entire chart retrograde because the entire chart is coming through your ascendant, is that is creates an evolution wherein you will develop a healthy respect for individual differences, cultural differences, belief pattern differences versus the need to convince and convert. And that is because there is such an emphasis on developing your own individuality.

Audience: With Jupiter retrograde in the 1st house, and Sagittarius on the 3rd house, would that also emphasize that?

Jeffrey: Yes. It would typically represent a tremendous degree of switching from the left to the right brains or visa versa. The 3rd house correlates to the left brain, and Sagittarius and Jupiter to the house of the right brain. It could be integrated to a total degree, but that integration is based on where the person finally decides to place the emphasis in their thinking processes. Are they going to allow the intellect to lead the intuition, or are they going to allow the intuition to lead the intellect? The answer with Jupiter retrograde in the 1st house, with Sagittarius on the 3rd house cusp, is to let the intuition to lead the intellect, not the other way around.

When Jupiter is retrograde at birth many of these Souls will feel as if they are always lacking something because of how they take in information. Sadly, many will then compensate for this lack. Compensation in astrology correlates to Jupiter, Sagittarius, and the 9th house. Thus, many will compensate for their perceived sense of lack by attempting to be like everyone else. They can attempt to latch onto the prevailing beliefs of the society of birth in order to feel like they fit so that they can be like everyone else. They can attempt to buy into the latest fad, of the most groovy thing to do as defined by most others around it. When this happens such Souls then create a living lie because they are not any of that. As evolutionary astrologers, when you see this in one of your clients, it is imperative that you help them try to see this act of compensation leading to the living lie. And, within that, to help them come back to their own natures, of that which they are that requires an independent examination of themselves. In turn, this can then lead to developing a life that honors their own specific individuality no matter if it does not look like anyone else's reality. As a result, they will be living their own truth.

Saturn Retrograde

Here we are going to have an individual, evolutionarily and karmically speaking, who needs to define their own sense of personal authority, structural reality, and ways of integrating into their culture as determined, Saturn, by them. Saturn correlates with consensus norms, customs, taboos, social regulations, and laws equaling consensus of any given society. In turn this then generates pressure from the consensus to any individual to conform so that the consensus can feel continuously secure within itself.

Saturn retrograde says "No, I am not going to do this", "I will do it in my own way, thank you". In other words, Saturn retrograde people must define, Saturn, their own laws, regulations, customs, taboos, and how they go about integrating themselves into the society of birth that honors who they are as individuals. The foundations of their circumstantial and inner reality cyclically or perpetually will change depending on the house, i.e. mutable, fixed, cardinal, or the sign that the Saturn is in and the aspects that it is making.

When Saturn retrograde people are born through parents who encourage individuality they will have no problem with those type of parents. In fact, they will have a healthy respect for such parents even if their own individual reality is diametrically opposed the reality of the parents. Conversely, if they come through parents in which one or both of the parents are authoritarian types, then there is going to be a problem. This is going to be a clash of authority. Of course, from an evolutionary and karmic point of view, it is essential of course to determine why any of us are born through the types of families that we are. And, at the same time, when we become parents it is essential that we understand the karmic and evolutionary reasons that we have the types of children that we have.

Saturn retrograde people will be very introspective type Souls. They are highly reflective. The very nature of this reflection is to examine the nature of their reality at any point in time. The intent in such examination is to determine, Saturn, what needs to be changed in their reality so that growth can occur, what existing dynamics may be in place that are causing some kind of problem or difficulty in their life, to become aware of the need to change something in their life that is preventing growth and/or new impulses that will allow them to grow or change. In turn this then causes them to become aware of what needs to change in their existing reality so that that growth can be accommodated.

Saturn retrograde Souls naturally brood. Brooding is very different than depression. This occurs because Saturn retrograde simply can not buy into what the mainstream of a society is calling 'reality'. These people need to define a structural reality that is unique to them. As a result, these people tend to question the consensus in terms of what constitutes real meaning in their lives, what is actually important, and which in not important. This then creates a gulf between them and consensus society in which most people live. The brooding and withdrawal is then necessary for them to do because it can lead to an inner awareness of what they can do for themselves that will create that sense of meaning, of what does feel important for them to do as individuals.

So, if the Saturn retrograde person is living with a certain kind of partner who interprets this withdrawal as threatening to the relationship it will cause that partner to issue all kinds of judgments and conclusions about the Saturn retrograde person. And, of course, those judgments and conclusions will all be wrong because they are all based on a reality within the partner that is being projected onto the Saturn retrograde person. These kinds of assertive and projected judgments will only have the effect of driving the Saturn retrograde person more deeply into themselves, of deepening the introspection and withdrawal itself. If this kind of pattern goes on long enough in such a relationship the Saturn retrograde person will then simply feel like they are going through the motions of the relationship versus being in that relationship.

The bottom line is that Saturn retrograde simply can not buy into what the mainstream is calling reality. They need to define a structural reality that is unique to them. In certain kinds of evolutionary conditions it can create a type of psychology in which they never feel like they fit into anything, that they never belong, even when they have a functional life in place that includes work, relationships, friends all of which has some meaning for them. They just don't feel like they belong to any of this. And this then creates the inner sense of just going through the motions of life itself without making any kind of total connection to it. This then creates this inner haunting feeling of social aloneness. It adds to the cyclic of perpetual brooding and reflection. It creates a strange feeling of 'mourning' for life itself. I remember reading a play by Anton Chekhov called *The Seagull*. In this book there was a woman who was always dressed in black. One day a person came up to this woman and asked why she always wore black. And her answer, a perfect Saturn retrograde answer, was "I am in mourning for my life".

Audience: There seems to be an alienation either internally or externally. People are doing socially approved things but they just don't feel that they fit in. They have no meaning. Or they are doing what has meaning in their life and other people are thinking that they are absolutely crazy.

Audience: I have experienced that but a little different. You can play the game that the traditional society is involved in, like being involved in a group and going along with it, but at the same time there is this feeling of not really being accepted by the group even though you haven't really done anything to offset it. You know that you have a feeling of not really belonging, but you also have that feeling that the others aren't really accepting you.

Jeffrey: What that is based on is the natural instinctual vibration of your Soul. Keep in mind that your Soul intends for you to make these redefinitions, of a necessary withdrawal from the consensus, in order to individuate yourself. This then creates your own unique vibration that emanates from your Soul. You are not really aware of it but the vibration creates the effect in order to induce the intent. That is what Saturn retrograde people fail to realize. Then they feel that they are feeling ostracized or falsely judged behind their backs. This is a common experience for Saturn retrograde Souls.

Audience: That's really true until you realize what is going on. But when you also realize that when you define your reality in such a way as to make a career that is reflective of you, and to structure yourself into society in such a way that it is reflective of you, then you will attract people that reflect that and then you feel complete acceptance.

Audience: That's true. Sometimes you can't change the whole structure so you find something different.

Audience: Saturn, as the most structured and crystallized of all the planets, is the most difficult, to change with respect to its reality. I think that the most common results would be to either feel spiritually bankrupt, and to go along with society, because it needs Uranus and Mars to work with it: to really break out of it because it is so structured.

Jeffrey: Again, it depends on the condition of the Soul. If it is in a consensus state, and the Saturn is retrograde, it is going to have a problem and it will typically compensate by creating the appearance of normalcy. If it is in the individuated state, and firmly into it, then it actually gets off at thumbing its nose at the system. So, it depends on the evolutionary state. Also, when you find Saturn retrograde in charts, from a family lineage point of view (that is one of the linkages of Saturn – family lineage), it is most common that the Saturn retrograde offspring will be more evolved than the parents.

Audience: If somebody was in a consensus mode and they were compensating, it would lead to sickness would it not over a period of time?

Jeffrey: Yes. Because of repressing the evolutionary intent. It will initially manifest as structural problems in the skeleton. One of the common symptoms is arthritis. That can degenerate into immune system problems relative to B and T cells being given false instructions by way of the thymus gland. Then it gets more severe. For example, once you have that, it can lead into leukemia for example, or a change in the red/white blood cell counts.

Audience: Could that also be someone who has Saturn/Uranus conjunct?

Jeffrey: That would emphasize it. The Saturn retrograde is virtually pointing to Uranus, the door is open to Uranus. From the point of view of consciousness Saturn correlates to the parameters of what you are consciously aware: the threshold of the unconscious. So the immediate sphere of the unconscious is the individuated unconscious, and Saturn is pointing to that: Uranus.

Uranus, of course, relative to the individuated unconscious, contains three specific forms of information. That which you suppress by way of Saturn: what you don't want to deal with or refuse to deal with. It correlates, in total detail, to memories of this and all prior lives. This is why Uranus correlates with long term memory whereas Mercury is our short term memory. And it correlates to abstract information which pertains to your larger, freer future. So, this is why Saturn and Uranus are inherently antithetical to each other. The bottom line is that Uranus is forever trying to revolutionize the crystallized structures of the Saturnian reality. Uranus, of itself, places a premium on individuality, a de-conditioned Soul that is only defined by its own unique nature. In Buddhist terms what is called the 'diamond nature'.

So, when you have Saturn pointing to Uranus, well, guess what? This natural threshold or barrier of the consciousness defined by Saturn retrograde is not very strong. This means that unconscious content is either perpetually or cyclically penetrating the consciousness of the Saturn retrograde Soul.

Audience: If the repression in a family exists and causes emotional troubles, the Saturn would not want to be part of it. I have Saturn retrograde and I had to go back to live with my parents for a while. I had to give up everything I had studied and knew in order to relate to them, but it imprisoned me for several months. Of course, I have Saturn in the 12th, so I really felt like I was in prison. So it is interesting to hear anybody else's comments if they went through anything sort of similar to that. It almost caused a nervous or emotional breakdown. It almost got there but I got out of there in time to offset that. So now, it is nice to have freedom! I can think the way I want and have no problems, no repression.

Audience: Can you say anything about repeating with the same parents, repeating or reliving with those same people?

Jeffrey: Yes, with Saturn retrograde it typically correlates with the need to repeat or relive other lifetimes with one or both parents in which something was not finished or resolved. And, of course, that is the intent in order to resolve that which was not resolved before.

Audience: Is anything excluded from the collective unconscious that is in the individuated unconscious?

Jeffrey: Yes. Everything is interlinked, obviously, but the individuated unconscious is its own dynamic. It is content that is unique to you as an entity. The collective unconscious is content that is unique to the entire species: Neptune.

Uranus Retrograde

So, Saturn retrograde points towards Uranus which really means an emphasis on freedom, and individually to define your own structural reality circumstantially, and internally, that reflects your individuality. When you have it pointing towards Uranus it point towards archetypical rebellion. Rebellion towards what? Anybody telling you what to do or how to do it. It places an emphasis on the need to experiment with reality structures, different forms of, in order to determine through experimentation that which is most reflective of you. Or to at least to inwardly contemplate different possibilities, to reflect upon them, to brood if necessary.

When Uranus is retrograde, this is now pointing toward Neptune, isn't it? So, Uranus retrograde emphasizes the Uranian archetype with respect to the emphasis upon individualization or individuation. Individuation correlates with the archetype of Uranus. There is a prevailing European esoteric thought form which states that you are not an individual until you do liberate from the consensus. Until then you are simply called a 'person'.

Audience: In some cultures, you take the name of the father until you mature and then you take your own name.

Jeffrey: That's why last names are commonly linked with social function. That is the actual origin of family names. You have to keep in mind that throughout most of human history one social function is passed on from one family member to the next. It was inherited, Saturn, thus family names have their origin in a social function.

Audience: Unless someone is born with Saturn retrograde.

Jeffrey: So, the retrograde emphasizes that side of Uranus because Uranus is that part in all human beings that makes us feel different than the next person. Every human being on Earth has a feeling of being a little bit different than the next one. The clearest demonstration of that is your physical appearance that equals your self-image. But, the feeling of being different can be emphasized: how different do you feel?

The most common denominator in all charts is to have Aquarius somewhere, Uranus somewhere, and a sign on your 11th house cusp. That occurs in all charts. Thus in every human being there is this archetypical linkage to feeling different. But how much is it emphasized, how many planets do you have in Aquarius, how much is in the 11th house, how many aspects to Uranus. This determines emphasis. So, relative to compensation, Uranus retrograde people may feel socially insecure relative to feeling different from everybody. This can lead into conforming or bonding with a segment of your overall peer group in order to feel socially accepted and secure: thus individually secure. Uranus retrograde people, as a result, tend to have to be a group of one. When responded to archetypically, these people are not group joiners. If they join at all, it will be a bunch of other mavericks who are honoring individuality, not dogma. Uranus does correlate to how whole groupings of people put themselves together in the context of the whole of a society. You can have a conservative grouping, or a progressive grouping, or a status-quo grouping of peoples. Within these groupings individuals make friends with others of like mind: Uranus. We tend to bond with others of like mind in order to feel secure not only within ourselves, but of course within the overall context of the society of birth so that we don't feel completely alone. When Uranus is retrograde at birth this will correlate to a Soul who intends to repeat or relive certain friendships from other lifetimes in which something was not resolved or finished. Within that intent lies the fact that such Souls also desire to reconnect, retrograde, to certain Souls that they have been traveling with for many, many lifetimes in which the intent is to simply carry on with one another.

Uranus retrograde emphasizes and creates all kinds of mental thought forms that occur in the consciousness of their own volition; thought forms that implicate and symbolize a larger and freer future. And that is because Uranus correlates to the Soul's inner blueprint for its evolutionary future and needs. Thus, these types of thoughts that symbolize the future percolate up from the individuated unconscious through the door of Saturn where

Saturn correlates to the structural boundary of what we are consciously aware of at any point in time. It is the natural boundary between our subjective consciousness in any given life, and our individuated unconscious that correlates by way of long term memory to all of our prior life memories, and contains the blueprint from within the Soul that correlates to our evolutionary future.

Typically, relative to most people, seventy percent, these ideas go un-acted upon. They are left as mental considerations only, and thus generate frustration because the person can glimpse different possibilities and yet, relative to the fear and insecurity linked with aloneness, they go un-acted upon. The message in the Uranus retrograde is to act, to act upon such messages. But the key is to only act on the ones that are repeating themselves: the ones that won't go away. The ones that appear one or two times are typically ahead of their time which is one of the problems with Uranus. The thoughts keep reappearing over and over are the ones to take action upon. They will typically symbolize the next five to seven years of the Soul's life to come if acted upon. These thoughts are only a problem when they are not acted upon. So, as a result of Uranus being retrograde, it is either cyclically or perpetually releasing into your consciousness the unconscious content that is unique to yourself.

That content will contain three dimensions. One is what we are discussing now: the thoughts that correlate to the Soul's larger, freer future that reflects the evolutionary intentions within the Soul. It also contains the content of that which we repress by way of the Saturn archetype. That which we repress can be all kinds of things. It can be anything that makes us feel insecure about ourselves, things that make us feel uncomfortable about ourselves for whatever reasons, parts of our individual history that we want to run from and/ or do not want anyone else to ever know about us, and memories of a traumatic nature that are repressed in order to create a sense of psychological stability because the nature of the trauma, or traumas, are so severe that it would lead to that instability until they are addressed: healed in some way. Uranus also contains the content, again, of all our memories from this and other lifetimes: the long term memory. This also correlates to the memories from this life that have been consciously forgotten. How many can remember in total detail, for example, what one did on a certain date ten years ago? Not too many can consciously recall such a thing and yet that memory is within us: Uranus.

When Uranus is retrograde in the natal chart this will correlate with a Soul in which all the dimensions of the individuate unconscious will surface into the individual's conscious awareness on a perpetual or cyclic basis throughout their life. The intent in this is for the Soul to review, retrograde, such content in order to learn from it over and over so as to be able to apply it to the ongoing reality, Saturn, of itself. And the intent in such application is to accelerate the evolutionary process of individuation. The intent is to learn from the past as such memories surface into their conscious awareness over and over, and then to not duplicate the past where that past is understood to be slowing down the evolutionary development of the Soul into its future. As the ideas surface into the Soul's conscious awareness by way of Saturn that correlate to its larger, freer, future that become repetitive, retrograde, the Uranus retrograde Soul will naturally desire to take action upon them. And, in so doing, they will then accelerate their own evolutionary development.

One of the most difficult correlations of Uranus, Aquarius, and the 11th house is that of trauma. When Uranus is retrograde at birth this will typically correlate to a Soul who has experienced various kinds of traumas that remain unresolved within the Soul. When a trauma that has been experienced by the Soul remains unresolved this then correlates in varying degrees of intensity to the phenomena of Post Traumatic Stress Disorder. As a result of this every aspect of the Soul's life will be affected by this unresolved trauma, or traumas. When this is the case then any manner of circumstances that the Soul creates for itself can trigger this PTSD. When this occurs the behavioral response is very disproportionate to the actual circumstance at hand that has triggered the PTSD. The core affect of PTSD is a fundamental disconnect manifesting as detachment from almost all of life conditions, or situations.

When Uranus is retrograde at birth the Soul intends to resolve this ongoing affect of the PTSD that has been carried forwards into the current life from the life in which the trauma, or traumas, took place. Because of this intent the Soul will perpetually or cyclically release fragments of the memories associated with the trauma or traumas into the conscious awareness of the individual so as to relive, retrograde, the trauma or traumas in the current life: reliving in the sense of remembering them. In some cases this intent to relive in order to heal and move on from the trauma, or traumas, actually manifests in the Soul as recreating in some form the original trauma that took place in the context of the current life. When this is the case the intent, the reason why, is the same: to heal them so that the Soul can move forwards in its evolution. Until that is done one of the affects, evolutionarily speaking, is keep the Soul 'marking time': frozen in such a way that the Soul can not move forwards. If you are counseling such Souls, or if this is your own situation, it is important to understand that the only real healing that can take place is when the Soul is able to determine the reasons, or the why, of the need of creating such a trauma, or traumas, to itself in the first place. This of course correlates with the Saturn lesson of learning how to accept the responsibility in our own actions, versus feeling like a victim to them. One of the great things about Evolutionary Astrology is that is allows for an awareness of the actual reasons or causes of anything, including why any of us need to create various kinds of traumas.

When Uranus goes retrograde through transit and/or progression then this will correlate with a time in which that content held in the individuated unconscious percolates into the awareness of the individual. And, at those times, it becomes an evolutionary imperative to act upon that information in order for real evolutionary growth to occur. As a result of this imperative the individual will suddenly begin to feel a detachment from their existing reality in every way. This detachment is necessary for it then allows for an objectification of their life conditions to take place. The detachment is essential for this to occur because it removes the Soul from the emotional dynamics that keep it bound to those conditions. Thus, by detaching from the emotional binds that keep it attached the Soul is then allowed to objectify its reality in every way which, in turn, allows for an awareness to take place that shows the Soul how to make the necessary changes in its life for real growth, evolution to occur.

Going back to where we started when Uranus is retrograde at birth it is pointing towards Neptune. In combination this creates a core alienation from the reality of Earth itself, of societies in general, from any sense of meaning for life that is defined by the majority of people on Earth, and thus gives rise to the inner questioning within the Soul of that which does constitute meaning: lasting meaning for life. Neptune correlates with the ultimate meaning about what life is, and is not. This is why it correlates, among other correlations, to Spirit, and the search for our Creator: God/ess.

Uranus retrograde natally correlates with Souls that are fundamentally detached from life itself, detached even from themselves: it is as if the

Soul is constantly observing itself, and not being truly engaged in anyway from within itself, or life itself. The actual intent in this is for the Soul to view itself, and everything else, without any emotional linkages so that it can objectify itself. The intent is such objectification is *self-knowledge* and knowledge about everything else that is not colored or conditioned by emotional attachment. As a result of this kind of evolutionary process the Soul then can become aware of exactly what it needs to do in order for its own evolution to proceed, and what any life condition needs in order for those conditions themselves to change so that growth can occur.

Neptune Retrograde

Neptune correlates to the very nature and origins of consciousness. As a result, it correlates to what we want to call God, or the Goddess. Within this Neptune correlates to that which constitutes the ultimate meaning of life itself. Of itself consciousness is very analogous to water. Water, of itself, is formless. Yet we can put water into any form or container and the water, consciousness, thus assumes the function of that form. It is then defined by the nature and function of form. Consciousness in human form thus correlates to the nature of consciousness in that form: the human form. When Neptune is retrograde at birth it correlates to a consciousness, the Soul, who will progressively reject or rebel against that which constitutes the real meaning for life as defined by temporal values emanating from whatever society or culture of birth. The underlying desire in Neptune retrograde is to discover, to realize, what the ultimate meaning for life is. And that ultimate meaning will be linked with timeless values, not temporal, where timeless values correlates the cause of life itself: the cause of the manifested Creation. Because of this underlying desire the Neptune retrograde Soul can inwardly experience, cyclically or perpetually, a deep inner existential void in which nothing in life means anything to it. This will be true until the Soul has makes choice to commit to that which will provide for that ultimate sense of meaning: to a spiritual life in which the desire to know God/ess within. Even when this is occurs to the Neptune retrograde Soul there can still be cycles or bouts of this existential aloneness because of the nature of the world in which the Neptune retrograde lives: how most are living their life. This juxtaposition of what the Neptune retrograde Soul is living by way of a life committed to God/ess and the vast majority of others who are not thus, creates this feeling of existential aloneness.

Within the evolutionary process of rebelling against temporal values associated with what life means many of the Souls with Neptune retrograde will manifest a diversity of thoughts of what does correlate with ultimate meaning. Thus, they can create any manner of desires in which the initial reaction to those desires is to feel that whatever the desire is will connect them to this sense for ultimate meaning. And this can be literally anything that the Soul can imagine that is then infused with the projected ultimate meaning by the Neptune retrograde Soul. And, of course, it may be entirely possible for the Neptune retrograde Soul to actualize whatever the desire is that in now infused with the projected ultimate meaning. And, for a time, this can create a real sense of that ultimate meaning, a real sense of satisfaction in which the Soul feels that it has found or discovered that ultimate meaning for itself.

Yet, in time, this feeling will give way, and revert back to, the inner sense of meaningless: the inner existential void. This occurs of course because of the real intent of the Neptune retrograde Soul: to commit to a spiritual life in which the real ultimate meaning is realized. So, from an evolutionary point of view, the Neptune retrograde will necessarily experience these cycles of disillusionment that are caused by the projected ultimate meaning into some desire that is not linked with what the core intent of Neptune retrograde requires: a life committed to God/ess. These cycles of disillusionment will continue as long as the Soul tries to chase down any desire that is infused with the ultimate meaning in which that ultimate meaning can not be realized.

Neptune also correlates with the nature of the collective consciousness, and the collective unconscious. The collective consciousness means the totality of what all humans on Earth of inwardly feeling, of what they are thinking, of how they are reacting to the events on Earth at any point in time. The collective unconscious correlates to the memories that are held within the human species in terms of its past. Within this there are other forms of the collective consciousness/ unconscious. For example, there can be a racial collective consciousness/ unconscious: the Jewish race, the gypsies who have their own unique genetic codes, the North and South American Indians, the Eskimos, and so on. And, within this, there can be areas on the planet that can be termed regional collective consciousness/ unconscious. For example, the South part of the USA, the Bavarian region of Germany, the tremendous cross currents within consciousness in Jerusalem because of the history/ unconscious in that area between the Jewish peoples and the Muslim peoples. And so on. As humans of course we are all part of this collective consciousness/ and unconsciousness. When Neptune is retrograde the Soul is much more inwardly sensitized to the impact of both the collective consciousness, and the unconsciousness. And this increased in sensitivity can then deeply affect the psychological state of the consciousness of the Neptune retrograde Soul.

Neptune correlates to the awareness within the human species that all of Creation, all forms of life, all forms of humans no matter what their race, religion, societies of birth etc., are *interrelated*. It is this interrelatedness of the human species, of all of Creation, that the Neptune retrograde Soul is attuned too. Thus the impact of the collective conscious/ unconscious upon their psychological state of consciousness can be so deeply affected.

Relative to Uranus, and its correlation to traumas, Neptune correlates to hysteria as a function of certain types of traumas can occur in any given life, and the hysterical reaction that occurs due to the nature of certain types of traumas. When those traumas remain unresolved, with the attendant hysteria, they will keep moving forwards with the Soul in each life that takes place after the life in which the traumas took place. This is called hysteria dysphasia. In some Neptune retrograde Souls this unresolved trauma, and the hysteria associated with it, will be present from birth. When this is the case the chemical composition of the brain itself will be in a state of imbalance. A variety of psychological affects will then be present within the consciousness of the Neptune retrograde Soul.

These will include 'irrational' behavior linked with specific kinds of stimulus where the behavior being triggered is utterly disproportionate to the nature of the stimulus itself. Whatever the stimulus is has the affect of igniting the original reaction that took place when the original trauma occurred. It can include dissociative behavior which can also manifest of split or multi-personalities. It can include creating an imaginary reality that is considered to be the actual reality of the Neptune retrograde Soul. It can include all manner of eating disorders, phobias, and neuroses of all kinds. It can include an absolute inability to take responsibility in any way for life itself leading to a psychological state of being a perpetual victim who blames anything or anyone for that which it is responsible for. It can lead to various types of autism due to the intense sensitivity within the Soul that causes the Soul to want to hide. In certain of these cases it can also cause the phenomena of being a 'savant' who has capacities and abilities that are typically labeled as being a genius. When this is the case it this will occur as a direct reaction to the deep inner compression within the Neptune retrograde's consciousness where that compression is in direct proportion to the withdrawal from the circumstantial life around it. That compression thus ignites the Neptune retrograde desire to connect with its core intention: to seek ultimate meaning. Thus, this compression creates an inner doorway to the source of Creation itself. When that doorway is then opened in this way this then causes the Soul to have these savant like qualities because they are coming from much larger forces that the Soul itself: the affect of the doorway leading to the Creator Itself.

Neptune also correlates with the phenomena of sleep, and the dreams that can take place while we are asleep. The primary intent of dreams within consciousness in human form is to purge the Soul of all kinds of data and information that it takes in during its waking life. As a result it keeps the Soul stable by way of this purging. This is why the majority of people dreams are what can be called 'junk dreams' that mean absolutely nothing. We can also have highly symbolic dreams in which the nature of the symbols in those types of dreams are signaling to the Soul that it is processing, needing to look at, various areas within its life that correlate to the major evolutionary intentions for the current life being lived. When those intentions, and the life circumstances that symbolize those intentions, are being carried forwards from other lifetimes into the present, this can then also manifest as past life dreams. We can also have what can be called 'super-conscious dreams' in which the Soul can leave its physical body during the sleep state. The Soul will then 'dream' that it in some place from on high, the astral plane for example, in which is it is then having some kind of instruction or teaching from an entity that is not on this Earth. This is also associated with what is called 'astral traveling'.

When Neptune is retrograde the Soul will typically have dreams in which the nature of the dreams is to review, retrograde, the nature of its current life in a variety of ways. This can include having past life dreams in which something in whatever life was not resolved. For some this will also manifest as a penchant for the super-conscious types dreams. When Neptune is retrograde at birth this can also correlate to Souls that have trouble sleeping because there is such a high degree of energy within their consciousness that is continually processing, reviewing, its life. For some others however when Neptune is retrograde it can correlate with the feeling of needing to sleep all the time. When that is the case this is typically a reaction to two dynamics. One is a Soul whose recent prior lifetimes have been so traumatic, or so full due to the nature of the life itself, that the Soul comes into life in a state of exhaustion. Thus, this feeling of needing to sleep all the time. The other dynamic correlates to Souls who simply do not want to engage their life because life seems too heavy. Thus, the reaction is to remain as unengaged as possible, leading to this feeling of wanting to sleep all the time. A variation of this with some Neptune retrograde Souls is to want to avoid or escape life in the form of drugs, alcohol, of any manner of activities that have the affect of avoiding any real engagement in their lives.

Pluto Retrograde

Now we come to the apparent phenomena of Pluto retrograde. We will consider Pluto retrograde from a purely evolutionary perspective. Pluto is retrograde roughly six out of every twelve months. Approximately half of the population will have a retrograde Pluto in their birth charts. What does it mean?

Relative to the four natural evolutionary conditions, Pluto retrograde means that half the people are not accepting the status quo, and will question the status quo in such a way as to reflect their own natural evolutionary condition and state. This process allows collective evolution at all four evolutionary levels or conditions. Pluto retrograde, then, allows for collective evolution to occur because half the people at any one time are questioning the status quo in some ways. This is utterly necessary from evolutionary point of view because it allows for growth of the entire human species. It prohibits stagnation, non-growth and crystallization.

From the above it may be understood that the retrograde Pluto tends to place the emphasis on the desire to return the Source of the Soul, Soul, or to evolve in a more accelerated fashion. Because of the individualizing effect of Pluto retrograde, the person must do which they must do in their own way. At the deepest possible level, the Soul, Pluto retrograde promotes an internalization process, a relative need to withdraw from external activity. Because Pluto correlates relates to the deepest reaches of our unconscious, this impulse may not be actively implemented given other factors in an individual's total makeup. The need to withdraw may simply be sensed as a wistful desire that remains unfulfilled. Even if it is not acted upon, the individual will still feel a sense of distance from within itself, and others in a fundamental way.

Because the retrograde Pluto tends to emphasize the desire to return to the Source, or the need to accelerate the elimination of separating type desires, the sense of cyclic or perpetual dissatisfaction is deeper in these individuals than in those who do not have Pluto retrograde. Keep in mind that all of us, with or without Pluto retrograde, will have this experience to one degree or another. Dissatisfaction is directly linked to the interaction of the co-existing desires in the Soul. Until all separating desires are totally eliminated this sense of dissatisfaction is the psychological symptom or effect that originates in the desire to return to the Source. Dissatisfaction allows for the progressive realization of 'not this, not that'. Through this process we will someday realize what it is that creates ultimate satisfaction. The point is that those with Pluto retrograde will experience this sense of dissatisfaction more deeply and consistently that those who have Pluto direct. Pluto retrograde accelerates, in its own way the evolutionary process: individually and, therefore, collectively.

Thank you all for coming today.

Also by The Wessex Astrologer

www.wessexastrologer.com

CPSIA information can be obtained
at www.ICGtesting.com
Printed in the USA
LVHW081128030822
725097LV00008B/198

9 781902 405520